THE WEDDING WITHIN
THE WAR

THE WEDDING WITHIN THE WAR

MICHAEL ROSSMAN

PARIS REVIEW EDITIONS

Doubleday & Company, Inc., 1971, Garden City, New York

Acknowledgments

I owe thanks to the following folks for permission to reprint these writings:

"The Fourth Night of Cambodia" originally appeared as "The Day We Named Our Child We Had Fish For Dinner" in the *New American Review 11*.

"The Vigil at Chessman's Execution" originally appeared in *The Daily Californian* of May 6, 1970. "Memo From Spaceport Berkeley" originally appeared as "From Moonshot Berkeley" in *The Daily Californian* of August 1, 1969.

"Civil Rights and the Free Speech Movement" originally appeared as two articles in *Occident*, fall 1960 and fall 1964. "The New Radicals" originally appeared as part of an article in *Occident*, fall 1964. "All Things Come to their Change" appeared in *Occident*, fall 1961.

"Barefoot in a Marshmallow World" is reprinted courtesy of *Ramparts*, Volume 4, number 9, issue of January 1966.

"The Movement and Educational Reform" appears courtesy of *The American Scholar*, Volume 36, number 4, autumn 1967.

"Cooling It: The Adventures of Garbageman" appears courtesy of *The New Review of Books*, Volume 10, issue of February 15, 1968.

"A Violence Sequence" originally appeared in three sections in *The Village Voice*. Reprinted by permission of The Village Voice. Copyright © 1968 by The Village Voice, Inc.

"Ode to Benny Spock" was first published in *Green Flag, Journal For the Protection of All Beings* #3, 1969. City Lights Books.

"Letter to Jerry Rubin" originally appeared in the *Berkeley Barb*, 1968.

"Reflections on American Theater" is an expanded version of "Typhoon Season," which appeared in *Activist* #22, Volume 9, number 1, fall 1968 issue.

"The Context of Campus Violence" was first published by Straight Arrow Publishers, Inc., in *Rolling Stone*, #30, April 5, 1969.

Fragment of "Poem for a Victory Rally in a Berkeley Park" appeared in the *Marijuana Review* #5.

Fragment of "Poem for a Victory Rally in a Berkeley Park" appeared in *The Whites of Their Eyes*, CONSUMPTION, Volume 3, numbers 1 & 2.

"Declaration on the Birth of the Child Lorca" appeared in the *New Schools Exchange Newsletter* as a prepublication excerpt from the RASBERRY EXERCISES. Reprinted from New Schools Exchange Newsletter, Issue #47, 301 East Canon Perdido Street, Santa Barbara, Ca. 93101.

Fragments of a song by Carl Oglesby, published by Fennario Music Publ., Inc., ASCAP, is used with permission of Vanguard Recording Society.

"The Fear That Precedes" by Robert Duncan was originally published in *Evergreen Review*, Volume 1, issue No. 2. Reprinted with permission of the author. Copyright © 1957 by Robert Duncan.

"A falcon circles with his eyes" is used with permission of the author. Copyright © 1971 by George Csiscery.

"Claiming Turf in Berkeley" first appeared in the *San Francisco Express-Times*, Volume 1, #25, issue of July 10, 1968. "Huelga KMPX" appeared in the *San Francisco Express-Times* in 1968.

And larger gratitude to Mary Dick, Erica Weiner, and Karen McLellan for sharing the numbness of typing; to Mike Kenney for his help in editing; and for the grace of their art to Jan Worthington, Michael Alexander, and Deborah (God's-Thumbprint), whose linoleum-block birth announcement provides the cover.

CONTENTS

THE WEDDING WITHIN
THE WAR

Blessing

I wrote these words to bear witness
to birth, sweet seed in its husk
of sorrow. Now their pain and foreboding
stagger me, editing. Am I merely a man
with a dark vision? Or is it that we live
truly in the Belly of the Beast,
where exploitation breeds, where the Yang
rules all of the captive lands
and the Capitalist armies of Night
forbid us to take their name seriously,
here in the kitchen of Death where we gather
at first light with torn cloth banners,
unpracticed hands, and prepare,
as our energy heats the waters,
to accept the new child
with his badge of blood.

This book is for you who were beside me there, in all
the lonely places.

12 February 1971

After I got out of jail in 1967, I set out to write a book about change. Along the way it grew into three, of which two are now finished—this collection of journalism, and a book of theory for new education, called On Learning and Social Change. *The third book,* Making the Changes, *will be a more intimate speculation about the nature and practice of the broad transformation our lives and our culture are undergoing. Each reflects upon the others. All are political, in that they spring from the struggle to be an active agent of social change, a conscious swimmer in the blind river of History.*

This is a volume of personal journalism, spanning the decade during which we began our struggle to change Amerika. This is not a history of what came to be called the Movement, but a series of views from its perspective—windows into time, key moments as they seemed at the time *to one young man growing up through them. I wrote most of these pieces spontaneously, from the need to grasp what was happening at the edge of conflict, see it in context. Most deal with our public theater—or* demonstrations, *in which we came together to show ourselves to each other and the world.*

As we who were its life grew and changed, so did the Movement which was ours. And as its vision deepened and expanded, so did mine. How strange it is, to edit at thirty-one what I wrote during my twenties! Retracing a decade of Movement history, I fall into my personal well of time, meet myself as a nineteen-year-old kid trudging a picket line, starting up the years toward the future, looking for a people to belong to. Many of my reports from this quest seem naïve and raw now. But I haven't materially revised or updated them. For whatever they reveal about the slow, timid growth of consciousness is more than my private story—as the essence of our Movement is not a sequence of events, but a progression of consciousness.

1970

The Fourth Night of Cambodia

The night we named our child we had fish for dinner.

"What shall I do with the filet?" asked Karen from the kitchen, "there are bones in it."

"Cook it," I said.

"I don't like it with bones."

"They come out easier after it's cooked. That's the way fish are."

"Oh, never mind." Clatter of pans, water running. Indistinctly: "Screw you, anyway."

"What was that?"

"I said, never mind."

"And what else? What after that?"

Clatter of pans, running water. I pulled myself up again, weary, and went into the kitchen. She was standing over the stove, stirring instant mashed potatoes. I couldn't read her back. I held her. "I think we're tearing ourselves apart because the world is coming apart," I said. "I think you're right," she said. "Water the plants," I told her, as I went back into the front room, grimly ignoring the radio, the phone, "that's the thing to remember now, remember to water the plants."

It was the fourth night of Cambodia. I was watching the ferns when our brother Lonnie from San Diego came in. "Carol called to find out when you're coming back," I reported. "She says they're working for a school-wide strike on Thursday. The English Department already voted to go out. Farber brought them round, and the paper's agreed to support it."

"All up and down Telegraph they're talking about Kent State," he said, his face still flushed from walking, intense through his spectacles. "There's little knots of freaks just talking, all along the street. It's true, four were killed, the National Guard shot them down in the parking lots. I can't believe it."

We want to run a training program this summer, for public school teachers in the San Diego area: learn them a little political smarts to protect the learning they're learning. But Carol can't make the planning meeting, too busy with a crisis in the Woman Studies Program she's organizing in the college there. And she's hard to get hold of now: with the Minutemen at their door, they don't go back to the house much, and are learning to travel armed. Lonnie and I fumble to fix time for another meeting. Nothing will come into focus. He drifts out the door. I say, "Wait." We embrace.

Later Tom calls from over in the next house, to tell me that Reagan has ordered all the state colleges and universities closed, through Sunday at least. Another first for California, the Golden State.

Three years before Cambodia, I visited Kent, Ohio. That was spring 1967, the media were just discovering the Haight and the Hippy. I was on my first round of visiting campuses, just starting to sort things out, to adjust my perspective from Berkeley-provincial to a national scope, and learn what work I could do in our ghetto. For the moment, I was writing a story on what the War was doing to what we then called the Student Movement, and I wanted some unknown dreary large public campus to play off against Antioch and Oberlin. So I chose Kent State, found a contact, and spent a couple of days there.

I mostly remember the flat apathy of the faces I met wandering the campus, these students of lower-class blood slack weary from the mineral-drained hills of upland Ohio, serving time for the upward mobility of the teaching credential. And the buxom girls chattering in the morning Pancake House, as I sat over fourth coffee, road-grimed, hugging my sleeping bag. Flat, that campus, flat. Some months earlier a first hiccup of antiwar protest had turned out a hundred for a lonely march. Now I found all told maybe a dozen committed to keeping active, trying to find a way to move it on. Isolated, embattled, lonely, embittered, taking refuge in an overtight group whose talk was laced with hurtful humor and flashes of longing.

They took me home for the night, the house was old and they had made their warm mark upon its surfaces. They lived in what would become a commune, and then a family. Over late coffee we talked about organizing, about guerrilla theater, about holding together for warmth. Hang on, brothers and sisters, I said to them, some Spring is coming. And I left them the large *Yellow Submarine* poster I designed for Mario's birthday—an anarchist pro-

gram for a disruptive festival of joy, "a generally loving
retaliation against absurd attack." The poster commem-
orated the 1966 Second Strike at Berkeley—for us in the
West, the first time freaks and politicos joined in public
ritual, in song and an elaborate masque. We discussed community programs, wild with the energy of coming together, and broke into spontaneous joy, singing chorus
after chorus of "Yellow Submarine"—imagining all our
friends on board, the blue sky, the life-green sea.*

Then next October, before I left for my second round
of traveling campus work, we put on our feathers at
dawn and marched down seven thousand strong into Oakland to block the doors of the Induction Center. After
we got the shit clubbed out of two hundred people, we
tied up downtown Oakland for the rest of the week,
dodging the heat and chanting, "We are the people!" in
the intersections.

So long ago. *Saturday in Kent they trashed the town
in protest, breaking fifty-six windows.* I was in Rock
Island, Illinois, with brother Russell from our troupe, talking about the death of a culture and teaching college kids
how to begin to play again, to live in their bodies.
*Sunday in Kent they burned down the Army ROTC
building.* I was home at the house we call Dragon's Eye,
sixteen of our family were learning to play a holy Indian
gambling game together, a ritual for pooling psychic
force, handed down through Stewart Brand of the Prank-
sters. *Today in Kent on the fourth of Cambodia two
thousand turned out, and they shot four dead in the parking lots.* O let us laugh and canter. O I will play the

* *The Beatles wanted $50 for permission to quote the lyric.*

Fool, grant me my mad anger, I still believe that Art will see us through.

October evening falling in 1964, I was standing in Sproul Plaza beside the police car that held Jack Weinberg captive; I was changing in the crucible that formed the Free Speech Movement, the first campus explosion. It was the thirtieth hour since a thousand captured the car and Mario stepped on top to begin the first open public dialogue I had heard in Amerika. Behind Sproul Hall six hundred cops were preparing, around us the Greeks were chanting drunk, "We want blood! We want blood!" We were sharing our green apples and bread, waiting for them to wade in clubbing, and singing, "We are not afraid," in voices shaking with fear, betrayed into life by our longing for the pure radiations of community which we first there kindled among us, bright as imagination. And I had a heavy flash, and said it to some friend: *"Five years from now they'll be killing kids on campuses, all over Amerika."* They began with the blacks, with the Orangeburg Three massacred in '68, and they killed the first white brother, James Rector, at People's Park in Berkeley nine months later. And now Kent State: only the first in this Spring when my five years come up.

(Rewriting now on the sixth of Cambodia, plastic underground radio turns real as it tells me how the girl's leg broke as they beat her and threw her off the wall, an hour ago up on campus, and how two thousand National Guardsmen have been ordered into Urbana, Illinois. I've spent ten separate weeks in Urbana, we have family there, Vic centers it, he works in wood and is making a cradle for the baby. Last month I saw him; he was organizing a craft/food/garage cooperative. The week before he had charged the pigs for the first time to help rescue a brother, was still shaken.)

But I had that flash and said that thing, I truly did, and have five years of poems to prove it, canceled stubs on the checking account of my sorrow, a long coming to terms. Sure, I'm a prophet, my name is Michael, I've shared total consciousness and seen the magicians summon the Powers. Prophets are common in Berkeley, and I've met quite a few on the road, mixed with the saints who now walk among us. What else do you expect to appear when our energy comes somewhat truly to focus? It is time to own up to what we are doing. Everyone knows or suspects a snatch of the holy language of Energy, via acid, confrontation or contact. The wavelengths of our common transformations flow strongly through Berkeley: for twelve years now what happens here and across the Bay happens a year or two later in concentric circles spreading out across Amerika. I've lived here all that time. Most leave. If you stay you close off or go mad. Or you stay open and are transmuted, transformed into an active conduit for the common sea of our Energy: lines of its organizing come to flow through you. I think I am learning to feel them in my body. It is frightening, it is always frightening not to have a language in which to wrap the nakedness of your experience. Cold wind of new, hanging on the tip of the rushing wave.

For three years, linked into a growing net of comrades in work, I wandered from Berkeley through our involuntary ghetto. Four hundred days on the road, 150,-000 miles: I visited seventy campuses, worked on forty, training and organizing, trying to follow the Tao of transformation in furthering the change that is happening through us. Call me an action sociologist, a specialist in learning and student of change; color me proud to be supported mostly by my own people, freaks and radicals, plus some rip-offs from adult institutions and the media. I hustled to be free to put my energy where I draw my warmth, and luck was kind. And my trip is one among many. Our own and our best are staying with us now, instead of being bought off by the stale rewards of a dying System, and our change accelerates the more.

And I know where it's going, for a little way at least. For Berkeley is truly a barometer. Every college in the country is undergoing an evolution in the culture and politics of its captive transient population; and each evolution is essentially like Berkeley's. I have watched it happening on every kind of campus, from upper-class Catholic girls' schools to working-class junior colleges. Activism begins, diversifies to departmental organizing, anti-draft work and guerrilla theater; the dance of confrontation proceeds in growing ranks; the administration gets slicker but finally blows its cool; dope culture spreads, the girls chuck their bras—wow, you wouldn't believe the wealth of data. And then beyond the campus the voluntary ghetto forms. Freak community seeks roots and begins to generate communes, families, head-shops and food co-ops, freak media, friendly dog packs and dog shit, links with the farm communes—there are ten within fifteen miles of Rock Island, micro-sample of Amerika. O, it is happening everywhere just like in Berkeley, only faster now: long-haired kids on the street, merchants' complaints, heavy dope busts, teachers fired, kids suspended, leash laws, narcs and agents and street sweeps and riot practice for the neighboring precincts and dynamite at the farmhouse.

Here now in Berkeley it is the fourth night of Cambodia, Kent State is catching up fast, we shall have to go some to keep ahead. But like the University we have broad strength in our Departments, their lintels display the Tao of Life and Death. The Free Bakery has opened, capacity two thousand loaves a day, put together by a family of forty living mostly on welfare: people drop by to pick up bread or learn how to bake, linger. The city government is trying to get $175,000 for two helicopters to maintain a full-time patrol over the city; the City Council has decided not to have its meetings public, because of disruption; we will shoot their birds down, I am sure. A thousand tenants are out on rent strike, now the evictions begin. Governor Reagan is calling for a blood-bath. Gay Liberation flames buoyant in the front lines of demonstrations. Our medics are special targets, speed and smack are spreading like crazy. Six hundred Berkeley families are linked into the Great Food Conspiracy, buying cooperative spinach and cheese. The campus has the third largest police force in the whole county, the leaves are beginning to wilt from the tear gas. The people who hand-deliver a high graphic newsletter to 150 communes in Berkeley and the City, cycling goods and needs and lore and advice, come by and leave us a rap on planting and compost. My kid brother by blood was busted on campus last week, charged with assaulting a police officer with a deadly weapon, i.e. chucking a rock at a cop, $5,000 bail. He didn't do it, no matter: the Grand Jury's seeking indictments. The leaflet from the Berkeley Labor Gift Plan says, "*Together*, brothers and sisters, we can build a new community of labor

and love." Each time we go into the streets they test
some new piece of technology upon us, last week it was
cars spewing pepper-fog from their exhausts. The leaflet
from the Leopold Family begs the community not to rip
off records from the people's own store; they are selling
checks imprinted with the burning bank in Santa Barbara.
On the radio a brother is reporting from Kent, he says
he had to drive forty miles to get out from under the
phone blank-out the government has clamped over the
area. Berkeley was an exemplary city, you know. She had
a progressive form of government and an overtly liberal
party in power for years, she dazzled the nation with
thoughtful, advanced programs of curricular enrichment
and racial integration, active support for the schools was
her proudest civic tradition, O, Berkeley was always noted
for how she cared for her children.

Cold wind coming. Sky turning black, the missiles sulk
in their cages, the green net of the ocean grows dangerous
thin, the terrorism of bombs begins, the Minutemen multiply bunkers, the economy chokes and staggers, the blacks
grow yet more desperate, the war is coming home. I
figure I'm likely to die in this decade, perhaps in this
city I love, down the street beyond the neighborhood
garden, in some warm summer twilight when people sit
on their porches and the joy of live music drifts out from
their windows. That's a cold political judgment, without
much to do with what's also true: that since I woke at
fifteen I've never been able to imagine past about thirty-
five, it's been only a blank in my mind, always the same
through the years, down to now, when I'm thirty. Do you
mind if I finger my intimate fragments in front of you,
awkwardly? I can't fit them together. But what else is a
man to do in this mad time, pretend that everything's only

at its usual standard of incoherence? For I have also been One with the great two-headed Snake of the Universe, and I have seen us begin to recover our bodies and share our will, seen us learn that realities are collective conspiracies. Now in the families forming and linking we are weaving the blank social canvas for the play of our imagination. I have seen the first sketches of group will, love and art, and a whole life, the first organized forms of human energy liberated one more degree. They transfix me with awe; I was never taught to dream so boldly, I had to learn for myself. I was not alone. For all our failures and unfinished business, what we are pulling together is bright and well begun. If we are let live through this decade and the next we will be strong, strong, our women will be powerful and our men beautiful.

So all of this is running through my mind on the fourth night of Cambodia. I'd just got back the night before from three months of hustling my ass around the country to pile up bread for the baby and the coming recession, in the process cutting through maybe sixty family groups in twenty cities, cross-fertilizing news and goods and paper and trinkets, a bee in the meadow of change. I came back stoned and mellow at how fast and strong it is coming together among us, even within the strain of the War, and bearing the love of a dozen fine women and men for Karen. All day now through the cottage people have been flooding with these atrocity tales, I wallow in the gloomy pleasures of verification. Diagnosis: Fascism, soft form turning hard, terminal cultural cancer. The radio tells me 258 campuses are out on strike, and then sings to me: "*Rejoice, rejoice, you have no choice.*" I take another toke, last of the good stuff: been running too fast to score, and summer's customary drought is almost upon us. The typewriter beckons. Torn between life and death I calm my chattering schizophrenic, refuse, and turn to the guitar, god damn! the sweet guitar who embraces all of me in her stroking vibrations when I touch her well, O, how I need to go to the sea!

Music is magical, music is my balm, music suspends me and aligns the frame of my spirit. O, shit, I wish I could sing to you, I am no longer ashamed, it is time to come out with it all, nothing less will do, the child will be born. I hate these pages, hate these mechanical fingers. Sometimes I pop for a moment above the surface of sanity and grab for the floating flute or guitar, manage to clear the breath of my energy for a time from the choking hurrying flow of vital and desperate information, rapping words healing words data words analysis words magic words maggots and birds on the acid wallpaper of my mind. And I water the plants, the ferns in particular. When I am broken jagged like tonight I think it is because I mostly cannot cry, and that I travel the crystal rapids of melody for this reason too, singing because I cannot weep. When I'm together I see it as a way of keeping in touch with the slower rhythms. Whichever, the ferns are grateful, and they sing to me with their green misty love, and the spiders arch their webs in the corners of the window frames.

And I sing to them back, and to the dog my familiar, and to the pregnant animal Karen crouched unseen in her den—to them all, but softly to myself—a song I have made for her from a fragment another singer left in my mind. Karen comes in from the kitchen, plate and bowl of dinner in her hand, sets it down, retreats from the shaken animal in his den. While the rock cod cools I sing the song again, for the first time loudly.

Slow, with a lagging rhythm

"Things might be
It might be

la — zy if they weren't so cra-zy" ___ he
bet — ter in some o — ther wea ther ___ I

tells you, I tell ___ you that too.
don't know, I'm do — ing it with you.

bridge between verses (freely):

(2)

Some say the city, a farm would be pretty,
the mountains refuse to be blue.*
Come, with me wander, while they seek us yonder;
what else could you choose to do?

(3)

But pray for the baby whose birthday is Maybe,
and meet me at two in the moon.
Keep warm if you're able and fight for the cradle,
we can't hide, let's ride this one through.

Keep warm if you're able and fight for the cradle,
we can't hide, let's ride this one through.

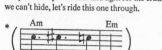

* fuse to be blue

"Now damn," I think, with bitter satisfaction, "ain't that a song to inspire pity and awe and all! Not bad for a first lullaby, opus 7. I sure would like to spend a long stretch of years writing some songs, be grateful if they just kept coming three or four a year, now that I know they're coming." And I rack the guitar, pick up the plate, and wander into the bedroom to eat with Karen.

In the next room my love is curled weeping on the black leather chair, the dog is anxiously kissing her, careful of her belly, I hold the song of her sobbing. "Ah, little princess," I manage to whisper, "you didn't know what it would cost to be my muse." Through my head spin Cambodia, Babylon, that five-year-old flash by the cop car, growing up during the McCarthy years with the FBI at the door, the times we have been in the street together, our trips, our campus travels. "But there's spin-off, you know," I say, "we're maybe better prepared spiritually for what's coming than most, advantage of foresight and practice, pay of the bruises. We've been making our peace for a while." No ultimate blame: culture changing too fast for its able. But the child will be born, though they tie the mother's legs. "Yes," she says, "but I didn't know it would be this sudden." And then: "But if the gods are stingy with time, at least they've been generous in other ways."

On my lap. I see. Wavering. The plastic plate with pink decal flowers from the Goodwill. Fresh fish filet our cousin family brought us from up the Sonoma coast. Cheese sauce, recently mastered, with chopped green onions. Dehydrated mashed potatoes. In the stoneware bowls Deborah made and laid on us for the anniversary —before she went down South again to the Army-base coffeeshop she helped start, to watch her successors get six years and then go off to help organize another—in my dear blood sister's bowls is fresh spinach salad, well-flavored; we are learning to tend our bodies. Anticipation of apple juice in the refrigerator. This is how it is, you see, I am sitting here eating this food, and Bull is watching us very intently while the puppy from next door chews on his dinner, and my feet are up cuddled around the ball of her belly, watermelon-hard in its last weeks. I sing to her, she cooks me food, the dog eats when we do, mostly. She is bearing our child; on the bed under the light and the ferns is the government pamphlet on how to raise a child during the first year; it's not bad.

And she says, "What do you think of Lorca?" "I think I can dig it, for a boy," I say, slowly, "I been thinking about it, and I can." "I'm glad," she says softly, the blush of shy triumphant pleasure crowning round her eyes, "your mother and I were having lunch, and we started to think of names of Spanish poets. 'García Rossman,' she said, 'no, that's impossible.' 'Federico . . .' I said. And then we just looked at each other, and we *knew*. And it has a nice sound."

I sink into the thought and mirror of her love, reach for the resonances, roots in the soil, and start to cry. Is it for the first time or the tenth, on this fourth night of Cambodia? Lorca was my first song teacher, the man who opened the keys of Metaphor to me: for ten years I relived his poems into my American language. "I have lost myself many times in the sea," he sang, "with my ear full of freshly cut flowers, with my tongue full of love and of agony. Many times I have lost myself in the sea, as I lose myself in the heart of certain

children. . . ." Hold on, dear heart, jagged at this four
A.M., now is not the time to tear. From Federico's arms
I passed through those of grandfather Neruda, and then
into Vallejo's volcano, which finished for me what acid
began and gave me open form to integrate my fragments.

But Lorca began me, long before I learned how death
found him in a Fascist trench, how he went to sleep
forever in the autumn night of the gypsies, beyond the
lemon moon. Mercurial brightest spirit of the second
Golden Age of his tongue's power, murdered in Granada
by Franco's highwaymen, in the first summer of the Civil
War. All the poets, all, all the singers were on one side
in that great division, perhaps as never before since old
Athens. And the schools and the hospitals of the brief
flowering of Republican Spain went down under German
planes and Italian artillery, the dogs of Church and
Greed. And all the poets perished or fled.

Torn, my father watched the Fascists rehearse, with
their scientific grace; stayed to organize at home with his
trade of words and a red perspective. I was born six
months after Madrid fell, while he was editing the Mine,
Mill and Smelter Workers' union paper in Denver. Pablo
Neruda was in exile from the Fascists in Chile. César
Vallejo was dead of hunger and heartbreak for Spain.
Lorca's grave was never found, in a hundred lands and
Franco's jails the poets of his race who survived sang
him their tenderest elegies. Lincoln Steffens began a new
family and life at sixty, his *Autobiography* instructed my
father. When he died the last lines in his typewriter read,
"the Spanish Civil War is the opening battle in mankind's
struggle against Fascism." Steffen's son Peter taught my
sister Deborah before she went South; I have touched

his children. Even the high school babysitters I hitched home from the airport with know what's coming down.

A week before Cambodia I was at a conference in Boston, thrown by some church folk and book people, on "the religious dimension of the Movement." Indeed. It was quite a happening, believe me: a bunch of us freaks from the families got together behind some mellow mescaline and opened up some free space, some Chaos. And then someone asked about Ritual, and little incredible Raymond Mungo opens up in a musing country style, speaking the sainted baby babble.

Well, we get up in the morning, he says, and we look at the light and we eat, we eat together. And we go to sleep when it gets dark, sometimes alone and sometimes together, for there is no light. But sometimes at night we watch the moon. During the day we plant. We chop wood. We use the wood for fire. We eat when the sun goes down. From April to October there is very much food. We have to find ways to give it away. We have to, there is very much. There is the summer solstice, and then there is the autumn solstice, and so on. Is spring the solstice was very cold, very cold. We chopped some wood and put it in a box. I made a mantra: *Equinox / sticks in box / soon it will be warm / big dog*. And a big dog came, and it grew warm. And sometimes we go out when there is no moon, and run around in the grass. And then we come back to the houses we build. Last week one of our houses burned down, it was very warm. We lost four brothers and sisters. I think we're going to learn to build better chimneys.

O, I met a little saint in Boston, he organizes energy, used to be a founding Czar of Liberation News Service, then he figured out the cities were dying, now in his Vermont town of eight hundred over a quarter live in communes, and he studies the government pamphlet to learn to build better chimneys. We're met on the fifteenth floor, overlooking the river of death called the Charles, the plastic pastries and draperies are poisoning our bodies, our minds, we've come to talk about rituals for living with fire. Mitch Goodman loves us and he's frantic with terror, sees the black sky looming, MIRV's lurking, etc. etc., he's positively yelling at Raymond, half his age and weight, scarecrow child in oversized coveralls: *But what about Fascism!?* And somehow we can't quite get it through to him there that Raymond is not simply talking about farms, pigs, dinner, etc. but about the house burning down and learning to make better chimneys and going on in season, and about Lorca and Vallejo and my brother and my sister and two of each dead in Kent and my lover lazy with child, whose belly my baboon feet grip as if I stood on the round of the world, spinning through all time.

I was translating a poem of Lorca's when I got the call that my grandfather was suddenly dead. It follows a brief skit for puppet theater, in which the gypsy whose name is Anything is captured on the bridge of all the rivers while building a tower of candlelight. He is brought before the Lieutenant Colonel of the Spanish Civil Guard to be interrogated.

He, Harry, my mother's father, was a Bolshevik; he organized a strike in the machine-shop, was jailed, loved his tutor, she died of consumption, he fled here in 1906 to dodge the interrogations of the Czar, clerked and warehoused to send Mother through college; he wanted her to learn. I have his blue eyes. He taught me to carve, cried with memory when I told him in '60 during that Spring of Chessman and HUAC how they beat us and hosed us down the steps of City Hall in San Francisco. "That was how it started, you know. . . ." he said. And three years later the phone call came and was, and I put down the receiver and thought for a moment, and said somewhere inwardly and quite distinctly, I will file this for future reference, I will weep for you some day, grandfather. And I turned back to finish reworking the poem, for there was nothing to do but go on; I knew it would take years to comprehend that grief.

Sitting in my rocker, plate on my lap, our eyes intertwining and my feet on the future, the ferns turn to oleander and the cottage to a patio, and the song of the beaten gypsy rises up in the well of his absence.

>   Twenty-four slaps,
>   twenty-five slaps,
>   then at night my mother
>   will wrap me in silver paper.

>   Civil Guard of the roads,
>   give me a sip of water.
>   Water with fishes and boats.
>   Water, water, water.

>   Aii, boss of the Guard,
>   standing upstairs in your parlor!
>   There'll be no silk handkerchieves
>   to clean my face!

And the tears rip through me grandfather deep and out everything open and echo in hers, and we touch and cling and are shaken. And the dog our first child and familiar pushes up anxious between us and offers her his nose and me his nads, which we take to complete the circle of energy, love and time around the child to be born in Cambodia. "Yes," I say, "Lorca, if it's a boy." "Maybe even a girl," she says, "it has a nice sound." "Maybe a girl," I say, "yes," and she says *I'm glad* with her eyes.

And the radio sings, *"Rejoice, rejoice, you have no choice,"* and the acid magic of those moments, of that state we once called existential, goes on and on forever, and I go off to set down the brief notes of these thoughts, like the rib-thin eaten skeleton of the dinner fish, to flesh back out later. And then we take off for the City, to try to be with our people, our theater troupe in rehearsal coming suddenly real. For it is clearly a time for coming together with those we are dear with, and we must take care that the Wedding go on within the War.

May 1970

1960
The Birth of the New Left

The Third Sunday in May Was a Beautiful Day

I can't sleep because I am cold and hungry.
I have no money for food. I sit and smoke
my last cigarette: my head spins and I cough.
The people going to church look clean and well-dressed.
My pants are torn and dirty. My stomach hurts.

Yesterday I marched in a parade for peace.
A hundred of us walked along empty streets
holding signs and trying to hand out leaflets.
Even the sun stopped shining when we started.
Today there are three-inch headlines about war.

I am nineteen years old. The Army wants me
even though I am hungry and need a shave.
The Army will give me food and let me march.
If I joined the Army I could get new clothes
and wouldn't have to worry about money.

My friends say I worry too much about things.
Last week a man shot himself in this building.
The papers said he worried about money
and war like I do, but he was unstable.
He died Tuesday. His blood is still on the stairs.

15 May 1959

Later, people would say it began in 1960, with the events I'll describe. But I think the New Left was well begun by 1958, when I came to Berkeley, drawn by the music of her twilight streets and by the news of a new activism quickening on the campus. The year before, the first broad-spectrum student political organization formed at Berkeley: TASC, Towards an Active Student Community (soon renamed SLATE). Out from under its umbrella we tiptoed, a few dozen strong, to nibble at the issues of the day: civil rights, capital punishment, nuclear disarmament.

The chill of the long winter of McCarthyism was still upon us. During the early Fifties its glaciers had ground the American Left down to demoralized disintegration, leaving radicalism to be born again, and differently, through the young. Our pickets announced its springtime. We were in the unfolding bud of a new consciousness, an Awakening in white America, touched off by psychic contagion from the black Awakening. But in 1959, when

I wrote the poem above, we were still very cold and lonely. Ours was still called the Silent Generation. We had no way to know how many were coming to feel what we felt—or that already a dozen groups like SLATE were forming at campuses up and down the West Coast, and some in the East.

In May 1960 we came together for the first time, from all around the San Francisco Bay, in two major demonstrations. In our protests against an execution and a witchhunt hearing, History was to discover the birth-cry of the New Left. For us, the discovery was of each other. We began to realize we were not alone—and then began the arduous process of finding out who we were and entering into a Marriage, still scarcely begun.

But that is a long story. Here are accounts of our first experiences of coming together in force—records from the moment itself, before we realized its implications. In this my accounts are typical of the consciousness of the white Movement at the time (black consciousness was always somewhat more developed). Our attention was still all focused outward, on what we were protesting. We had not yet gotten interested in who we were and the changes our actions were putting us through, or realized how weirdly different we might be—we were not yet engaged with the introspective core and vision of Revolution.

So perhaps the true testament of these accounts is the way their consciousness is limited. But I include them for a different reason. Since their time a million kids have gathered in force to protest, have failed or won partial success, have encountered the police, have lived the first bright flare of moral indignation transcending into social action. I don't know how else to say this: younger brothers and sisters, these tales are scraps of our common history, you will recognize their experience, archaic as some of its aspects may seem. You are not alone, least of all in Time. You share a heritage of developing struggle which stretches back continuously through these events, and through earlier roots we have all but forgotten— we who were born in the landscape the glaciers scoured clean.

I think it is time to remember, well beyond the memories written here. As much as our difference, our roots are our strength.

The Vigil at Chessman's Execution

Was it eight times in twelve years or vice versa that they tried to kill Caryl Chessman, for a child-rape that many came to feel was unproved? All the while he lived on Death Row in San Quentin, doggedly compiling the legal briefs that won him stay after stay of execution at the last possible moment, and writing books of some caliber and wide readership, that saved him from an anonymous death. The public spectacle of his being readied for death so many times in indefinite torture roused wide indignation. He became the focus for a world-wide crusade against the barbarity of capital punishment. On the eve of his execution thousands demonstrated in Rio de Janeiro.

Here some were moved to action. At first they were a vanishing few. The action was mostly silent vigils, organized by local Quakers, held during the night of each scheduled execution. Students started coming, the vigils continued, our numbers grew, especially when Chessman came round again. But our protest remained silent witness, and only flickered toward disobedience in the moment before Chessman's death.

As in tactics, so in spirit our protest was typical of the politics of the time. Our opposition to capital punishment was a pure example of "issue-oriented" activism: an immediate problem seen, an immediate solution sought

*by some simple act, all running on a pure surge of moral
indignation, untroubled by ideology. But I think we were
feeling more than simple distaste for society's murder
rituals when we stood outside San Quentin's gates and
listened to the wind. Our eyes were opening, a mystifica-
tion was breaking, we were beginning to see the acts
of Official America as ugly, wherever we looked. This
was a chance to express our growing revulsion, in a quiet
way. And as we did, the acts grew uglier.*

We reached the prison at nine that night, walking and
hitchhiking. There were seven hundred people crowded
into a short section of road, held back by a barricade and
a dozen guards. A public address system was distorting
the middle of a long speech; most of the crowd was gathered about the microphone, listening thoughtfully or talking in small groups in the gathering dusk. To the left of
them, a chain-link fence lined with carefully propped-up
posters: "PSYCHIATRY, NOT CYANIDE"; "DOES
BROWN HAVE CHESSMAN'S COURAGE?" To
their right, a steep rocky hill half buried in grass, and on
it, silent watchers, huddled in blankets and sleeping bags.

We left our books on the hill and went for coffee.
Beyond the crowd a mobile canteen was doing a brisk
business, though the night chill was just beginning. The
gentlemen of the press relaxed beside it, sipping coffee
and watching the demonstrators. Occasionally one would
move with his camera to a vantage point, and a bright
flash of light would startle the crowd as he shot the current
speaker or a "human interest" photo.

We made our way through the line, bought coffee, and
scrambled up the hill again. Seeing us shivering, a group

of students offered us extra sleeping bags. We scuffed a small part of the slope free from rocks, wrapped ourselves up, and listened as they told us of their protest march.

They started from San Francisco in the morning, crossed the Golden Gate Bridge, passed through Sausalito, and proceeded as directly up the highway to San Quentin as the police allowed, covering almost twenty miles. They spoke of the people met on the way: blank stares, taunts and insults; cameramen driving carefully abreast of them as they crossed the bridge, retiring to bars, and driving to the prison in time to catch their footsore arrival. Except for Sausalito, they added, and their voices lightened as they described how receptive the Sausalitoans had been. It was strange, they said: no one in the march made any reply to the jeers.

Almost a hundred made the march, most of them students. As photographers' bulbs flashed they pointed out marchers sunk in the nearby grass. Twilight gave way to night as they spoke, and the crowd began to dwindle.

The continuing rasp of the loudspeaker hung harsh and brittle in the cold air. Members of the Committee for Chessman spoke, taking turns with other groups and people from the crowd.

They spoke of Chessman and Brown, the Supreme Court, other trials and deaths. A retired guard said haltingly that he didn't believe the death penalty was a deterrent to murders or rapes. The former cellmate of an executed man described the surroundings of the condemned men, and his voice cracked as he said: "God, god . . . twelve years, a man can't take it . . ." Committee members called attention to the wastebasket circulating through the crowd, asking for donations to support the life flame burning on a nearby ridge. A student from India assured us of his homeland's support in an earnest, heavily accented voice.

Suddenly all eyes swung to the fence atop the hill: the sound of a portable generator disrupted the air, and two powerful lights bathed everyone present, even those huddled in the grass. A guard preempted the microphone and gave an unintelligible explanation: ". . . for security purposes . . ." We turned our backs to the glare and listened again to the speakers.

The night wind sprang up, sweeping damply off the Bay. Everywhere people offered extra blankets, or took shivering strangers under their own covers. Despite the cold, those who remained standing did not pace about but held their clustered position around the microphone.

After a long delay, Marlon Brando and Professors Burdick and Drinnon arrived, and stepped to the microphone in a blaze of photographers and autograph-hounds. They had lunched and spoken with Governor Brown in Sacramento. Drinnon in particular seemed convinced of Brown's sincere opposition to capital punishment; and when the three finished their accounts the air seemed so freed of tension for a time that we left our warm cocoons and joined the main crowd, anxious to talk more with them.

The night drew on. The curious, the publicity-hunters and the reporters went home to their sleep, driven out by the cold and the monotonous pleas for donations. The stream of cars honking their way through the throng slowed to a trickle, ceased. The guard at the barricade was cut to six men, secure in stiff khaki uniforms and patent-leather holsters. Only the glare of the floodlights broke the darkness. The p.a. system fell silent, and we returned to the slope, waiting for the dawn.

By two A.M. our ranks were reduced to their minimum. A contingent left for Sacramento to picket Brown's mansion, after an impassioned plea over the microphone. Another group departed for the Quaker prayer vigil in Tiburon. Maybe 150 of us were left to stand vigil during the dark hours.

People roamed the hillside, gathering grass for protection from the rocks. Some clustered beside the barrier and the guards: drawn by the sight of the guardhouse just beyond the barricade, with its warm lights and fragrant odor of coffee, or perhaps by some unspoken agreement to be as close as possible to the prison. Some crouched on the roadside singing folksongs, but the cold wind and their tired bodies soon discouraged them.

A family of six huddled around a portable stove. Inspired by their example, a small fire flared on the hill. After a moment a guard came hurrying out of the guardhouse, a cup of coffee steaming in his hand, and sidled up the hill through the blanketed bodies. Curtly but politely he told the fire's kindlers that it would have to be extinguished, and, his duty done, turned and slid down the dew-coated grass to his indoor post. Three students tore apart the neat border of rocks and stamped their fire out.

A cold calm held. The only sound, save for the wind whipping off the Bay, was the persistent chugchugging of the generator. Again a guard charged up the hill, this time to threaten two students who tried to change the floodlight's angle so they could get some sleep. He restored the lamps to their full glare and again slid down the damp hill, this time to a chorus of hisses. Stiff from the cold and the rocks, unable to sleep, we abandoned our blankets and went for a stroll.

We crossed the highway and scrambled down to the littered beach. Someone had left a small bonfire, safe from the prowling guards. We stoked it again and sat before the flames, discussing the long vigil and Chessman's chances for reprieve. The speakers had left us hopeful, and we spoke, half in jest, half sadly, of attending the next Chessman "party." The fire blazed high; and one by one other strollers were drawn by its warm beacon to come and sit beside it. But not for long: after a few minutes soaking in its warmth, each rose with a groan and the comment: "I must be getting back . . . ," and returned to the vigil, to stand and shiver against the barricade or sit body-with-body with strangers on the hill, sharing warmth.

A strange crowd, this one that spent the night beside the prison gate. A blonde freshman from a city high school, with blistered feet; a withered old lady with an artificial rose, silent the whole night. A shabby group of beatnix with beards and guitars; three businessmen in grey flannel suits and attaché cases. A Negro carpenter with his family, staring silently into the flame of the Coleman stove; a group of Stanford students who had come to watch an hour, and stayed on. How many held through the long hours solely out of curiosity or a desire for publicity? Why were the teacher, the truck driver, the youth with the swastika, the young mother and child here?

Sleeping, pacing, whispering, huddling morose and silent, most people did not speak of why they came.

The reporters and photographers began returning, harbingers of dawn. Slowly the watchers bedded on the hill came to life. Soon a buzz of conversation filled the vacancy left by the generator's silence. The mobile canteen returned, causing a general rush for coffee and snails; and soon the entire crowd was astir again.

We returned to the base of the hill with our coffee, swinging our arms and pacing to drive the night stiffness from our limbs, picked up discarded signs and paraded experimentally. A few early newcomers swelled our ranks. As the sun rose, the press arrived in full force: "Carry this sign, not that . . . Stand a little closer to the noose those guys set up and start it swinging; this is a motion shot, not a still . . . thaaaat's right!" A student swore and said something about monkeys getting at least peanuts to perform, and a workman spat and looked away. We did not speak to the American press: during the night papers had been passed around documenting their distortions of the case, and each new press car that disrupted the slowly milling demonstrators was greeted with grimmer and grimmer faces. A young woman jeered in an open window: "Come to watch the zoo?" The four well-dressed gentlemen inside withdrew their cameras hastily and looked confused.

As the sun rose higher, clouds came, denying us this bit of physical warmth. We crowded around a tinny portable to hear a 7:30 news broadcast: "No change in the Chessman case . . ." A guard drove by, his shift finished, and leaned from his car with a smile: "It won't be long now, kids." No one even bothered to curse him.

Stiff and grubby after the long night, we came to life slowly. We waited anxiously for word from the Supreme Court, set to convene at 8:00. Another broadcast came over a car radio, and we drifted over. "Brown says the decision is out of his hands," someone relayed, and a sudden gust of cold wind made us shiver again. Someone else said, speaking to no one in particular, "I want to see the guy who pushes the button." No one answered him, but one by one we began to pick up signs and trudge in a slow circle along our section of the road.

New arrivals swelled our ranks, and the line grew longer. A strange tension hovered in the air: nobody spoke, not even to hound the guards. The hillside crowd grew thicker, and for the first time since midnight a sizable proportion of people were there for the sole purpose of watching us. Cars honked through our line, disgorging photographers and cameras on trolleys, sound equipment and reporters with eager notebooks. Only the European press treated the marchers with deference.

The chill lessened and our pace increased. Someone announced the hour of nine with a shout: "One hour left," and we began winding in and out of the oncoming line of cars, led by several high school students, holding our signs before the windows. People came down from the hill to stand beside the road. One by one marchers took them by the elbows and brought them in. A band of thirty youngsters climbed the hill, hurling catcalls, snickers, and shouts of "communists." Someone struck up a song, new words to an old tune; "Brown, where is your conscience? It has been removed . . . The papers are against us, they should be improved . . ." and for a time the sound of off-key but earnest voices filled the air.

At nine the guards at the barricade and along the road were increased to twenty or thirty. They stood in silent groups of two or three, watching the demonstrators. Cars pressed past in increasing numbers; a guard would halt our line for each one until its papers could be checked and the barricade removed and replaced. The long march went on, slowly, and just as slowly the feeling grew that we were marching not for Chessman alone, nor even against capital punishment, but for something much more important, something transcending politics and laws. A student who had marched from the city said, "I keep feeling that what we're doing is helping each one of us more than it can possibly help Chessman." No one disagreed.

Minute by minute the tension grew, and each time a radio picked up a broadcast hasty shouts relayed the news. Suddenly the loudspeaker erupted into sound for the first time in hours. "May I have your attention, please? The State Supreme Court has voted four to three to refuse to recommend clemency . . ."

A long moment of silence hung like a clock-stroke above us all, guards and marchers and spectators alike. Then, as a large press car started down the road toward our stunned circle, the cry went up: "Sit down! Sit down!" Once started, it was echoed again and again: "Keep your hands in your pockets! Put down the signs, keep your hands in your pockets, sit down!"

Immediately marchers and spectators sprang to the center of the road and sat down. The car tried to edge past on the side, but a dozen seated figures appeared before it. Thirty of us sat there, acting in unison, without leadership, as if by instinct. Then the guards came charging from behind the barricade, shouting and cursing. They picked us up one by one and tried to carry us off the road; but as soon as a sitter was released he walked back onto the road and sat down again. Frustrated by twenty hours without incident, the guards grew angrier and angrier and finally discovered a way out: they began to kick several of the seated demonstrators, kick them in the legs, groin and kidneys. One man lost consciousness. We gathered around the guards, who jostled him and another limp figure to a squad car down the road. The press car pulled hastily past, somehow neglecting to take pictures, as we ran after them. A marcher lay down before the squad car, blocking its passage; the guards jerked him up and threw him in the back seat. The squad car pulled away with a squeal of rubber amid cries of reassurance for the imprisoned demonstrators.

Chaos. A young girl sobbing uncontrollably, helpless with fright and anger: "They did it. They did it. With their big fancy guns and their boots. We didn't do anything. We didn't *do* anything." Cries of shock and outrage in the air, mingling with curses and warnings from the guards. Hearst photographers fiddling nonchalantly with the lens-covers of their cameras. A KPFA reporter scurrying around, trying to find where the men had been taken.

We stood shaking with rage and frustration, looking silently at the guards, unable to find words; or comforting the crying women. Suddenly the amplifier blared again: the sheriff of Marin County was speaking, "Now listen. I want everyone to listen to me. We've had no trouble here before . . . we agreed that you could come here as long as you weren't violent . . . we're here to protect you . . . let's try to keep it orderly . . ."

Immediately words came, and bitter replies rang through the air: "See how the fascists protect us!" "Violence? Violence? Who's violent?!" "Police brutality . . . go on, kill Chessman, you bastards!"

Suddenly a calm fell on us again, and with hands trembling beyond control, we picked up our signs and began to march again, slowly, on shaky legs, in the same circle. The watchers on the hill came down to join us, and the guards stepped back to let us pass. Ahead of me a sobbing girl was walking, the arms of a Negro marcher and a white marcher clasped behind her back, one saying softly and intensely to her: "Don't cry. Don't cry. Tears won't do any good. Look at this and remember it. Remember it, and don't ever forget it. Stop crying and look at them, and remember what they looked like when they were doing it." Someone started a song, and slowly our shaken voices picked it up and carried it to the silent catcallers on the hill. Around and around we marched, in silence save for the song, until the girls stopped sobbing and our legs stopped threatening to collapse.

A quiet voice came over the p.a. system: "Please form in ranks by the south side of the road. It is ten minutes to ten. Please keep calm; this is a tense moment for us all . . ."

We lined the side of the road in silence, faces set, holding our signs tightly, as the photographers balanced atop cars to catch us at the proper angle. A woman crying on her husband's shoulder choked: "Don't let them take pictures of me, don't let them . . ." A photographer shoved a marcher aside and knelt to focus on her; another marcher blocked the lens wordlessly with his sign, glaring at him until he left.

Someone held the microphone to a car radio, and KABL's syrupy voice rose and hung above us: "We are at San Quentin, waiting for Caryl Chessman to be executed, just outside the main walls. It is a clear day; there are wild flowers in the grass. The sun is shining brightly now, the prisoners are at their jobs, totally indifferent to the tense drama being enacted here today. In just a few minutes Chessman will take the famous thirteen steps to the gas chamber and receive his cyanide before sixty witnesses. Across the bay lies the great concrete block of San Francisco, forming a backdrop to this scene; most of its people are totally unaware of the spectacle at hand . . ."

We stood without words, too numbed by what had already happened to protest against this. The microphone was pulled away from the radio, and a high voice rang out: "Leave it on, let us hear, let us hear and remember what the bastards say . . ." No one moved. Six minutes passed, completely silent.

Suddenly there was motion in the center of the crowd around the car, and half a dozen marchers came walking slowly out, their faces contorted and hardened into masks, crying unashamedly. More drifted out. A student laid his sign down in the middle of the road and walked away without a backward look; the sharp slap of the wooden handle on asphalt echoed interminably. More and more people began to leave, still in silence, their heads bowed, and a voice near breaking came over the amplifier: "The meeting of the Citizens for Chessman is over . . ."

We walked to the car in silence, drove home in silence. By the time we reached Berkeley the first papers were already on the newsstands, their headlines three inches tall.

3 May 1960

How do we judge what is in vain, or learn what is won by our presence, beyond one chance to be together in despair? No one has been executed in California since 1964, nor condemned to death since 1967.* The custom lingers in disuse. Yet the laws have not changed, and public temper is growing more passionate. Right now our attention is off the subject of formal murder by the State—no one expects the My Lai defendants to be executed, and the pigs kill Panthers on an informal basis. But ritual murder is traditional in the theater of Amerikan politics. As with Sacco and Vanzetti, and Ethel and Julius Rosenberg, it comes into practice in times of heavy repression, every twenty years or so. We should expect it. When the next act begins, the principal victim may well be a woman or gay, if not black, and the action of protest much more complex.

* A month after this paragraph was written, in March 1971, Charles Manson and three women companions were sentenced to death in California. Whatever their crime and guilt, clearly the politics of cultural repression had much to do with the sentence.

The Protest against HUAC

Even before Chessman's death, we were getting ready to meet the Un-Americans.

What do people know today about witch-hunts, the public dramas of the time we blamed on Joe McCarthy? For six years, all over America, committees and vigilant citizens were hard at work, ferreting out suspected Commies and pinko sympathizers, exposing them by letter, insinuation, and television. If you moved in any way that seemed dissenting or strange, you were liable to be branded as a "fellow traveler," and to have your life destroyed wherever it was exposed to the mercies of society. This was as true if you dressed funny in grammar school as if you spoke up for Negroes at the office. So I entered adolescence in the ice age of conformity, a member of the Silent Generation, groomed by the glaciers to become a "man in a grey flannel suit."

The Cold War froze us to the marrow, as the Depression did our parents: as they still seek safety in material possessions, so we still struggle against our conditioning to find it in anonymous silence. Now historians see those years of repression as imperialist Amerika's inner response to the specter of postwar Soviet communism. But I think the general hysteria was as much our national reaction to the realization that, in the nuclear game, we were playing with the tools of absolute death. In a time when evil spirits have been set loose, no theater is more appropriate than a witch-hunt. (Its sacrificial climax was the execution of the Rosenbergs for atomic treason.)

The most feared agencies of repression during those years were the Senate Internal Security Subcommittee and the House Committee on Un-American Activities (HUAC). Long after McCarthy was toppled from power in 1954 by a sudden flash of public revulsion and shame, they continued to summon suspected subversives to Washington for interrogation, and to send delegations on periodic tours to conduct local witch-hunts (and drum up support for their yearly Congressional appropriations). Their power to condemn was informal but great, and helped maintain the climate of frightened silence. For most of that time, in fact, the only power of protest their victims had was silence, usually under cover of the Fifth Amendment.

Silence was stamped so deeply upon our spirits that even the young who were growing into social activism took it for a primary strength at first, in the North as in the South. Looking back, I'm struck by how proud we were at being mute and restrained. Yet despite our contradictions, our mood had changed decisively. By the end of the decade HUAC's members were apprehensive. Increasingly in hearings victims had abandoned silence to attack the Committee with aggressive rhetoric. Demonstrations were beginning to organize against its visits in some Eastern cities.

In May 1960, a HUAC subcommittee came to San Francisco, for the first time in several years, to hold investigative hearings. By then, heady with the resurgence of political dissent, many of us were partly eager for their visit and the chance to confront one surviving head of the hydra Terror of the Fifties. A week later, I told a loved friend in New York what happened.

20 May 1960

Berkeley

My Dear Kathy Greensleaves:

Enclosed is a letter I wrote you months ago, and never mailed. I can send it now because I can write this letter now. I hope that when you finish it you'll understand what being able to write it means to me. I am writing now to try to clarify what has happened, for myself, as well as for you. I will try to write carefully enough that you can show this to people around you.

• • • •

About two weeks ago we heard that the House Un-American Activities Investigating Committee was coming to town again. Last year the same announcement was made. Such a furor arose that they postponed the scheduled hearings again and yet again, until they dropped them entirely, explaining that the Bay Area was such a nest of Communist activity that further study and subpoenas were necessary. Their unfulfilled visit was not without consequences: over 100 teachers in the area were subpoenaed, and HUAC took great care to send copies of their files to their local school boards. Most of the teachers were fired.

This time the Un-Americans announced their arrival in a less glorious fashion. A week before the hearings, small stories appeared in the back pages of local papers.

Nonetheless, reaction began immediately, on campuses and off. All around S.F. Bay, meetings were held, generally small but determined to prepare a proper welcome.

In Berkeley we organized a group called Students for Civil Liberties, and set up a petition table at the usual place, Bancroft and Telegraph. By the time HUAC arrived, over 1,600 signatures had been collected. People wrote letters to the *Daily Cal;* sent postcards to Congressman Cohelan; spoke at noon rallies (we were in the election-campaigning time); and just talked and spread the word. During the week before HUAC's arrival, the *Daily Cal* also ran excerpts from the official Committee records (which I had the pleasure of assembling after reading 300 pages of transcript to refresh my memory).

And during this week other things were happening in the community. Two subpoenaed grammar school teachers were summarily fired by the Berkeley School Board. A vast outcry in their behalf arose. I did not make the meeting in their defense, but the papers reported the crowd at an unprecedented 1,000. The Board was forced to delay the firing of one and to rehire the other. But I was present at an open meeting of the East Bay Ad Hoc Committee, an organization formed last year to combat HUAC. It maintained a tenuous, dormant existence, until the Monday meeting. The subpoenaes from the East Bay, some thirteen persons, were there to speak. There were also 500 people from Berkeley, almost none of them students—the meeting had no publicity on campus. I have not heard such sincere applause since I heard Walter conduct *Das Lied von der Erde* in Chicago three years ago. I remember saying to Richard, that the term "grass-roots" has long been out of favor in American sociological jargon, but that perhaps it is time to consider it once again.

For some reason, HUAC's arrival was postponed two days; the announcement was again buried on the back pages. One can only guess why. Since HUAC neither issued more subpoenas nor left town, it was probably an attempt to throw us off balance, as one steps back before an oncoming punch. This was a mistake on their part; it was not a punch, but a wave; and they stepped back just far enough to receive the full crest on Saturday.

It's hard to say what the Committee's nominal purpose was. Last time they were investigating "Communist infiltration into schools," and only teachers were called. Some of these were subpoenaed this time too, but only if they had not lost their jobs the first time. But this time students, longshoremen, commentators, and others were called. Among the subpoenaes was Doug, an eighteen-year-old Berkeley student. When we thought of what his summons meant, the first inkling of what was really happening began to dawn on us.

You might know that Willis, chairman of the visiting subcommittee, comes from the Third Congressional District in Louisiana. He has a constituency of over 300,000. Many are Negro. It is said that 10,000 names were dropped from the registration roles shortly before the last election, and that Willis was elected by 8,000 votes. Similarly, Arens, HUAC's Counsel, also serves as adviser for a wealthy textile manufacturer in the East. Arens earns his keep by helping the textiler award large grants to people who seem to have an avenue for proving Negroes genetically inferior. And so it goes.

Obviously Doug was not called up because of his strong, hardcore political past. With the Committee's voluminous files, surely they could find someone in the area with more of a past and more to tell them. But Doug had been very active in CORE and the picketing of Kress/Woolworth stores in Berkeley to support the sit-in strikes down South. He also participated in Peace Walks, and worked against capital punishment. But I think his CORE activities were the deciding factor, for many of those subpoenaed had been similarly active.

Anyway, the purpose of subpoenaing him was clear. A slow tide of student activity in matters political and social has been rising in the past year, in conjunction with immense doings in the rest of the world. Doug was spotlighted as a clear warning to the rest of us: "Do as he has been doing, and you may be sure that we will take note of you." And there is a less obvious conclusion to be drawn from the list of subpoenas: those who run things are hurting as a result of the semiorganized picketing against discrimination that has sprung up around the country.

The hearings opened at 9:30 A.M., Thursday, May 12, without fanfare, in San Francisco. I got to City Hall at 9. A crowd of 150, half students, stood in line to attend the hearings. Outside there was a slow picket of maybe fifty. During the morning it grew to a hundred, while the crowd inside the rotunda swelled to 400. We went up and down the line passing out leaflets and copies of the current *Daily Cal*, which had a front-page story on the Committee.

We found to our dismay that Willis had issued a number of white cards permitting entrance to the hearings. They were given to members of the DAR, and also to the American Legion and to the Southern Baptists, who had just passed a resolution commending the Committee for its vigilance. Resentment began to grow among the people who had hoped to attend the hearings. Legally they are open to the public. But the Supervisors' Room, which seats almost 300, was largely filled by holders of white cards.

Photographers and reporters were sprinkled sparsely through the assemblage, and a few police were on hand to handle a routine situation. Despite the packing of the house, perhaps 100 non-card carriers managed to gain entrance. The rest were relatively silent during the morning, standing patiently. I left early to help set up loudspeakers in Union Square for a rally featuring local Assemblymen and an Episcopalian minister. When noon came, most of the crowd followed, leaving a hundred or so at the door waiting to dispossess the carded ladies.

The rally was a success, which surprised us. We filled Union Square, maybe 2,000 people, and the speakers were very well received. We marched back to the Civic Center along Market Street; I was one of the monitors. I stayed in the Square until the whole line had filed past, then walked and ran as fast as I could to reach City Hall, hoping to get into the hearings in the afternoon. The line was so long that I couldn't catch its head. By the time I reached the Hall, winded, there were 300 in the rotunda, talking in eager whispers and awaiting the 1:30 opening of the doors. I joined them right before the main entrance, as several girls had held my position, and waited also.

Then things began to happen. We found that the white-card carriers had resumed their seats, in even greater force than in the morning, through a *side* door, and that a small number of us, perhaps seventy, were to be admitted. By early afternoon the crowd was in a mild uproar. Irritated by the injustice of the cards, tired from walking and picketing, and packed body-to-body in the great rotunda, everyone striving to be as close as possible to the door, we began to chant: "Let Us In   Let Us In   Let us in Letusin Letusinletusin . . ." Chanting alternated with singing, mostly songs such as the National Anthem which everyone knew. An attempt was made to get everyone to sit down, but unrest was so great, and the packing so close, that this was impossible.

Meanwhile, the hearings inside had not been proceeding in the most orderly fashion possible. In the morning most of the time had been devoted to the ritual invocation of the deities (God, Mother, Ike) and to the testimony of several trained seals. There was grumbling from the non-card spectators during this, but peace had held.

That afternoon was different. "Unfriendly" witnesses were called to the stand and greeted with the usual harassment, badgering and pointless questions, unveiled insinuations. In past hearings the normal response was silence. This time they kept trying to read statements questioning their presence there, the legality of the committee and of Willis's election. They kept demanding that the hearings be made open to all, as had been legally promised. And so unrest on the inside grew in proportion to that on the outside. Soon the back half of the room began cheering the witnesses—Doug was testifying at this time, and of course his response was very partisan—and jeering in disbelief whenever Willis or Arens made a particularly outrageous statement. The peace was not aided by the forcible ejection of several people, in particular Archie Brown, a Communist labor man, who was hauled out yelling "I want white cards too, Mr. Willis. I want to see my friends here!" Outside, he gave an account of what was happening within the chamber. The feeling of "sellout" grew.

Nor was the peace inside aided by the passing-out of anti-Semitic pamphlets by members of the DAR, several of whose girded damsels applied patriotic kicks to students and others being escorted forcibly from the room. And so it was that the uproar grew inside, and soon, as the chant "Let us in" filtered through the thick doors, the answering chant filtered out: "Let them in." At one point the back of the room rose spontaneously, stood on their chairs, and sang the National Anthem, while the entire front of the room and the Committee itself sat stonily, looking neither to right nor left.

Outside the chant progressed. More press arrived, eagerly photographing and interviewing. Suddenly the riot squad arrived also, in white crash helmets, baggy breeches, with guns and billies, and polished boots. Without warning they began to drag a rope before the door, pushing their way through the people gathered there. One woman had a heart attack, a pregnant dame was knocked down and kicked, and general confusion prevailed for a minute. When the air cleared there were over thirty cops before the door and behind the rope. Singing and chanting began anew. The noise was kept in relative order by those of us who were monitoring but kept recurring spontaneously. A number of people were roughed up by the riot squad. I was almost smashed in the face for attempting to pacify an officer who was shaking a young girl, and accidentally brushing his black leather jacket. The riot squad was particularly noisy and nasty, and immediately earned the label "storm troopers, SS men." The sheriff came and spoke to us in a very politic tone, promising that small groups would be admitted to the hearing room. His promises never materialized, but by the time this became clear it was late enough that no new uproar began.

Meanwhile, inside the room, things quieted down. A full complement of cops appeared along the walls, and the ejection of still more protesting spectators kept the disturbance at a minimum. In defense, the students inside began humming *America the Beautiful* very softly, ceasing whenever an officer came near. I was told that the impression was very beautiful.

We went home determined to return to the hearings, although no organized demonstration had been planned for Friday. Despite the occasional disorder, which never exceeded noise, our protest had gone quite well. Our reception in some newspapers was hysterical, babbling about a riot being barely averted by the quick action of the police force. This was not the case: the police did much more toward inciting riot than quelling same. Their actions added a new factor to the crowd's emotions, that of resentment toward the cops as well. Not the cops themselves, but the riot squad; but this was a distinction that easily blurred.

I was not at the hearings on Friday—Black Friday, Friday the 13th—and, all things considered, I am sorry. I'd been awake for three days running, and went Thursday night to hold vigil at San Quentin, on the eve of yet another execution. I got home shortly before noon, wrote a story for the *Daily Cal* on the vigil, and passed out. Charles came and woke me at 10, told me to call my parents because they were worried about me, and to get the hell over to Stephens Union to an emergency meeting.

In the week since, I have pieced together what happened at the hearings Friday. The morning was like the previous afternoon: singing and chanting, newspapermen, and discontent. The picket outside was over 200 strong and continued the whole day long. Many more police were present. The barricade was in place before the demonstrators arrived, and the "friendly spectators" were already in their seats. A loudspeaker was set up outside, in the Civic Park, to broadcast the hearings, and a large crowd gathered around it. Only about ten demonstrators were admitted to the hearing room. News of this quickly got around and increased the tension among the 200 or so who still waited in the rotunda.

The clamor for fair admittance grew to such a pitch that the sheriff came around at 11 and asked the demonstrators (who were largely students) to return at 1:45.

He told them that people, including card-holders, would be admitted on a first-come, first-served basis then. He was heeded, and things became less noisy. Little happened inside the hearing room, save that the witnesses were raking the Committee over the coals as best they were able; the crowd at the loudspeakers heard this, and cheered often.

Willis had given the sheriff and other police a tongue-lashing, describing them as "panty-waists" for the newspapers and saying that with a well-organized force the previous day's disturbances would not have happened. During the late morning in the hearing room men came in with large pictures just out of the developer's room, trying to pick out those who had been particularly troublesome the day before from among the few students there.

Active demonstration within the building ceased entirely at noon, as people awaited fruition of the sheriff's promise. Let me quote you from two eyewitness accounts—we have been collecting them as an aid to the defense of the arrested students, and in preparation for a history of the three days:

"By the time the doors opened, our line contained two hundred persons. As we stood, quietly and respectfully, the earlier denizens of the chamber began filing back into the hearing room. A cordon of policemen stepped in front of our line and pushed several students away from the doors to make way for the card-holders. They were admitted through the side doors, doors inviolate to our group. A girl shouted, 'They're letting in the white cards.' Another voice from the line replied, 'Shut up, let's give them a chance.' Finally the card-holders were inside the chamber. 'We've got room for fifteen people,' a voice said. A shout, a cry, arose from the line: 'No, no, no!' Another voice attempted to quiet us. 'Shhh, give him a chance to speak,' people said. 'There's room for five people.' 'No, no, no,' was chanted again. Then the group beneath the rotunda chanted and sang. Suddenly we were flanked by additional officers; they formed a cordon between ourselves and the chamber entrance.

"We stood on the landing, stunned; they, behind the barricades. Someone started a song; at once we were all singing the old song, 'We shall not, we shall not be moved . . .' A shout: 'Sit Down!!' As it re-echoed, we sat, in a pattern which reminded me of a flower.

"The water struck out at us without warning. The police, in seeking to disperse us, had turned on a high-pressure fire hose. It had the opposite effect. The demonstration surged forward, not to seize the hose or the attackers, but to defy them. The singing rose over the sound of the spray and we pressed together. The police were prepared for this and charged us, their clubs swinging. I turned and saw a youth lying face-down on the upper step. He was moving slightly and several students tried to reach him. They were knocked back by clubs. The police were holding him down. He somehow managed to stand—blood had already covered a third of his face. About sixty persons huddled together in the face of two heavy streams of water and about twenty policemen. We sang the National Anthem. The water stopped. It looked like we had won.

"A new phase began. More policemen filed into the rotunda from every door. They pushed and pulled people down the steps. Again the cry to sit down. The stairs were filled with demonstrators. The hoses were turned on again. The police were using the hall as a sluiceway for human beings. A girl was lying unconscious on the hall floor, a policeman dragging her limp form onward.

A man rushed out to the officer and hassled for a moment. He stopped, and the man opened the girl's eyelids. 'She's alive,' he said. At my side a man laughed."

—Joel Brewer's and Alan Shelly's accounts

Everyone save the police testifies to the following facts: there was no violence from the students at any time, and almost all of them were seated with their hands in their pockets or behind their backs when the "riot" started; promise was given of fair seating, and the demonstration was conducted peacefully on that promise; no warning was given to clear the rotunda before the hoses were brought forth and turned on; the demonstrators at no time "charged the door" or the hoses; the police in general, and the riot squad in particular, were guilty of what can only be described by a badly overworked word: "brutality." The particular tales are too many to give in full: unconscious students were dragged down sixty-some steps *by their heels*, their heads bumping on the marble and the girls' skirts over their heads; a riot squad man detoured a few feet to step on the outstretched hand of an unconscious demonstrator, spraining or breaking a finger; men were held down and clubbed or kicked in the groin. The scene has been described as the Odessa Steps and few who were present can speak of it calmly. Sixty-four students and others, including five minors, were arrested and jailed. They included picketers, spectators, and passersby.

The newspaper reports were biased to the point of incoherence. UPI sent out a dispatch initially accurate and favorable to the demonstrators; but within half an hour reversed their ground totally. The final consensus by the papers was that the riot started when a student grabbed a cop's billy and slugged him with it.* No mention was made of the card-pass system, of the promises voided, or of the actions of the police in detail. Two eyewitness stories said explicitly: "I saw no evidence of police brutality . . ." Yet the papers betray themselves: they say 400+ cops were at the scene when the riot was on (most already there), and offer as a peak estimate of the demonstrators within the rotunda, 250.

The rest of the day passed in relative peace. No one was allowed inside the building, and the picket line—which did not waver during the "riot"—maintained and increased its order and strength. When the hearings ended, people went home to spread the word.

And so it was that I was roused to attend an emergency meeting to plan for the last day of the hearings. It began with fifteen people; by the time I got there, it had been moved twice, finally ending up in the basement of a co-op, and had grown to 800. Eyewitness accounts of the day were given, Doug spoke, a defense fund was set up in the form of a wastebasket passed around the room. It took in $450 from the students present (few of whom had been in San Francisco that day, or, indeed, the day before). There was an air of great excitement marshalled into order by the sense that something of extreme importance was afoot.

The meeting itself was unbelievable: on this campus, where you can't raise fifty people for a poetry reading, when only 1,000 students will sign an anti-ROTC petition in two weeks of circulation, where attempts to organize peace programs, discussion groups, and similar things have met repeated failure, 800 people came to an informal,

* This was later disproved in court.

unpublicized meeting. It was not the violence alone that brought them, or that made them stay past midnight; they knew what was afoot.

Afterwards twenty-five of us met in a nearby apartment to finish planning the demonstration, taking upon ourselves the task of organizing and controlling the picket lines. That our protest was to take solely the form of picketing is testimony to the feelings of the crowd. Overriding our sense of shock and outrage was this sense of responsibility for the coming day. We realized the necessity for maintaining a strong and orderly picket, and the grave possibility of the worst bloodbath in the city's history. The tactics of the police had made it clear that we could expect no aid in disciplining the line.

We tried to plan for all contingencies: police violence, integration with ILWU pickets, interference by American Legion goons, reinforcements from SF State, agitation for violent protest from within our own ranks . . . We chose a steering committee of six, laid plans for liaison with press and police, and drew up picket regulations and sent a group off to mimeograph 1,000 copies. Three hours later we adjourned, after providing for a meeting before the demonstration began and setting up rides for the carless monitors.

I was present all the next day, as a monitor on the line. People were barred from the entire building. A line was formed ending at the steps, containing potential spectators. They were admitted in small groups throughout the day. Though the white cards were still packing the chamber, a fairly large proportion of non-card carriers got in. The line conducted itself at all times in an orderly fashion, waiting patiently for admittance. Several hundred police were there, including thirty cavalry and forty motorcycle police (riot squad), who kept circling the building. Most of the garden-variety policemen stood silently during the entire day, neither making comments nor attempting to interfere with the proceedings.

The loudspeakers were again set up in the park. Three or four thousand people came to listen to them and watch the picketing. Most stayed the entire day. As a whole they were amazingly partisan, and grew steadily more so as the day progressed. One reason for this was that the microphones were placed so that the whispers of the Committee members to each other were clearly audible, and most damning. The crowd's sympathies were very clear: they booed the trained seals, cheered whenever a subpoenae managed to say something, and reacted loudly to the testimony of Sheriff Cahill and Inspector Maguire, who gave sterling, whitewashed accounts of the police action the previous day. There were few students in the crowd, so the noise cannot be held to their account. Nor were there any agitators.

But the picket line was the most significant part of what happened. We began marching half an hour early, because there was no other way to keep so many people in order. The line's strength never fell below 400, and in the early afternoon there were 1,200, many with signs. A large percentage were students, of course, but there were labor men, mothers with children, businessmen, and a general sprinkling of the surrounding community. We had tried to weed out signs explicitly referring to the police violence the day before. Most of the pickets complied gladly when we explained that we hoped not to inflame the situation still further, and that we wished to focus attention on the main aim of the demonstration— the protest of the Committee's activities. During the day girls ran out and brought Cokes back to the monitors, who never left their posts during the nine hours. When people broke to grab a bite of lunch they often brought back drinks which were passed, hand to hand, down the line. At 3, when legs began to really drag, I started giving out the remnants of a roll of Life Savers. The response was so heartening that I took a couple of dollars and went for more. We passed them out one by one. By the time the hearings ended we distributed over 120 rolls. People lit up like light bulbs, and the humor of the act combined with the small lift it gave, helped maintain morale in those slump hours.

This line was our triumph. Its behavior was flawless. Through the whole day there was not a song, not a shout, not a cheer, not a boo. Many in the line had been there the day before; many others had heard first-hand hysterical accounts. Picketing is hard work; an hour on the line is at least the equivalent of an hour of hiking: the steady, constrained pace and the windblown signs combine to make it extremely tiring. Thus the picketers were irritable, resentful, and tired—and, being mostly young, filled with the kind of energy and emotion that is so hard to repress, which usually finds outlet in shouts and singing—or in the traditional panty raids.

Saturday the line was dead silent, save for scattered conversation, and its order never broke. We started strong, we held strong, and we finished strong, maintaining the line almost half an hour after the Committee left the building at the close of the hearings. The line was single file, doubled around the large block, and spaced almost militarily. And it held, it held! When six police jumped a bearded photographer on the steps and hustled him into the paddywagon amid boos from the crowd, the line continued. When Arens appeared on the balcony, the crowd greeted him with jeering Fascist salutes, and sang "Arens is a Fascist . . . Committee go home . . ." The line, a thousand strong, marched in silence. Police jerked a Negro out of the admission line and began pummeling him and dragging him off, and a cry of protest arose. The line held. The horsemen started toward the crowd, and the crowd gathered itself and came forward shouting to meet them. The line slowed down. During the closing speeches, the pickets and crowd were explicitly described as Communists. A vast boo arose, the sort of sound a hometown baseball crowd will make in the midst of a hot pennant race when an umpire makes a flagrantly outrageous decision. Our line remained slowly marching, in perfect spacing and perfect silence. I cannot describe the sound; it had a knife-edge behind it, the most ugly sound I ever hope to hear. I think it was at that moment that all of us had the frightening vision of just what the crowd's attitude really was, and of what it could do if anything began to happen. I know I had this feeling, I can call it up now, like the chill that remains in your bones after standing long hours in the cold. Yet the line held, without a sound, without a break in pace.

The police watched all this in silence, and I think they were impressed by what they saw—the normal squad, at least; the SS men kept looking for trouble. The closing speeches went on for close to an hour, and it was then that the real feeling of triumph began to hit us. The line tightened its formation and increased its pace, and we began to smile. Some students had gotten inside, either awaiting their turn in the hearings or not having left afterwards. They were singing and chanting. We heard them, loud and choired. Then Willis began cursing us in his closing speech; you can imagine what that did for our morale.

The Committee left without fanfare, with no announcement until ten minutes after their actual departure. And the manner of their leaving was interesting. Not in the fancy Cadillac of previous days, smiling Committeemen pausing at the door to flashbulbs and the cheers of the DAR. No. In a small white car, flanked fore and aft by cop cars, unannounced, through a side door, without pausing for photographs . . .

Writing now, so much later, it is hard to convey the feelings we had. During the whole closing speech I stood at my corner, policing the line, relaying word of the testimony and Willis's rantings, words of encouragement: "It's almost over . . . they're in the closing speeches . . . keep ranks until the crowd has dispersed . . . Willis is cursing us now . . . five feet apart and slower, please (but it was impossible to slow them!) . . . that's our boys in there, yes, ours are singing . . ." I stood, sunburned of face, as were most of the marchers, smiling, proudly feeling my white armband with the black M for monitor on it, smiling and smiling till my face was fixed in that expression. And crying, without control, crying with love and pride for the people and how they had handled themselves and what they had done. Two weeks ago, when they killed Chessman, I had come close to crying from sheer rage and frustration. This time it was different, this time we had won. And all of us knew this. We did not dare to say it, did not dare break the rigid control that had kept the line going all day. But I was not the only one crying.

That night in Berkeley we had a small party, attended mostly by the "hard-core, experienced agitators" as we had been described. And it was a victory party: we sang "We shall not be moved" as I have never heard it sung, as a saga of the three days, event by event, and we sang it for a full half-hour of intensity and enthusiasm, stopping only when the guitarists could play no longer. We had the first papers then, the big headlines: "5000 AT CITY HALL," and the references, the forced references, to the discipline and deportment of the line we had held. And here too was another sign of triumph: the headlines had changed. Friday morning we were "a screaming mob," Friday afternoon "Communist rioters," Saturday morning "agitated demonstrators." And Saturday night and Sunday morning? "People." Just that.

• • • •

I have told you the events. Now let me tell you their meaning.

It is hard to know where to begin; I think I will plunge right in. These three days as a whole were almost certainly *the most significant political event in this country in the past fifteen years, and possibly for the whole previous quarter-century.*

These days show that HUAC and its kindred spirits have reached and passed the point at which they begin to evoke more anger than fear by their actions. The testimony is clear: the vast majority of the crowd, and almost all of the picketers, were there not for the spectacle, but because they knew what was happening. They were there for protest, and the deportment of the line, that wonderful line, makes this statement unshakable. There were friends whom I never would have expected to see, marching silently, without complaint, for the whole day. There were people from the community who had not even signed a petition for decades. But it is the students I am most concerned with. We set up a table on campus to help raise a defense fund for those who were arrested. Contributions have been coming in at a rate of over $200 a day. From the students who before would give money only for Greek Week or Spring Sing. The editorials have been saying about the riots, "too bad . . . they have clinched the survival of the Committee for another twenty years . . ." If testimony is needed that the case is much the opposite, it is to be found in the gallon mayonnaise jar that is emptied and taken to the bank every few hours.

Meanwhile, elsewhere in the City, picketing of Woolworth's and Kress's was continuing in force as it has for several months. And a peace parade, the Little Summit March, was marching toward Union Square and a meeting of 3,000 people. Conservatively, at least 8,000 people were actively demonstrating throughout San Francisco that day. Do you remember my poem, "The Third Sunday in May"? I wrote it a year ago, after another peace walk. Only a hundred of us marched that day.

I keep wanting to dwell on the determination of the people in the picket line. They were mostly students, and for the first time in many years, students who knew what was happening and why. I've been in college four years now, active in political affairs, a close watcher of the atmosphere in the community in general and among my coevals in particular. These three days have furnished a solid base on which to set the hopes which I and so many others have carried so long in our virtual solitudes.

Student apathy is, by now, legendary on the campuses. Yet here is the sign that we were not in a condition of death, but one of stasis. Oh, there have been portents, most notably what has been happening in the South. But the Southern incidents are not overtly political in the sense that the San Francisco incidents have been. This is not to take away the rightful honor of the Negro (and white) students there—but the fact remains, the expression here was essentially different.

What has happened here is partly a product of the locale, a fairly liberal community by tradition, though not particularly so in the past decade. But it is primarily a product of the times. We knew on Thursday, and said as much, that the mere physical sound we raised in the rotunda was a sound that has not been heard in this country in connection with a political situation since the middle of the Depression. The days that followed confirmed and strengthened this knowledge. Two years ago, one quarter the number of people could not have been rallied to oppose the Un-Americans. Two weeks ago the "hard core" of students on local campuses who were willing to drop whatever work they had and strive toward organizing a "reception" could not have exceeded 100. But tomorrow, or five years from now, the number will be ten times that: everyone who was there Friday or marched Saturday, or has friends who did.

And I see something of more significance even than the coming death of the Committee and the reawakening of students. I see the rise of a new Left in this country, a Left of a nature that has not been seen within this century. It will be a Left unconnected with the past. The Communists as a group are dead, though the Committee will go on flushing phantom dragons for quite a while before it expires. The Socialist movement is split into many small groups, and the movement so headstrong among its younger elements several years ago for a United Front has come to very little. I think the new Left will rise, is rising, almost without influence from the splintered old Left. The remnants of the old Left are looked upon almost as curiosities, with no one wanting very much either to emulate them in their verbal violence or to hate them.

Instead a new Left is coming, a Left of "independent radical activity": non-partisan, indiscriminate in its condemnation of reactionaries and old-style radicals, not inclined to organization (which will make it difficult to trace its rise), and uncapturable by either the splintered old Left or by progressive elements in present major parties. The Democrats had their chance with Stevenson after '52. They muffed it badly, and I do not believe they will regain it. A strong position as a peace party might have captured this new movement had it been taken in preparation for the '56 election or even, possibly, for the coming one this Fall. But I think matters are beyond capture now.

It is hard to predict what the course of events will be for this New Left, if indeed my surmise as to its existence and development is correct. I think there will be little or no permanent organizational tendencies, few or no alignments with established forces, much confusion as to its real nature, futile attempts made both to capture it and to stamp it out, much seemingly grass roots activity on the pressing matters of the day—disarmament, bombs, peace, witch-hunting, capital punishment, integration. I think all the elements are here and clear for those able to read them, and I regret that I am not myself more skilled in doing so.

But I know—and I am not alone in my feeling—that this decade will make a great deal of history. And I believe also that this new Left is an historical/social inevitability. Rather than delay its birth, the events since the war have been most necessary and have gone a long way toward shaping what will come. So much silence will have an out, and a peculiar and potent one indeed.

It is one thing to say that we are living in the middle of history; everyone is aware of this. It is quite another thing to *know* that this is so, to participate in actions that one knows are in the growing-bud of the historical tree. Pardon me if my surmises as to the significance and implications of what is happening seem to overreach themselves. I have given them much thought. You might show this letter to some of those embittered, defeated people you write me about. California air does not bring political action on such a basis, despite its other salutary effects. Have heart: the Revolution is coming faster than we knew, though it will be a very different sort of revolution indeed from any that have preceded it.

Love & Heart,
Michael

Sometimes, in the intensity of Coming Together, Time's weather clears, and you can see for years and years.

Even the newspapers caught a version of the flash that time, and in an avalanche of editorials first began to recognize America's youth as a threat to ultimate law and order. In these 1960 demonstrations you can also see the early stages of our relationship with the police, and how we emphasized passive self-restraint in the face of violence. We had—dare I say it?—a certain sense of civilization then, enough even to be distressed by girls' skirts being rudely uplifted. But surely the signs of violence we were given on the marble steps of City Hall told us what to expect for our pains, and for later in the decade.

Whatever's proved true about us, we were right about HUAC. In those three days—and in the informational campaigns we carried on for the next few years—the mystique of HUAC's unchallenged omnipotence was shattered. It hasn't visited the Bay Area since, and it cut out traveling altogether for a few years. By the time it summoned Jerry Rubin to Washington for his Vietnam Day Committee activities, in 1966, America's climate was maximally Liberal, and HUAC was fair play for mockery—

Jerry appeared in a moth-eaten American Revolution uniform, drawing a wide and appreciative press.

But HUAC is not dead, it has only been renamed; and a new chapter has already opened in the annals of witch-hunting. The victims now are "agitators," the attacks less comprehensively organized but increasing. Since 1967, Federal and local judiciaries have been drumming up conspiracy trials, and since Cambodia and Agnew, ad-hoc committees have been springing up to purge college faculties and welfare agencies of subversives. After the sentencing of the Chicago Eight in 1969, we held a protest in dozens of cities, called The Day After. It marked our resumption of organized opposition to witch-hunting—which we will need to develop more strongly, given what we're headed into.

1964–66
The Turning Years

Later there would be confusion. Many would come to believe that the "youth revolution" began in 1964 with the first major campus disruption, the Berkeley Free Speech Movement. For those who got their comprehension from the mass media, and for the young who turned active after the New Left had come to seem simply one among many currents of change, a sense of the earlier roots would be lost.

But the FSM marked a turning point, rather than a beginning. By fall 1964 white involvement in Civil Rights was at its height, and the student movement was seven years old in Berkeley. This was four years, one under-graduate generation, after the HUAC "riots" made Berkeley nationally notorious. During these years many came to Berkeley, as I had earlier, to grow in its ambience. But already the context had changed. The Movement itself had become a presence, forcing all the young to begin in some way to define themselves with respect to it. Rock and psychedelics were still newly rising: through 1963, student action was the only major expression that clearly belonged to the young. And in the Movement, many of us came to feel that at last we had something worth defending, besides our naked souls.

In defending it, in the FSM, the energy and anger of the white youth of Affluent America turned for the first time against our parent institutions. We revolted against the university, long felt to have gone awry in its function of nurturing, because it tried to kill what was being born in us. This made for heavy symbolic theater, whose images saturated the nation and changed minds many ways. From this conflict emerged the motto, "Don't trust anyone over thirty"; and after it, talk of Generation Gap began.

We were turning: not so much left or right, and not only against, but into . . . something else, without a name. During the next two years we grew older, and easier about rejecting our parent institutions now that our anger was out in the open. We began to experiment with the seeds of alternate institutions: in communes, free universities, underground papers, rock events, be-ins and street theater, and so on. By 1967, when the Haight—our Mark I ghetto community—was exposed, it was clear that the Movement had expanded beyond all political bounds and recognition, and was on some verge—perhaps premature, but real enough—of carrying us through deep transformation into a new human culture.

I stand at the edge of the next decade. Already the lives of my friends are torn with agony, attempting this transformation, what little we can grasp. Looking back on the FSM, its symbolic value is clear now, and justifies its enshrinement in our legends. For the first time, we acted collectively on a condition of our own immediate life, acted on behalf of ourselves as a class whose responsibility is the future, rather than on behalf of oppressed minorities, or of humanity in the abstract. It was as if a signal had been given: after this time began our deliberate attempts to construct new conditions for our becoming.

• • • •

Insofar as this book is a history, it is not so much one of events as of the perceptions and consciousness that attended them. Please understand how limited our consciousness was during the FSM. Some of us already called ourselves hippies, with a small "h," but what was on our minds was a simple longing for community, and not the suspicion that we might amount even to a counter-culture. When it came to action, we still saw ourselves simply as American citizens fighting for our rights under law.

Suddenly what had been a somewhat unorthodox movement for social reform began to mutate wildly. We who were caught up in these changes struggled to find or make new terms to comprehend them. Always the Movement was a process of redefining ourselves. In reflecting that, this book is faithful. The pieces that follow come from these years of early confusion when new images were dawning.

The process was amazingly rapid. Thirty months after the FSM, not only we but all America were trying to grasp the presentiment and terms of a new culture. Hastily the media codified the devitalized icon of the Hippy—flower-child innocent and ecstatic, but shorn of his roots, political and other. A year later the Yippies put balls on the image—help us, sisters, our icons still are sexist—and came to Chicago hand in hand with radical politics. We are still searching for a next image, both harder and softer, to guide us.

But from the FSM till the Haight nothing was even this clear. We were just coming to feel the broader effects of our turning on, just realizing our need for new icons.

These pieces from the Turning Years are an index to some of the stages our consciousness passed through as we puzzled over our behavior. They are my personal index, but the quick progression of their perceptions was shared by many.

Civil Rights and the Free Speech Movement

The perspective of these perceptions is pretty weird. They were written in a state of controlled hysteria, after the FSM climaxed in 800 arrests and the first successful campus strike, as background material for an ACLU group preparing briefs for our legal defense. Yet the view of new radical activity with which they open is abbreviated from a paper written in 1960 (for a SLATE-sponsored conference at Mount Madonna, which turned out to be the first national meeting of New Left groups). For the character the white Movement would have through the first five years of the Sixties was already clearly defined. It remained to be elaborated, and this article goes on to trace its development in connection with Civil Rights.

All that I wrote then is true enough. As I explained when the article was published in the campus literary magazine,* "It has recently become fashionable to explain away the events of the FSM in terms of alienation, the Multiversity, etc. Surely such factors are important, and my own thinking runs more or less along such lines. Still, a balanced explanation should give proper weight to the political atmosphere in which FSM occurred."

But it's also true that I was leaning over backwards to

* *Occident*, fall 1964. See also "New Faces on the Picket Lines," *Occident*, fall 1960.

*give a rational account, and to not appear a raving apoc-
alyptic tormented by visions. I was a young intellectual
acid-head, my mind absolutely shattered by a new experience, trying to speak plausibly about what led up to it, to
a pretty straight group of liberal lawyers. At that time we
had scarcely any words of a new vocabulary, other than
"trip" and "community," and I think it was as much for
my own reassurance as for theirs that I tried to explain us
so familiar.*

The new radicals

The "new radicals" came out of a landscape of fear.
They had a moral ideology and were willing to take action
to support it. In post-McCarthy America, to do more
than send a letter to a congressman was to be "radical." To
picket or to sit-in was to protest with a new voice.

The trademark of old radicalism was a political ideology
with historical roots and structural goals. The trademark
of the new radicals is a primitive, moral ideology. Their
activity is aimed at issues, not at political or economic
goals. And the issues are moral ones: peace, Civil Rights,
capital punishment. This is often mistaken by onlookers
whose thoughts are tied to the past, since some issues
(like HUAC) have political overtones and are still the
concern of the old radicals. But always, if one listens, one
hears the simple, naïve, and stubborn cry that distinguishes
the new radicals: "This is *wrong*, it must stop!"

The old radicals are still here, though the pressure of the
new radicals has made them less programmatic, more issue-
oriented. Their numbers have grown: at Berkeley now
(1964) there may be 200 members in the splinter Socialist
groups, of whom perhaps fifty are active. The record of

the past five years of student activity shows that the new radicals set the pace and choose their own tactics and specific goals. In general, it seems that the old radicals have been co-opted by the new, rather than conversely.

Why the new radicals?

They are young, and come from a grab bag of backgrounds. Of those arrested in San Francisco and Berkeley in 1962–1963, over half were twenty or under, and most came from politically inactive families.

Why do they appear? The answer seems to lie in their education, in the broad sense of the term. Mass media have left marks on them. Newspapers and television brought them, inescapably, a childhood of scandal: McCarthy, contaminated cranberries, Bobby Baker, fixed fights, the U-2 flights, Stevenson lying in the U.N. . . . the list is endless. The paperback revolution brought them *Walden* on the one hand and, on the other, *The Organization Man*, Baldwin, *The Hidden Persuaders, Growing Up Absurd*, and dozens of similar books, in millions of copies. An improving educational system, and the growing willingness of teachers to speak out again after the McCarthy Era, made discussion of social problems commonplace in the high schools.

Other factors are involved. It seems reasonable to connect the eight televised years of Eisenhower's Presidency with the lack of faith the new radicals have in purely political solutions, or to link civics classes at the time of the Southern sit-ins with the recent Civil Rights arrests in San Francisco. However complex the factors, the new radicals are a force on the American scene, and the size and frequency of their protests will continue to increase. Dramatic events like the HUAC and Sheraton-Palace demonstrations are not isolated incidents, but are part of a moving and growing social change.

The beginning: a new kind of silence

Strong forces built up the potential for the sudden emergence of the new radicals in the North. Their appearance was triggered by a new kind of silence in the South, the silence of young people in buses and at lunch counters. It was a waiting silence, not a fearful silence; and it said, "Now it is time." The bus boycotts of 1955, the sit-ins at lunch counters, and the students waiting lonely at classroom doors were visible to the whole country. They carried a special message for the new radicals.

By the end of the McCarthy Era it seemed that no effective action toward social and political goals was possible: in particular, the young had never known any. But suddenly, in the South, people were taking action. It was a new *kind* of action, morally unquestionable, and often illegal. Its tactics were dramatic and unprecedented. Its goals were limited and clear. It produced instant and dramatic heroes and leaders. It broke with all the established frameworks, and the spectacle of the NAACP trying to hold back the bus boycotters made a lasting impression.

What happened in the South between 1955 and 1957 left an indelible stamp upon the new radicalism of the North. It said what kind of action was possible, and that such action had for the first time a fighting chance for success. This lesson took some years to catch on: Southern tactics were not adopted until the chanting of the 1960 HUAC protests. At present new radical activity in the North follows the Southern pattern. It is issue-oriented, it depends heavily upon the drama of its protests, and its voice throughout is one of moral outrage. It uses civil disobedience as a tactic, not as an ideology. It has little faith in the established institutions of social and political change, even though it often functions within them, as in doing precinct work. It is resigned to having to step outside the legal framework.

Drama is a constant element of the new radical protests, South and North, and causes much criticism. Many people find it distasteful and claim that emotion in not a "legitimate" weapon of protest. But drama is essential to the organizing of some activities, and to their success. Its emotional component is not aimless. The sight of seated demonstrators waiting for police to descend is meant to evoke the moral nature of the protest.

This dramatic aspect is usually criticized for being "socially acceptable," i.e. faddish. But to the extent that many feel such action to be the *only* effective ("acceptable") form of action, the drama has a moral and an historical sanction rather than a "social" one. For this reason, the dramatic aspects of new radical action are more likely to increase than to decrease in the future.

The consequences of action's being possible

The new radicals' continual concern with the Civil Rights struggle is more evidence that the Southern protests continue to influence the Northern ones. Throughout the North action focuses more consistently on this issue than on any other. Participants are led to take action on other issues, and their sense of purpose and tactics shapes this action. Conversely, Civil Rights ranks are swelled by recruits from other areas of new radical activity. There is, in short, a continuum of activity, in which it is impossible to isolate Civil Rights. Many organizations which participate in Civil Rights activity—SLATE, DuBois Club, YSA, Young Democrats, SDS, etc.—have equally intimate participation *as organizations* in other issues. In organizations which do not participate formally (e.g. Women For Peace) most members are frequent Civil Rights activists.

Thus the Civil Rights struggle interlocks with and binds together the whole spectrum of new student activity. The most obvious reason is the seriousness of the problem and the extent to which it has penetrated the nation's consciousness. But there are subtler reasons. Clancy Sigal says, "The liberals, unable to solve the priorities on their plate, . . . have turned to the one problem that does look as if it *can* be solved within the context of contemporary American existence." (He goes on to speak about broader problems that are being neglected in favor of this one, e.g. how to live a human life with the things we've created.)*

The moral legitimacy of protest and action is most clear on this issue. In a society with a recent history of crushed protest, and no recent history of action, this is important. The fact of *any* action having an effect is tremendously impressive. So far new radical activity has had little effect on other issues (perhaps it can't?), and the new radicals keep turning to the Civil Rights issue for reassurance.

But not only the radicals are concerned with Civil Rights. Many students who have never walked picket lines have an active and vital interest in the Civil Rights movement. They have followed it closely for years and were deeply involved in the recent trials in San Francisco. They

* If you want to learn what happened to the last American Left, read Clancy Sigal's novel *Going Away*, recently reissued in paperback—the only book I know that paints a broad portrait in human depth of the effect of the midcentury Repression.

see, in student involvement in this movement, the best and
most vital expression of their generation. That students
form the core of the struggle, and make unprecedented
changes, is for them a promise, and the only such promise,
that they will be successful in the broader struggles they
may in the future undertake (and on which, in many cases,
they are already embarked).

The Civil Rights movement represents a symbolic promissory note upon their own futures, upon the chances that
their own lives (in areas seemingly far removed from Civil
Rights) will be less futile than they feel those of the
previous generation to have been. The strength of this
feeling must not be underestimated, though it is subter-
ranean. Many students who do not normally participate in
the Civil Rights movement will fight for it when it is
threatened, not only because it is meaningful *per se*, but
also because it is a promise of meaning in their own lives
and work.

Civil rights: 1957–1964*

The involvement of Berkeley students in Civil Rights
activity proceeded in three phases. The first depended on
traditional tactics: resolutions, investigating committees,
and, at its end, pickets. The numbers of students involved
were generally small.

In 1957, the year of the Montgomery bus boycotts, the
student government introduced its first bill concerning discrimination (in the fraternity system), and SLATE began
to organize. SLATE sponsored forums and discussions,
and led the first real student activity in Civil Rights: sup-

* I am indebted to Stevie Lipney and Linda Chown for the material on which this survey is based.

port of a 1959 Fair Housing Ordinance. As if to set a precedent for later years, the first real difficulties between student political activists and the Administration began with this issue, when the Administration tried to take disciplinary action against SLATE for holding a rally on campus. Student protest quelled this action, but the further disagreements between SLATE and the Administration led to SLATE's being thrown off campus in summer 1961.

February 1960 marked the first adoption of the more moderate Southern tactics in Berkeley: a picket of Woolworth/Kress stores, in sympathy with Southern boycotts. Berkeley CORE took it on as a project, and lines of fifteen to sixty marched twice a week in Oakland until March 1961.

Spring 1960 saw the first general peak in student activity. In March, the student government formed Students for Racial Equality to collect money and food for Southern students. SRE tried to function for thirteen months, but Administration regulations totally crippled its efforts: despite raising several thousand dollars and a great deal of food and clothing, the regulations forbade using these fruits for their intended purpose. In frustration, SRE disbanded. Since then, with one abortive exception, student Civil Rights work has abandoned any effort to function as part of the University (though some "off-campus" organizations enjoy limited use of campus facilities).

For the next two years, the pattern of escalation of tactics, commitment, and membership was interrupted. There were many reasons for this. Student activity in general suffered a severe blow when SLATE was suspended in June 1961. New and more restrictive Administration regulations handed down during that summer proved a severe impediment to the functioning of extant

groups and the organization of new ones. Student groups
had to adapt themselves to a minimal dependence upon
the campus.

Perhaps the major reason, however, was the crisis in
world politics. The problems of disarmament and Cuba
fused during these two years, and the new radicals, sensi-
tized by previous crises which threatened nuclear action,
reacted strongly. Thousands gathered to protest the block-
ade of Cuba and the imminence of war. To speak personally, there were times when we half believed that our lives
were numbered in days. Such an atmosphere of trauma
and its aftermath were not conducive to active concern
with gradual social change—to put a deep matter briefly—
and serious Civil Rights activity resumed only after this
atmosphere of nuclear tension had been for some time settled.

This may explain the moderate nature of Civil Rights
activity during this period. The Freedom Rides began in
summer 1961. A SLATE conference that summer led to
fund-raising efforts and committees to investigate discrimination in local housing. A number of Berkeley students
joined the Freedom Rides, and interest ran high on the
campus.

A SLATE Conference in summer 1962 led to the formation of Bay Area Friends of SNCC, which later
branched into eleven chapters. During the next year Civil
Rights activity was largely confined to work for an anti-
discrimination Housing Ordinance and for candidates with
strong Civil Rights platforms.

Their defeat helped prepare the third phase, in which
the local Civil Rights struggle has, in its essential characteristics, finally identified completely with the struggle in
the South. In August 1963, 200,000 people, including many
Berkeley students, staged the March on Washington. The

next month the Birmingham bombing shocked the nation and galvanized the campus. One thousand students heard CORE's James Farmer at a rally, and several days later 5,000 gathered in San Francisco to hear him speak again.

A student referendum to send funds to SNCC failed narrowly. In October Campus CORE was formed, with fifty members. It immediately moved against discriminatory employment, picketing downtown Berkeley businesses. That month action was launched against Mels Drive-In. Of the ninety-three demonstrators arrested, thirty-seven were Berkeley students. Following the arrests demonstrations continued, forcing an eventual agreement.

In February 1964 demonstrations began in San Francisco against the Sheraton-Palace Hotel. From 300 to 2,000 people took part and well over 300 were arrested, many from Berkeley. During a marathon sit-in in March, the Hotel Owners Association capitulated and signed an agreement which resulted in a considerable number of jobs. Immediately the NAACP initiated its Auto Row campaign, which resulted in 330 arrests and another agreement.

Meanwhile there were sit-ins at the Richmond Welfare office, and demonstrations against the hiring practices of the Oakland *Tribune*. Not all of the activity has been this dramatic: one-to-one teaching programs in the Oakland schools have received considerable support from the students, and during the summer and fall over five hundred Berkeley students worked actively to defeat Proposition 14.

The problems of a new movement

The new radicals have created a broad movement of social and political action. Many of the movement's problems depend on its nature, rather than on its goals. It is centered on the campus because the students' lives are centered there. The campus is the center for communication, organization, and non-academic education: at Berkeley these activities do *not* exist detached from the campus. In this respect, the movement is overdependent upon the University, and is extremely sensitive and vulnerable to any change in its formal policies.

Since the movement is issue-oriented, its functioning depends on rapid and flexible means of communication and organization: sudden issues or crises will result in large gatherings mobilizing on several hours' notice. Issue-orientation also determines the educational activities it depends upon: speakers, forums, debates, and distribution of literature. These are directed to a broad audience and are, again, very vulnerable to interference.

The student groups which undertake these activities must function on or near the campus. They lead precarious lives. Their sources of money and facilities are slim and center on the campus; likewise, they recruit members on the campus, particularly at events they sponsor. Once a group's ties with the campus are weakened or broken, it ekes out a minimal existence or dies.

These problems affect all groups. The FSM protests this semester must be viewed in this light. Since the characteristics of the new student activity are embodied most clearly in Civil Rights activity, these problems, which stem from them, are most important for precisely these Civil Rights groups. Thus the "reinterpretations" of the Administration's regulations this semester (and in the past five years!) hit most strongly at the organizational heart of the Civil Rights movement on campus. Both the vehemence and breadth of the protest stemmed partly from this fact.

On advocacy and identity

The most important single substantive issue was the problem of advocacy. Though restrictions on the *form* of campus political activity are onerous, regulation of the *content* of speech is a death blow, since the movement depends so heavily on possibly illegal tactics. The students did *not* protest in favor of illegal advocacy, but in favor of the principle that determination of alleged illegality must be left to the courts. They particularly feared restraints by the Administration on speech which was *not* illegal but led to possibly illegal acts. Such speech was vital to the Civil Rights movement.

The Free Speech Movement and Civil Rights

The initial change in regulations came in mid-September at a time of unprecedented student involvement in election work (five hundred strong) which had gone on all summer. The immediate effect was to cripple the ten student groups working to defeat Proposition 14. Beyond this, it was clear that the new regulations would cripple the Civil Rights movement entirely, since SNCC and CORE were entirely dependent upon the campus, and other groups were largely dependent.

The feeling was widespread that this was *not* accidental. The entire campus was aware of the intense hostilities and pressures generated in the outside community by the events of this spring. Within a week after school began, it was the common supposition, supported by uncautious statements by the Chancellor, that pressure from the Oakland *Tribune* had caused the crackdown. Evidence of discrimination against the Civil Rights movement continued to mount, when tables were set up in violation of regulations. Only students sitting at tables sponsored by groups particularly active in Civil Rights were singled out for discipline by the Administration, and all eight suspended students were active in Civil Rights work.

It is important to understand that the students' concern with free speech was not abstract. The recent successes of the Civil Rights movement left a deep impression as to the immediate practical relevance of Constitutional rights: free speech had been *used*, and was (so the feeling went) being taken away because it had been used. Likewise, many students involved in new radical activity see it as being more relevant to their lives, and to the society, than the necessary evil of amorphous and a-moral formal education. The sense that new radical activity is properly a *student* activity is widespread. By crippling this activity, the Administration was striking at what many felt to be the only "real" part of their education. This feeling was reiterated throughout the semester and helped provide the emotional force behind the FSM.

December 1964

The Birth of the Free Speech Movement

I've said what I think the FSM signified for us collectively. For me personally it was a heavy turning, a re-beginning. It signaled the Tearing Loose—the active beginning of the end of my life within the old institutions, the start of my work as a man in helping make the seed of some Ways adequate and new. We lived a transcendent community into action for a few weeks, and in that light and intensity I just melted inside. I don't know how else to describe it. I had been so long split apart, so slowly and awkwardly trying to come together—drugs, mathematics, vocation, love, therapy, time. And suddenly . . . whap! an historical thunderbolt.

I stood there afterwards, stunned by a flash of some new reality, transient but firm enough to be really grasped. Undeniable. It took years for me to start to sort out what had come to fusion inside, years to figure out what kind of a man my stuff might become, in a place of shared longings. So slowly what has happened becomes real. For the moment of FSM itself, only this much was clear: I was involved to my deepest levels in saying NO to what I had known and was raised to become; and YES to an image half-grasped but at last enough shared that it might become real.

All that is a story for another book. Here is only a fragment, a precise slice out of time, the exact beginning of the FSM. It is as close as I've come to capturing in flight a moment beyond my private life. The morning after we ended our two-day besiegement of the cop car, while people were busy meeting to formally declare the Free Speech Movement and condense its initial structures, I sat down alone with a tape recorder. Torn open, everything boiling in me, I had to get it out some way. It was the instant before we had even grasped the fact of our community, save in action. And the way I know it was a beginning is that it was like dying and being reborn, I felt despair and hope flicker in wild oscillation.

My name is Michael Rossman. I am a graduate student in mathematics at the University. I will say this, because I feel defensive, because of criticisms we have gotten: my academic qualifications are impeccable. I am a teaching assistant, and a Woodrow Wilson Fellow. It is shortly after noon on Saturday October 3. I am making this recording because some journalism is needed, of a kind we have never had. These last two weeks have been very strange. I would like to say what they were about. Not so much what they mean, because I'm not sure what's going to happen after this. I have tried to write about what led up to these weeks before. I have never been able to: the magnitude and complexity overwhelm me. I can talk about it now because last night, after it was all over, an ex-girl friend of mine who was in it with us and whom I had not expected to see, picked me up and took me like a tired kitten to her place. And then she asked me what was going on. And I tried to tell her, and I broke down and cried. I cried because I was tired, because I was sick, because my heart was broken. If I show any "unseemly" displays of emotion, I should like it to be charged up to that.

• • • •

[*I talked about the McCarthy years, and how they had drained the spirit from a landscape.*]

Then things started happening. It started when the young kids down South sat on lunch counter stools, got beaten off them, thrown into compounds, and hosed down in freezing winter nights. They were doing something for all of us. But the NAACP said, "Not so fast." King's organization grew out of this. But when the young students started sitting in more, his people said, "Not so fast; not so fast." And the NAACP said, "Why don't you do it like King did it originally?" Well, it's an old tale, and we'll hear a lot more of it. Everybody saying, "Not so fast." "Don't be radical; don't rock the boat; be nice." Meanwhile the sit-ins went on, and civil disobedience became the main tool. The NAACP had been fooling around with legal things for years; they never got anybody anywhere much.

The only life in the country in those years was in the South. And then it started spreading to the North. There were a lot of us depressed by the silence, by the injustice, by the fact that the generations that should have been leading us—our parents and our teachers—quite simply had the spirit kicked out of them. And meanwhile, there were all these terrible things going on. And it wasn't just the radicals or college kids. Even my secretary friends who never participated in political stuff would sometimes wake up screaming, dreaming of atom bombs.

[*I sketched the early years of student activism, the way it spread, its first cresting in 1960.*]

Anyway, the conflict of these last two weeks began in

the '50s. As the interests of students up North, and particularly in Berkeley, mounted at an accelerating rate, so did the repressive measures directed against them. I don't want to speculate about motives; when I say repressive measures, I'm speaking purely phenomenologically, about the *effect* of the measures. Some of the motives were absolutely wretched, and some were in good faith, carried out by people who thought they were doing the best thing. Likewise I'm going to speak continually of the Administration here as a monolith, and I want to apologize. I know it's not; it's composed of individual men. One I've known for thirteen years, and I count others as friends; they have done me many favors. I think they are good men; they are honest, they are conscientious, they are concerned. But the effect of their work in the Administration is monolithic. And repressive.

I mostly remember the repressive things that happened here before late 1961, when I dropped out of politics. Like with the *Daily Californian*, the campus paper. In 1960 the *Daily Californian* was one of the four best college papers in the country and was perhaps the most responsible paper on the entire West Coast. Its people took Journalism seriously. They believed that a newspaper was a vehicle for issues of consequence to its readers. So they were very active in mobilizing support for things like the Chessman and HUAC demonstrations, and nuclear disarmament—not that they *advocated* these things directly, but they printed information. Just information. I can almost believe that all this business about free speech means something. These last years have almost beaten the belief out of me. I don't see that the First Amendment, all this nonsense, has anything to do with the reality I live in. And yet, the truth was that during those years, the *Daily Californian* was a good paper, and it printed good stories. It printed both sides of a question, and people read it and were moved to act. In fall of 1960, it endorsed the SLATE candidates for office.

The Administration was hurting from SLATE. SLATE had been the major organizing force on campus. A lot of adverse publicity came on the University for the HUAC hassle in San Francisco, as well as the other activities that SLATE carried on. And the *Daily Cal* endorsed a SLATE candidate. Now in previous years it had endorsed fraternity candidates for the student executive board. No stink was raised. This time, a stink was raised, censorship was instituted, and the whole staff walked out. They printed the last issue of the paper with a black border: "They are wiping out freedom of the press, we resign."

They tried to set up an independent paper.* It didn't work. Things like this never work; there are never enough people willing to give their support. That's just the way it is. That's what our world is like. The Administration recruited a scab staff, who started putting out the *Daily Cal* again. Well, nobody's read it much for the last four years; it's been a house organ. And so our main medium of mass communication was wiped out; we were left with occasional rallies. But you can't communicate things to people in twenty-four hours; it takes years.

The next thing that happened was the Administration says, "We've got to keep this place free from influence." They give us the Kerr Directives, they reinterpret them and reinterpret them. They set up a completely artificial distinction between "on-campus issues" and "off-campus issues." And it was a big joke at the time. A big and very bitter joke. We said, "Well, the fallout falls on the campus too." But we didn't get anywhere. So all of a sudden all

* [The *Independent Californian*, four years before the *Berkeley Barb* became the first underground paper.]

these organizations that were on campus since the fifties, since the beginning, they're off-campus. They can't use the University facilities. That practically wiped SLATE out. I was never a member, I hardly ever went to meetings, back when I was politically active. But SLATE was a vital educating force, a vital organizing force. It staggered along, downhill all the way, and hasn't had much effect since then. And notice when the Administration says, "They have to be off-campus." It's when SLATE started being effective.

Then there were the graduate students. They thought the Associated Students, the ASUC, was a sandbox government. And it was: the Administration dictated the resolution it passed to affirm the Kerr Directives. Some graduates objected to being forced to pay the membership fee. So those in power sent out a questionnaire. Nobody knows how they picked the particular graduate students they polled. They asked, "Do you want to be in the ASUC, or don't you?" Of those who returned the questionnaire, most said "No." So, the Administration said, well, it's very simple, and they abolished graduate membership in the ASUC. They did not make it voluntary, you know, which is what we would have wanted. They abolished it by fiat.

The effect of this was to wipe out graduate leadership in campus politics. The undergraduates are transients. They start very young, they stay here at best four years. The only chance for responsible continuous leadership in student affairs lies with the graduate students, who stay here for years and years, because it takes a long time to get a Ph.D., whether or not you're involved in politics.

So the Administration wiped the graduate students out of the action. Then they finished reorganizing "our" student government and its Executive Committee, which activists were coming to control. They changed Ex Com to the ASUC Senate, in a way that put it back in the hands of the Greek system and dorms minority and minimized "off-campus" representation.

And the Administration fired good instructors, who had been active politically. I'll talk a bit about that later. There were other things that happened; I forget them. The point is that as the students' interest in things grew, repressive measures upon their involvement grew in proportion, to cut down communication, leadership, power. That's how it goes. Most of the measures were passed like in the middle of second summer session, when there was almost nobody on campus, no one to make a protest.

At the end of this time I simply divorced myself from student politics. I mean from politics entirely, because I was never able to draw a line between student politics and politics in the big world. I don't believe there is one, I have never believed that. And it got to be too much, they kept beating us down, pushing us off the campus where we belonged. Each time it was heartbreaking, and I just got tired of fighting. Over the past three years I've been in very few political activities, been involved in more private things.

But I know the surface of what's been happening. There was a relative vacuum for a couple of years after that. Then things started picking up again. I don't understand why, but they did. The long chain of sympathy picketing of Woolworth stores started. After that there were sit-ins at drive-ins, shop-ins at stores, sit-ins at the Sheraton-Palace, at Cadillac, at Bank of America, at the *Tribune*—that was roughly the progression on the Civil Rights front. On the Civil Liberties front, there was fighting against the film HUAC put out, giving their doctored version of the 1960 "riot." There were protests for disarmament, and so on. Things started gathering momentum again, kept going, and kept growing.

These two weeks on campus, then, they were not two weeks. They were the culmination of six years.

• • • •

When we get back to school this fall, Dean Towle of the Administration hands down this order. For years there had been these tables on the edge of the campus, at Bancroft and Telegraph, where organizations handed out literature, solicited members, and collected funds. They were there, because they used to be on campus—right in the heart of campus, Dwinelle Plaza—but the Administration pushed them off. We used to be able to stand up under the Dwinelle Oak and talk, and advocate things. They stopped that too.

So Dean Towle said, "No more tables. They block the flow of traffic." So we say—I mean the students, because I didn't get into this until later—so we say, "Gee, we don't think they block traffic; tell you what, we'll put up the money to get an independent organization to make a survey of the traffic flow." The Administration doesn't reply to this. So we start to hold meetings. Suddenly, a week later, the reason changes. We can't have tables because of the Kerr Directives, which have always been there. Always for like three years! The tables had been on campus for at least fifteen! "They've always been there," they tell us, "and we're just getting around to realizing what they really mean." So just out of thin air, they give this additional thing—well, anyway, it becomes illegal, by the Administration's rules, to hand out literature there. Let alone advocate things, let alone collect money and members.

Meetings go on, more students keep getting upset. A

week later, suddenly, the Directives are reinterpreted again. The Administration tells us we can have tables at Bancroft to distribute information. Just information. Well, that suggested the tables hadn't blocked traffic in the first place. But the Administration never got around to admitting this.

But this wasn't enough, we still couldn't advocate things. There were so many contradictions. The University is spending quite a bit of money advocating Proposition 2, a bond issue, but they won't let us advocate against Proposition 14, a fair-housing ordinance. Insurance men come into the card files, which are open to the public, and collect our names, and try to sell us insurance, but we can't collect names of people who want to help in the South. The Peace Corps recruits members on campus to help overseas; we can't recruit people who want to help in this country. The University sends out United Crusade envelopes to employees—I've worked for it, your superior asks you for your envelope back. They keep check lists of who brings envelopes full of money and who doesn't. But you can't collect money on campus to send some clothes down to Negroes in the South who have been evicted.

So all this was rather upsetting, and people still weren't satisfied. So a vigil was held, all night, on the steps of Sproul, the Administration building. I finally got interested enough to go to a vigil again. It was the worst one I'd seen; I mean I didn't like the people in it at all. They seemed to be the young kids who hang out on Telegraph Avenue; there was a lot of wine, guitars, it all seemed pretty rowdy. I felt very alienated, so I went home at 2 A.M. Still, a hundred or so stayed all night. And the next day or so, the Administration got around to saying, "Well, you can advocate things." They reinterpreted the

Directives again. They never gave a reason for these successive reinterpretations.

Well, this still wasn't enough to restore our effectiveness. The University had shoved all these organizations off-campus and then graciously permitted them these tables in the last three or four years. And this is how the organizations kept alive. What it meant for them to be denied the "privilege" to collect money and to recruit members on campus—a right that exists at every state and junior college in California—was that they'd die. And in particular this meant CORE and SNCC.

The attack on the tables seems to have been triggered by the Oakland *Tribune*, Bill Knowland's reactionary paper. We heard that Knowland got very upset during the Republican convention when Scranton supporters were being recruited on campus here. And he got even more upset when members of an ad-hoc Civil Rights coalition started picketing his paper every Friday night between five and seven o'clock. So someone from the *Trib* called the Administration, to inquire about the tables where the pickets are recruited. And the Administration decided they were illegal. Of course, the University is supposed to be free from sectarian political influence from the outside.

So the effect of the last little points that the Administration wouldn't grant us—to solicit money and membership on campus—would be precisely to wipe out the organizations causing the most active distress in the community, the most effective student organizations. I don't want to belabor the significance of this: to anybody who's followed the Civil Rights events in the city, it should be obvious.

These, I think, are the real pragmatic issues involved. I didn't feel this originally, but there are some theoretical issues involved too. Like freedom of speech. The Supreme

Court says free speech alone is not enough. Like, fine, you can hand out literature, but you've got to be able to get the money to print it up to hand it out. In fact, you've got to be able to get the members to print it up too. So these two little remaining points are directly connected with the free speech issue.

For the first time ever, all the political groups on the campus united in opposing what the Administration was doing. Not only the various socialist splinter groups, and CORE and SNCC, and the Young Democrats, who have never been very radical. Also the Young Republicans, Students for Goldwater, and even the Intercollegiate Society of Individualists, whom my political friends think of as young fascists. It was really a United Front, very strange political bedfellows. Because after all, here was a Constitutional issue.

And people said, don't be unreasonable, be moderate. Compromise is the central thing in a democracy. The Administration has come forward to meet your demands a bit; why don't you give a bit on these last two things? But it wasn't a question of giving *a bit* on them. For six years they had been trying to wipe out the organizations. This was not a new thing, and these were not two minor points.

And I want to make a point about tactics. There are a lot of people around, even in this community, who look on the Civil Rights demonstrations in the City as very unfortunate. They say, "How terrible: these kids get a cause, and they rush in and they perform hasty actions." But every single civil disobedience thing that has happened was preceded by months, sometimes over a year, of patient negotiation. And it was like this here. We had been negotiating not for two weeks. We had been negotiating for six years.

In all those previous times, what we did, we negotiated. We did everything through the approved channels.
We wrote letters to our Congressmen, letters to the local
newspapers, letters to the *Daily Cal,* letters to the University administrators. We went in and saw them individually, and as group representatives, and in groups. Nothing happened. Nothing ever happened. We negotiated, we
set up committees, we signed petitions, sometimes they
had 5,000 signatures on them. We circulated petitions in
the faculty. The faculty set up committees. We picketed.
And what did we get for these six years, every time
there was a repressive measure? We got nothing. We got
back in those years not one inch of the ground that was
taken away from us. We were nice all the way; we
were very unhappy, but we were nice.

So it's Tuesday, I guess, that they say, "To hell with
it. We give up. We're going to set up the tables on campus.
We're going to set up the tables, and we're going to ask
for money. We're going to ask for members." So they
set them up, and some people sat down at them. And the
Administration came along and took their names, and
summoned them to see the Dean. By some coincidence,
the five students were CORE and SNCC members. By
some coincidence they were precisely the leaders in the
movement. There were a lot of people sitting at the
tables, but the Administration picked these. It happens, and
there's not much you can say about it. You learn to expect
it. You learn to expect to get beaten every step of the
way.

That afternoon, the Dean of Men wanted to see the
five students. But by this time over 400 students had
signed a piece of paper that said, "I sat at the table too.
I want equal treatment. Suspend me too." And somehow
the five got into their heads that they weren't five any

more; they were 400. And they all went and said this to the Dean, and asked him about all the other people who had been sitting there when the five leaders' names were taken. And he said, "Well, I'm sorry. We can only deal with observed violations, not unobserved violations." They said, "How can we negotiate if our leaders have been suspended?" So he canceled the negotiating meeting that had been set up for 4:00.

Well, what can you say? They stayed in Sproul Hall and began a small sit-in. There were a hundred there at midnight when they got word that the five had been suspended from school, "indefinitely," and three more too. The three weren't even notified; they didn't know why, people thought it was for helping organize the afternoon protest. It was very confused, and after a while everyone went home.

So the next morning I was sitting around on the Terrace, wondering what was going to happen. Everyone felt sure something would. Lo and behold, they bring the tables out again and set them up right in front of the Administration building. And they sit down at the tables again and put out membership lists and start collecting donations.

This time, there's a "non-student" sitting at one of the tables. He's a member of one of the organizations, he graduated last year, in mathematics. And the University police come along and arrest him. He goes limp; what else can you do? And so four cops carry him to this police car that's sitting in the middle of the Plaza. And a crowd starts gathering, and some people sit down in front of the police car, and behind the police car. The police don't like this. Luckily at this stage it was only campus cops, and as cops go, campus cops are pretty nice. As cops go. In a while it is noon, there are 3,000 people around this police car in Sproul Plaza. Around the car hundreds are sitting down; they don't want it to be moved.

Then somebody gets on top of the car—the cops let him—to talk to the crowd, it was unhappy. And then this incredible dialogue began. People got up on top of that car from before noon Wednesday, they were talking until two in the morning. All different points of view were offered. The top of that car was a platform thrown open to anybody who wanted to come up and say what he had to say. I have never heard anything like this in my life. It was a continuous dialogue that went on for fifteen straight hours.

And people stopped and listened to it. And people voted. If you've never seen 3,000 people voting, it's a very strange thing; 3,000 people in, as the newspapers described it, "a mob scene." So many people on a political issue had never been seen on campus, a large political demonstration on campus is maybe 300. Several faculty members told me that the Chancellor became absolutely hysterical —they used those words—and complained "he would not listen to reason." It seems to me that the rest of the Administration was pretty hysterical too.

Around three, some of us went into Sproul Hall and sat down in the corridor. We were going to block the Dean of Men's office. Why the Dean of Men? Well, he couldn't do anything, and the Chancellor said he couldn't and wouldn't do anything, and the President said he couldn't and wouldn't do anything. And you know, after six years of hearing this, you get tired of hearing it. And you say, by God, there has to be somebody around who can do something. So we sat down.

And crammed in in this hallway, we conducted a four-hour dialogue on who we should bar from the office and who we shouldn't, and what tactics to use, and what we were asking, and so on. Our general consensus was the following demands, which we considered very moderate: That the arrested ex-student be released; that the suspended students be reinstated, because they were our leaders and we couldn't negotiate without them; that while the negotiations were being set up and while they were in session, nobody else be suspended, before some final decision about on-campus politics had been reached. That was all we asked. And they wouldn't listen, they wouldn't grant us any of it.

While we were sitting there, some faculty members came and talked to us. The faculty got upset when they saw 3,000 people sitting in Sproul Plaza, and when they realized how hysterical and how intransigent the Administration was. So they formed a committee, and they went negotiating with the Administration, and they kept sending people back to us, reporting that they were not getting very far. And they told us, "Look, we're trying to intervene in your behalf, and we think it would be best if you'd clear out of Sproul Hall."

Well, I got very upset by their tone. I mean, their hearts were in it and all, and some of my best friends are faculty members. But why was it now that they were trying to intervene? What had they been doing for the last two weeks? And the last six years? It upset me incredibly. Whose fight did they think this was? We felt that the faculty and we were in this together. That this was free speech, academic freedom, things like that. And where were they the last six years while we were getting cut off?

But the faculty have always been like that, except for some rare courageous individuals. At best sometimes some get concerned and try to "moderate in our behalf."

They're always unsuccessful. But all along, we felt that we were fighting for the both of us. These are the men who should have been leading us for all these years. Instead, these were the men who have been saying, "Cool down, go slow."

They've been like this for a long time. I don't know when it started. During the fight over the Loyalty Oath, in the early '50s, a bunch of faculty got thrown out. Most eventually crawled back in, and some couldn't get back in, and a few fought it out. And why it all happened was, in my opinion—and I really do think that the time for being polite is past—that the faculty hadn't the balls to stick up for its own, and the students hadn't the balls to stick up for their faculty.

The faculty got crushed in '52, and they haven't had the guts to do anything since. They've registered nice respectable protests, while they watched the students get wiped off campus, and watched their own men get wiped off too. For example, Professor Drinnon in History. He came, because he believed that students and faculty were political animals too. He took a very active part, he and his wife, in the Chessman vigils, and he cheered us up an awful lot. After that, they decided they couldn't re-hire him. They said something about not enough money, and he hadn't published enough. He had two books out, and a third at the press. In the opinion of students and many colleagues, he was a brilliant teacher and a sharp historian. Did anybody stick up for him? The faculty circulated a petition, we circulated a petition, that's what it came to. Nobody walked out on a class. None of the other faculty up and quit or anything. Two years later, it happened again.

Very few faculty were ever seen with us in public. One walked the line with us at HUAC, many of us stud-

ied with him and loved him. Sometime later, after all
the press about the "riot," Goldwater stands up in Congress to give people ideas about it being the duty of red-
blooded Americans to go and kill Commies, and an anonymous hate pamphlet appears on campus about him. A
couple of days later somebody comes along with a shot-
gun and shoots him. Shoots him, and kills somebody else
in his office at the time, a poet, a friend of my friends.
One of the few men who had the guts to walk with us,
and they shoot him. We're all alone; we've always been
all alone, all alone on all these things. Nobody has the
courage to stand up with us, nobody has the courage to
say, "This is enough. There is a right and wrong, and
you've got to go all out for it, or you've had it."

So anyway, the faculty came and said, "Look, why
don't you get out of Sproul Hall; the Administration is
hysterical; they absolutely refuse to budge. They won't
even grant the most reasonable demands as long as you're
in Sproul—in fact, as long as this whole demonstration
persists."

Well, we didn't want to get out, even after sitting
packed to the gills with people walking over us. But we
said, "Look. Okay. We don't believe it's going to do any
good, but as a gesture of good faith, we'll make a uni-
lateral withdrawal from Sproul. As soon as we hear that
the faculty and Administration are negotiating together,
we'll withdraw for an hour and a half. Or until quarter
of 7:00, whichever comes first." And they go away.

Now the Sproul Hall doors have not been closed before
7:00 since 1942, supposedly by University law. So we
sit there waiting for word. And no word comes. Outside
2,000 students are sitting around this car. So at 6:20, the
Administration tells the campus cops to lock Sproul
Hall, so we can get out, but so no one else can get in.

It was a grievous breach of good faith. A handful of guys said, "You shouldn't lock the door," and then sat down in the door. The cops started dragging them away, to lock it, just as we started coming downstairs from the Dean's Office. We saw what was happening and went and sat down in the door too.

At first people are sitting there individually, and the cops are dragging them away, and then we start linking and locking. And there's this human lacework built into the doorway. There's maybe sixty of us in the doorway and extending on both sides of it. We're not just linking arms. We're holding onto each other for dear life. And we keep trying to contract the lace, to plug up the doorway. And the cops are grabbing people under the chin, with their fingers dug in, and pulling them.

There was this one girl; I counted, thirteen of us were holding onto her. And this cop has both of his hands in her hair, pulling as hard as he can. And she's screaming. And between screams, she's saying, "Hold me tighter! Hold me! Hold me!" and then she screams, and then she says, "Hold me!" I don't want to make a big thing of it, but this is how it happened.

And we're lying on our backs twined like an immense octopus, singing *The Star-Spangled Banner*, maybe because it's the first thing that comes to mind, and women are screaming, and the cops are kicking people and hitting people in the face. And this one cop comes jumping over, like last down, one yard to go for a touchdown; the two lines crash up, and the fullback tries to pile his way over the top. This cop comes jumping over, boots first, and goes out. Then he starts coming back, to go in. Like fools, you know, we say, "Take your shoes off." And then we take his shoes off for him.

I admit it was a very stupid thing to do, because almost

the only pictures that come out of all this day are of the cop with his shoes taken off. And we get these big headlines about how we pulled this policeman down a flight of stairs and took his cap and shoes off. But we wanted he should take his shoes off so he wouldn't step in people's faces. It's not nice, that's all.

So somehow we hold the doorway. Sometime later we vote—of our own accord, mind you—to leave. Because it was an empty position at that point: they had us blocked out from the upper floors. So we left and joined the main crowd.

So it's Thursday night, and there are still well over a thousand of us. And by this time we realize simply that we have to hold that car. That car is the only thing we've gotten in six years. It's our car; it isn't the cops' car any more. And so we start bringing sleeping bags. And the dialogue on top of the car continues. People are getting up there and talking, and people are listening. And people are voting on this, and people are voting on that.

It's almost enough to make you believe that if it were given a chance, the democratic process might work. It just might work. People quoted books as if books were relevant. They talked about the Greeks, and they talked about theories of politics, as if it all *meant* something. And listening to them, I almost believed for the first time in years that it did mean something.

And we're sitting there near midnight when this kid Mario Savio—he's twenty-one, I'm twenty-four, a kid too —comes running up; I had never seen him before the last few days. He was one of the leaders, one of the suspended students. He talked pretty good; I gather he's a junior in philosophy. He's got a good heart, he talks straight sense, and he's got an infinite amount of patience. Anyway, he'd been up and down on the car during the day, and now he comes running up because some people jumped him, right off campus. It turns out, this huge flood of fraternity boys has come down. The paper says there were 200 of them. But there were not 200, there were over a thousand. I have been estimating crowds for a long time. We're seated, packed in, and they surround us and stand around, yelling and throwing tomatoes and eggs. And throwing dozens of lit cigarettes into our ranks. When you're sat down like that you can't move, and they're trampling people at the edges. Some of their own people got up to the car and spoke to calm them down, and they threw eggs even at their own people, and Jew-baited them. And they were screaming at us, "Get off the car, get off the car." They wanted the car like freed, and I think they wanted blood. And they were calling us Communists, and, you know, we should go home and take a bath. God, would we have loved to go home and take a bath. A bath and a shave, and sleep. But you can't. Because if you go home, there'll be nobody there. And always before, we've gone home, and there's been nobody left.

Meanwhile, the Alameda County Sheriff's Department men are standing in the background in their nice blue uniforms. And some of them are egging the fraternity boys on. We appealed that they should form a line between them and us, they should stop this, because it was an incredibly explosive situation. And they yelled back, "We don't see that it's explosive." Faculty members appealed for the same thing and got the same answer. So it stayed on being explosive.

It was like out of a fairy tale. Mario and a girl named Jackie were standing up there on top of the car and trying to *reason* with them. Mario in particular, who'd been up I don't know how many hours and had been talking all day, is trying to explain to them our position. And they keep yelling and throwing things at him, and then he starts talking, and they start chanting, "Get off the car," so nobody can hear him. And he waits till they're done, and he tries again, and again, and again. This goes on for hours. To explain; to explain; to ask them to come up and talk.

And meanwhile we're sitting there, scared to death. I'm not particularly cowardly, but they grow them big in the fraternities, and there are an awful lot of them. Somehow, tension bleeds away a little, and then this priest comes and for the first time there is silence. He climbs on top of the car, and some of the fraternity kids yell at him. But others silence them. Roughly he says, "This is a bad deal. There's a lot of hate here, and hate is bad. If you hate enough, it means murder. I want you to think of that." Then he gets down, and an Administration representative comes and says, "Go away."

After that, after hours and hours of speaking, we just shut up. They would yell, "Get off the car," and this little ruffle of "Shhh!" would go through the thousand or so of us. We sat there with our mouths shut for half an hour, and finally they just went away. Next morning, of course, the papers recorded a lot of conviviality between them and us; talked about panty raids and such things. I just want to say, it wasn't like that.

There was very little chance for sleep after all that. There were few fortunate enough to have sleeping bags. Some of us tried to sleep on the lawn, and got sopping when the automatic sprinkler system went on at five. Most got an hour and were grateful. I went and got my recorder and played with some guitars on the steps. When the sun came up people folded their blankets, picked up leaflets, and swept up all around the Plaza and the steps; it's a thing with us.

It's eight in the morning and it's a beautiful day; it's a beautiful Friday. And the sun starts coming up. And the sun keeps coming up. And the sun keeps up there all day, and we melt like wax. There's just nothing to protect you, you sit there, and you stink; you sweat; you feel faint; and you just sit there, packed around the car, and there's nothing else you can do. By now there were maybe 400 of us, and hardly any more all day who sat down. But by God, we had that car. It was all we had, and we were going to keep it until we were forced to give it up.

As soon as day begins the dialogue on top of the car resumes. Everybody gets up and talks about our three demands. And people give history; and people give facts. At noontime, when the crowd of onlookers swells to about three thousand, we ask them, come sit down with us. A few do. Meanwhile all this time Jack, the guy, is still in the cop car, they give him a beer can to piss in.

I finally leave for the first time I'd been away from this thing since Tuesday. So I come to class, and I say to my teacher, "Look, I was supposed to see you yesterday about a problem set I missed; I've been penned up in Sproul Hall all yesterday, I was there all night, I've been there all day today in the sun; can I have a stay of execution until Monday?" And he stands there with the NO ON 14 button on his lapel, which he very well might have picked up at one of our tables, and he says "No." Well, I was too tired to argue with him; I was too tired to say, "Why don't you come out in the sun too?" Because I knew he wouldn't.

But there were some good people in the sun. We were

pretty tired and pretty grubby, but the cream of the University was there, a good part of it. Teaching assistants, people with fellowships, scholarships, the Department's prize undergraduates. I don't know if it's ever been done, but if you were to take the grade point average—an absolutely silly criterion—of people who stood on these bloody lines, you'd find it to be awfully high. Maybe there are some people who flunk out of school because they get too involved or are in these things for hung-up reasons. But a hell of a lot of the best students of the University were there.

So we sat in the sun, and the dialogue continues, and there's so much information: historical résumés, California State Supreme Court decisions, and such. And somebody who'd been active in the old days, a law student, Michael Tigar, got up on top of the car. Those of us who had been active with him were very glad to see him. And he tells us about this book that Clark Kerr wrote in the late fifties, called *The Managerial Revolution*, and he gives us a summary of Kerr's thesis: There are the managed and the managers. The University is part of the managerial society. It's this big ship; and the ship has got a captain; and the captain is the President; and what he says goes. And Tigar says, "We thought the only place this kind of thinking was left in the world after the 1920s was in Mussolini's Italy." But he goes on talking about this book, as if it really meant something to talk about a book, as if these ideas and a rational counter-argument to them had some real use, which is very hard to believe after you've been around a University for eight years and gotten concerned about things, and had the spirit beaten down in you. At the end, Tigar says, "I don't want to be coarse, but there's one thing that's got to be said. People have been talking like this is just a little thing.

But I want to say, even if they cut 'em off one at a time, it's still castration." And that's the truth, and it was good to hear someone say it in so many words.

I was ready to drop, everyone was. I went to lie down on a lawn for a while, but I asked a friend to wake me because the word was that something was going to happen that night. The next day was Parents' Day at the University. And, wow, publicity for the University was bad enough without all the parents coming along and seeing a crowd of 400 beatniks sitting around a cop car and this guy still in it.

But I couldn't get to sleep, because I was too keyed up. Because the only way you can keep going after you've been going like this for a couple of days, is on nervous energy. And the moment you let loose of it you're dead, and so it takes hours to unwind.

Forty minutes later, a friend comes over and says, come quick, something's going to happen, and I go to the car. There are very few of us, and slowly other people start collecting around us, but they're standing. We're the only ones who are sitting. And we scrunch up close to the car, because the word is that they're going to come and try to take Jack away. Meanwhile all day there've been these negotiations maybe going on; we've heard nothing, we figured they'd break down. We sit there for two hours. People are passing out sandwiches; both days we collected money and outside people made sandwiches and brought them in, and offered other help. And people bring us reports of sympathy demonstrations in other colleges. All this is very nice when you feel very much alone.

Comes 6:30, 7:00, there's this incredible scene. There are 500 of us at most seated around the car, and maybe 3,000 spectators. Some of them are with us but afraid to get arrested, maybe another 300, we can't tell. But the great majority are the kids who were heckling us the previous night, the Greeks and others. They fill the steps of Sproul; they're clustered in the Student Union; they're on the roof of the cafeteria; they're perched in trees. I have never seen so many at one time. And they want blood.

Meanwhile, in back of Sproul Hall, there are 500 policemen, with boots, with night sticks in hand, and with steel helmets. And the hecklers are there, screaming for blood. "We want blood," they yell. I'd seen this sort of thing before, but never in such magnitude, never 500 cops gathered together. And we're there, and we're singing. There are 400 people willing to go to jail; we're singing because we're scared to death.

Well, the jail part doesn't so much bother me. I mean, I've got a teaching assistantship to lose and a career and things like that, but these are minor points. And they really are. Somebody was going to get killed. This is not a melodrama. Somebody was going to get killed, if the cops came in. That's why I was there. I didn't realize at first how many they'd have. Then when I found out, I figured—somebody's going to get killed.

Because there were all sorts of people sitting there, these ninety pound girls and pregnant women, no kidding, pregnant women, packed in, unable to move. And we try to tell them what it's going to be like. "If you're wearing rings or you're wearing pierced earrings, take them off. Don't leave buttons pinned to your chest. When they get to you, go limp. If you lock arms they'll club you apart." In between the fraternity boys are yelling to bring on the cops. If that had started, I do believe we would have had not only 500 cops on our backs, but 2,000 fraternity boys.

But what can you do when you're in one of these

things but lie there and take it? You tuck your chin to your chest so they can't get you under it, and you pray very selfishly that you're not going to be the one that gets hurt. And you hold on to the guy next to you for dear life. But you don't feel anything. You don't even feel hate. You know you dare not raise a finger to them.

It's sort of symbolic of the whole thing, these last six years. They take away everything, your papers, your rights, your friends, and you put up a polite protest, but you've just got to lie there and take it. And you walk a picket line clad in the same clothes that you went to your fellowship interview in, and they taunt you and spit on you. And you smile. And you don't get mad at them. Not because you're such a nice guy. You don't get mad at them because you can't afford to, because if you let what they're saying reach you, you'll crack in half. You can't do a damned thing about it. You've just got to sit there and take it, lie on the ground and let the cops tromp on you with their boots.

So anyway, like the eleventh hour plus, Mario comes running up to the car, and he's got this agreement, and he says, "I feel like I've betrayed you; it's the first thing that's been signed; you haven't got a chance to vote on it." How ridiculous this is, to talk about 3,000 people in this situation voting! And yet we'd been voting. We got some of the things we wanted. The arrested student wasn't arrested.* The suspended students weren't reinstated, but they were remanded to the faculty for discussion.* And there's some sort of mechanism going to be set up that may produce something about freedom of speech. We may possibly get a piece of land—and we probably won't. I don't know what's going to happen.

But it was very far from what we wanted, and from

* [We were deceived in these beliefs.]

what we started with at the beginning of the semester. Which was far from what we started with six years ago. I don't know about Mario, I feel sorry for him, he's a lovely guy. I don't know how he took the responsibility that was thrust on him, how he didn't crack during this whole period, and kept talking sense, from a good heart, and with a good tongue. I've been around for years, and I would put myself in his hands again. Though we didn't get what we wanted.

If we had had 3,000 sitting down there, I think our representatives might not have signed the agreement. Things are worth doing for 3,000 that they aren't for 300. I don't know if this makes sense. I would never sit down alone. Not because I don't believe in it, but because looking at how America has been running, one man sitting alone just doesn't come to much. Maybe I'm wrong on this. But we tried sitting alone, or nearly alone, on this capital punishment thing; it's one of the things that nearly broke my heart. We sat and we sat and we sat, many times and many places. And not a goddamn thing came of it.

Maybe I give up too easy; but how long can you keep going on having your heart broken? Sometimes I think what we need are more martyrs; sometimes I wonder if it helps us in the end. I feel very pessimistic about all this. But it was damn good to see those 300 there last night. Because the least thing you can say about them is that they believed enough to sit there if there were 300. And we've never seen that before. If we had had 3,000 . . .

But we didn't because of the last six years, because everything that helped us learn from each other was beaten down. You can't communicate things to people in twenty-four hours; it takes years. There's very little dialogue that

goes on; that's one of the troubles of the country: nobody talks to anybody else. That's what was so nice about
that car. It was our car; we fought for it; and while
we had it we stood up on top and we started a dialogue.

The university in America is a very bad scene. There's
no communication. Nobody will say anything. I mean,
you can point to incidents where people do, but when
you draw a line under it and add it all up, what do
you get? You get that there's no communication between
students and faculty, between faculty and Administration,
between Administration and students—it's all totally disjointed. And by and large, no communication between
faculty and faculty, or between students and students.
And the Administration only communicates with a tiny
section of the "outside world." We've got no communication, and we're all alone.

And all you can do is hope that next time a few more
will be aware that there are some issues around, and be
willing to sit down for what they believe. If you don't
know there are issues around, that's your tough luck;
the "powers that be" try to keep you from learning.
But I know enough to make me so sick at heart, so that
for a long time I wasn't interested in learning any more.
I couldn't take it. That's all there is to say. I know why
there weren't 3,000 sitting down. I'll be damned if I
know why even 300 were there waiting to get mashed.

I'm not even sure why I was there. I was there because I couldn't not be there, but that doesn't explain it.
We were sitting there, they were shouting for our blood,
and people were being very nice to each other, holding
each other's things, handing each other sandwiches, bucking
each other up. And I suddenly remembered, in the last
three years I've walked maybe five or six picket lines,
one of them was not too long ago, in Oakland, around

the *Tribune*. There were maybe seventy kids, not particularly well dressed. The cops were there, giving them a hard time, and so were the hecklers.

And these goddamned kids were singing; they were singing, "There is love in that land." Did they believe it? I don't know. Then they sang, "There's free speech in that land." We sang that last night. God. These are maybe the only people around who believe *anything*. But can they really believe there is love in that land? After reading the *Tribune*'s editorials?

There's so much hate around. There was so much hate yesterday, and so much last night. We were sitting there surrounded by hate, and singing about "There is love in that land." And after you've been at it two or three days, after you haven't slept, after you've sat there in the goddamned sun, with people yelling for your blood, knowing that you've been getting the boot steadily for the past six years—you get delirious. You honest to God get delirious. And you can almost believe what you're singing. You can almost con yourself into believing that these things mean something. That there is love in that land. That there is free speech, and all those other crazy abstractions, in that land.

3 October 1964

During the next nine weeks we developed the momentum, apparatus, and discipline to complete what was begun around the car. Finally the Administration did one outrageous thing too many, and a thousand of us marched into Sproul Hall "to bring the machine to a grinding halt." Our sit-in was broken by arrests the next day, whereupon 10,000 went out in the first mass student strike. This did in fact bring the University to a standstill, and the faculty into a panic in support of our demands. We got our tables back, and more besides. And one rare moment of clear victory, before the long struggle of Movement went on.

Already we are deep into the years of Nixon and Reagan. Repression is old news now, and we grow forgetful of its Liberal antecedents. The FSM shook the political structure of the State and unmasked the benevolent façade it wore during the Kennedy years. By the second month, University officials were phoning to threaten to have us indicted on felony conspiracy charges. That tactic didn't become popular for three more years. Still, it's *worth remembering that the first man who ordered State troopers onto a white college campus to bust and beat students was not nasty old Ronnie Reagan, but that kindly Liberal, Governor Edmund G. "Pat" Brown (Dem., 1958–66)—the same fellow who refused clemency for Chessman, in both cases choosing to act "against his conscience."*

But before the Governor's order and an army of cops jerked us back into reality, we brought to a first completion the image begun around the car. Into Sproul Hall we trooped, with all the thread-and-promise weight of what we were doing, and all the bag and baggage of our selves —with Mario's words about the Machine now spoken for us, and singing, so help me, about the love in our hearts.

Once inside, we set up projectors to show Chaplin movies on the walls. A Chanukah service was held. After it the folkdancers wound their way through bedding, study lamps and candles, down corridors to the stairwell niches where musicians and singers clustered. They avoided the study hall into which the top floor had been converted, and also the improvised infirmary and the kitchen. Eager hands hoisted food-flow through the windows. We ate terrible baloney sandwiches and then established the first Free University, conducting some of its dozen classes cross-legged atop the Civil Defense disaster drums stored in the basement. People smoked grass in the corners (1964, mind you), and at least two women had their first full sexual experiences under blankets on the roof, where walkie-talkies were broadcasting news to the outside through the local radio net and coordinating with Emergency Command Central. The Steering Committee met in the women's john, spontaneous organizing proceeded in the corridors, mimeographed bulletins passed around, and we went up to the roof to look for the moon, wonder whether they would use tear gas on us, and speculate about how to sabotage computers and power lines.

In those fifteen hours before the cops came to drag us off to jail and into the confusions of history, in that quarter acre of territory liberated by our presence, we acted out our universe in miniature. An icon came to flower—the compact panorama of our community, newly revealed in the bud of its growth.

Barefoot in a Marshmallow World

A year or so later, in accord with natural processes and the schedules of Eastern publishers, the main wave of books about the FSM washed over us. If you want to read its literal history you might try them,* for what else I have to say has been six years brewing and will wait a while longer. The briefest, most reasonable account is Hal Draper's, and a few essential or insightful pieces are scattered through the others. Much later, Max Heirich's more reflective and academic book appeared.† But the single work really to embody the spirit and living complexity of the FSM—Ken Sanderson's joyous and turbulent epic poem Multiversity Lost—*remains unpublished, save for a few disjointed fragments.*

Taken all in all, though, the early glut of books about FSM was pretty dismal. From this distance I can shrug it off as just another classic case of academic irrelevance; or examine its deeper implications in the scheme of concept-cooptation which maintains one-dimensional society. But at the time I was still capable of some amazement.

---

* *Berkeley: The New Student Revolt*, Hal Draper (Grove Press, 1965). *Revolution at Berkeley*, Miller and Gilmore, eds. (Dell, 1965). *The Berkeley Student Revolt*, Lipset and Wolin, eds. (Anchor Books, 1965).

† *The Spiral of Conflict: Berkeley, 1964*, Max Heirich (Columbia University Press, 1971).

*I mean, here we were, living on, fumbling to grasp what-
ever new had struck through us, when this avalanche of
stale language and old perceptual frames came down on
us, from the people we hire to illuminate our experience.*

*I had not yet got my own first terms together; I don't
know how many of us had by then. I felt defensive and
angry because I had nothing coherent to offer in rebut-
tal. But something needed to be said, about how far they
were off. Ralph Gleason pushed me to try, and got most
of what follows printed as a book review in* Ramparts.

"What do you feel about the FSM books?" I asked
my friend Steve Weissman, who was on the FSM
Steering Committee with me.
"The Academics are at the dung-heap with their for-
ceps again."
"You can tell the bird by his droppings?" I suggested.
"Maybe. But you can't tell the way he flies."

Those who were FSM will understand this, will understand how I struggle without poetry to say something
about these books that is not in their image and dead
names, missing the point as they miss theirs. How to
describe the terrifying sense of irrelevance they leave me
with? The conflict was cloaked in that fog: were they
talking to us, hearing us, even seeing us? How ironic, how
fitting, to find it again, from the same sources and for the
same reasons. I can only say—echoing the Chaplin humor
that infused every action of the FSM, yet finds no notice
in these books—that their Failed Seriousness Quotient is
very high.

FSM happened at the locus of Modern Scholarship. The
entire armament of analysis hung poised, desperately avoiding contact with the Perfect Chance that shook a fist

in its face, while we sang: *"I write theses/about feces/ and it greases/my way up the line."* Were we unfair? No sociologist finds it relevant that the novels Berkeley most quickened to the past decade were Kesey's *One Flew over the Cuckoo's Nest* and Heller's *Catch-22;* or that we lived the semester in their grim worlds. Heller says: *"There were terrifying, sudden moments when objects, concepts and even people inexplicably took on an unfamiliar and irregular aspect never seen before which made them seem totally strange."* That's how it was, though you'll find no trace here. These books are unwitting texts, as the semester was a laboratory, on the human need to reduce Events to safe comprehensibility by rendering them in familiar names. (The need is never mentioned; but maybe the psychologists' contributions were late.)

With the familiar, the writers succeed. We see a corporate portrait of the Administration's personality: torn between honest liberal rhetoric and plural pressures; unable to speak to or even control the students, and later the faculty; caught off-balance by our every reaction, and able to respond only by a panicked sequence of blunders based on the premise that civilization was crumbling, which revealed a total inability to understand who we were. It is a human portrait, which emerges in jigsaw fragments. And given it, one can half comprehend a truly tragic fact. The "high official (who) simply did not understand the issue about advocacy (and) had to go out in the hall to have the University lawyers explain it to him"—after three months of struggle and 800 arrests—was the University's President, Clark Kerr.

But only half. What is missing, besides poetry, is our face; and with it any real understanding of what the whole affair meant. Why? The unknown is dangerous by definition: explain it away, kill it, by naming it familiar. The evidence that this happened is indirect but compelling; the face of FSM appears by its absence. For these books leave a few questions unanswered.

Who were we? "Intellectual lumpen-proletarians, lumpen beatniks, and lumpen agitators . . . advocating a melange of narcotics, sexual perversion, collegiate Castroism and campus Maoism," Feuer charges. "Intelligent students who were novices in political action," defend Wolin/ Schaar. "Alienated non-ideological radicals," analyzes Draper. "68% had no organizational affiliation," confirms a survey. Plowing through this telephone book, one almost doesn't notice that the face above it is featureless: there's no sense of identity. And is the reason simply that only 80 of 1,200 pages were written by FSM members? I think not. Nor do I find it strange that hundreds of articles have been written on and around FSM, but only a bare handful by us. Everyone's quick to speak of us, but no one asks us to speak. . . .

Why did we do it? Everyone who doesn't think we were all Neurotic Dupes agrees: Civil Rights, Civil Liberties, Educational Alienation. (The surveys tend to contradict these views, and are thus ignored.) But this is the great University, 1965 Model: we're all alienated-civil-rightist-libertarians. Why now? why us? why this way? why so intensely? why, simply *why?* The explanations are so convenient, so glibly plausible, so circular—like a psychosomatic nostrum—that it's easy to escape the frightening fact that they explain nothing.

What did we do? The wealth of chronologies and descriptions, spangled with errors and contradictions, makes little sense. Comprehensiveness substitutes for relevance. No one warns that the most significant events are not discussed. But how could they be, without dealing with the *who* and *why?*

For example, the Police Car Episode. Draper alone devotes a few pages to it, his description's as refreshing and unsatisfying as Coke. Understand it, and you understand FSM. For FSM was forged around that car, *not* at the later "convention," and those two days were a miniature of the entire conflict. They furnished the emotional impetus for our fight; they were our signature on a promissory note of the heart. Given the nature of the participants, events thereafter unrolled with the Greek inexorability that fascinated us all (and is unmentioned, unexplained in these books). But *why* should up to 3,000 students surround a cop car for two days, and risk expulsion, arrest, and violent injury?

No one answers, no one notes that every theme later developed was huddled with us around the car. We used 4,000,000 sheets of paper to expand those barefoot thoughts (and *only* those) spoken atop the car in the first true dialogue I have heard in America. It was all there: the "non-negotiable" issues; the unexpected intensity of our commitment and community; our strange honest humor; the absent estrangement of the faculty; the Administration's refusal to speak to us save via 500 cops, or even to see us, encamped under its nose; our desperate spontaneous democracy; and the total loneliness . . . You'd never know this from the books, never know that no single new element—phychological, tactical, dialectical, compositional—entered the controversy from then till its climax: all that we were, all that we faced, were there full-fledged around the car, in every sense.

Is this merely a curious fact? Or does it lead to an idea: that around the car an irrevocable commitment to the creation of an Event was made, that the stalemate of nothing new had to ensue until the Event dropped its other shoe—or was made to? And if so, what was the nature of the Event, and why the commitment? No one asks these questions because they're truly terrifying: they demand an explanation perpendicular to all the framework of these books. I have no glib answers; those frameworks are mine too, which is why I have trouble suggesting the questions. But this book on FSM that will be relevant to our lives, and not merely a winter pastime, must deal with these questions in some way. And the quality it must have I can only and inadequately call "poetry."

Let us go back to the nature of the participants. I don't have an easy bag to put us in, but let me make notes on our strangeness by examining another key incident: the Abortive Sit-In. Two months after the Car, FSM sat, 5,000 strong on a Friday lawn, to hear our representatives denied audience before the Regents, the Highest Authority. Instead, they rejected the central technical point (on advocacy) of our whole fight, by a policy formulated well before the "negotiations" with which they calmed us; and they visited gratuitous punishment on "hostages" from before the Police Car Epsiode.

Our Monday response was remarkable. To begin with, we *sang*. Not the tired, self-conscious protest songs of the thirties, but our own felt words to the Beatles and Beethoven. We serenaded the IBM card from the steps of Sproul Hall; the death of responsibility, caked in liberal rhetoric, that stalked the campus like Heller's plaster-caked soldier come to life; our loneliness in a pluralist marshmallow world. Those songs are a gold mine for the anthropologist, folklorist, social psychologist. Let me examine just one, because you won't find any in the books.

As background, three sets of words that everyone knew, fog that we flew through: *"Property of the Regents . . ."* —a brass plaque fixed in the sidewalk where our tables once stood; *"49% of the hard-core (demonstrators) are followers of the Castro-Mao line*"—Kerr's quote to the papers, which he claimed months later was a misquote, but never bothered to retract before the public in whose name we were later arrested; "*The university and segments of industry are becoming more alike . . . The production, distribution, and consumption of knowledge in all its forms is said to account for 29 percent of the gross national product and . . . is growing at about twice the rate of the rest of the economy*"—Kerr's description of the institution to which our lives were committed.

And so we sang an early carol:

> Joy to U.C., the word is come:
> Clark Kerr has called us Red!
> If you are 49%
> you can't work for the government:
> the knowledge factory
> turns out more GNP
> without your subversion
> on its property.

And sang it *joyously*. For what other sane response was possible to a bankruptcy of the heart whose dimensions were inexpressible in analytic prose? Certainly we were seriousness personified; we've jail sentences to show for it. But faced with the absurd, in every sense, there is a dimension of response without which seriousness is meaningless. We had it; it is hard to examine; but our ubiquitous humor is an essential testimony to our sanity. That humor was also an indelible stamp on our use of words like "democracy" and "moral commitment," which—for the first time in our American lives—had become alive and real. In a rhetoric fog of words without substance, we often

treated ours lightly, as if leaning on them too seriously
might again crush the life from them.

After the songs, we held a sit-in. To a man the commentators dismiss it as signaling FSM's death. True, we
were dispirited in the remarkable Executive Committee
meeting that followed—in which a hundred people aired
grievances and analysis, speaking in strict rotation from
the doubled circle of face-to-face without which we could
not meet. But our dispirit was, I think, the realization that
the other shoe still hung, and would have to be forced.

No one observes that the movement had been steadily
gathering momentum: that the process in progress was
fueled, not killed, by Friday; that we left the sit-in singing; and that the working apparatus of FSM continued
its activity unchecked. Everyone attributes FSM's "mirac-
ulous revival" to the "ill-timed" action of the Administration in calling up students for fresh new punishments
on stale charges. But was what we called "the Inevitable
Atrocity Theory of Administration Activity" only a metaphor? No one really discusses that sit-in—nor the Big
Sit-In two weeks later, surely the oddest one this country
has seen, which landed 800 of us in jail and fulfilled the
promises made around the Car.

Such unanimity is charming, and suspicious. No one
finds significance in the fact that the penultimate sit-in
was preceded by a *formal debate*. During it, a highly
respected professor asked to speak against the sit-in. Steering Committee—which had kept the movement resolutely
free from faculty tampering—debated the proposition then
and there, and agreed to substitute him for the weaker
of the two speakers against: those who were *for* the
sit-in prevailing in this view over those who were against.
This is a hell of a way to run a movement, no?

I could go on, but why? Something's wrong here. All

the descriptions are subtly askew, subtly irrelevant. There are signs of dissatisfaction with the models: Draper complains we aren't ideological, Goodman complains we aren't analytical, Wolin complains we aren't cautious, Hayakawa complains we aren't Ghandian; and those against us just complain. Everyone wants to put us in their box, and we just don't fit.

Yet these books are relevant in a deeper sense. They are a landscape peaked by humaneness and fissured by spite, drifted deep by leaf-skeletons of words and the winter weathers of the heart, with no blank area marked "Here there be Tygers." These contours were the mold that shaped FSM. They were the trace of the ambiance we struggled within and against. The largest of them, and the most representative of the Academy, is modeled after Kerr's view of his role as President-Mediator. All the leading organized interest groups are represented—but a critical part of FSM's nature is that it wasn't *organized* —and the book succeeds in being distasteful to every constituency, a sphere bristling with views that balance each other hopelessly. But there's another dimension without which everything is flat, and it's absent.

In these books taken together, FSM appears in reverse. There is no humor, no poetry, no community, no contact with the real, no collective sense of value, no sense of the strange. The atmosphere is one of analytical structures that refuse to become relevant, to function properly. Ironically no one notes one of the most characteristic themes of FSM's dialogue on education, politics, scholarship, etc.: not that the structures should be changed, but that they should function properly and relevantly: We did not want new channels, new methods, but the proper functioning of those that were.

To function properly involves contact with reality. Is

this why the political scientists do not tackle the subject of FSM as political organization? Here are some notes. Who were "members" of FSM? No one ever knew, or defined what "membership" meant. When work was needed, you walked onto campus and grabbed the first person wearing an FSM button, and told him what was needed. His response would be *"Why?"* and then you had to explain patiently why you thought it was necessary. If he bought your explanation, he might devote stupendous amounts of energy and time to the task, taking it as his own. If he didn't, he'd just walk away. This was the attitude which spawned the loose maze of thirty autonomous Centrals—with the funny names everyone took so seriously—that were the working structure of FSM. If a need for a function were clear enough, people puddled like rain to fill it, establishing Legal Central, Press Correction Central, or Nexus in any convenient corner. We on Steering Committee—the Master Tacticians of the movement, hah! —often learned of new Centrals days later, or rang frantically for ones that had vanished. Is it any wonder that, leading the final sit-in into Sproul, our estimates of how many would follow ranged from 200 to 3,000?

And what *about* Steering Committee, that mysterious body that everyone—save some of its members—agrees "ran the movement"? Surely some social scientist should have been tempted to examine its function. Was it a tactical group or a policy-making body? Or an aesthetic symbol (the idea is fruitful)? Or simply irrelevant? But this again raises questions that lie at the heart of FSM. Why was the Steering Committee reconstituted four times in the first month, and then left to its own devices for the duration? What had this to do with the question of democratic responsibility on all of our minds? Why, in months of almost daily eight-hour meetings, did Steering Committee operate by discussing each detail down to exhausting consensus? Why was there only *one* vote taken on any substantive issue during this time—about the abortive sit-in—and this vote announced publicly? What caused our fanatic commitment to flexibility: no single tactical decision was made more than twelve hours in advance, and most within three? Surely these are questions that, were analytic tools properly applied to them, might begin to illuminate the nature of FSM. But here is a proper irony: with this irreplaceable experiment at hand in the heart of the Multiversity, to the best of my knowledge only two students (one an undergraduate) are investigating it in depth by talking with the people involved, and one faculty member by a series of questionnaires. *I write theses/about feces*, etc.

So strange. One survey ferreted out another strangeness, because surveys cannot turn their faces. "We asked those who affirmed the importance of off-campus political activity why they felt it important to a student's education, and the principal reason given . . . was its informative value in providing an understanding of the political process, rather than the duties of citizenship or the necessity for accepting responsibility for social problems." Pondering this unexpected answer—and what it portends for Education—I cannot escape feeling that, in a way we only dimly sense, FSM's strangeness was due to our seeing the world perpendicular, with new eyes in a new relation to it.

We had no theory, no elaborate justifications for our actions. We alone did not mourn the lack. But perhaps our aphorisms were more than cute. "*Fiat Lex*," our mock of the motto "Fiat Lux" of the Multiversity that met petition with police: were we not saying, "the letter killeth, but the spirit giveth life"? "Don't trust anyone over thirty": did this refer to age alone, or to a feeling that

few not branded from childhood by post-1948 America
could view the world with our eyes? That view, I think,
is reflected best in the meteor songs of Bobby Dylan, now
enormously popular in Berkeley, who sings for us about not
needing a climatologist to know what weather's in the air;
and about something happening which Mr. Jones can't
quite grasp.*

In fairness, we can't either. I think we were not prepared to accept our human voice coming like a new known
light to illuminate the actual landscapes that flicker into
existence at the edge of our flowing train of illusion. Perhaps we created FSM out of nothing, out of a need to
shield our eyes from the naked strangeness of those landscapes, a need to say: "It wasn't I who did it, it was FSM."
This view might help to explain the paradoxes of FSM.
Perhaps FSM did not exist at all, was only a *name*, a
handle for us (and others) to grab. And here we are at
the frightful abyss again: if FSM did not exist, what *was*
happening during that dense semester in which we tried
to mobilize our distant souls, make contact with the real
again, talk to each other like human beings, and lay our
bodies and hearts on the intangible line of the sane response, the perpendicular response that fitted the absurd
stimulus?

The answer lies in a poetry I cannot give, does not much
yet exist, but is begun. There is a new poetry in America,
the prose of the SNCC workers in the South, who are our
kin. That prose is lively, and unsettling to read; we have
not seen it before. It has spread north to Berkeley: in the
incredible dialogue atop the cop car; and a second time,
ten months later. After the conflict and its personal costs,

---

* *Robert Zimmerman & representative asked $1,000 to quote two
lines of song; but graciously came down to $200. Pardon my
clumsy paraphrase.*

there came a devastating three-month trial: a Catch-22 nightmare with no relevance in our hearts to that for which we had fought. At its close, the judge—whom everyone had assured us "would be defending you if he could"—did not look up at a single defendant, as he sentenced us to fines and jail terms ranging up to four months. Before sentencing, the judge asked for letters explaining why we did it. The 800 solemnly complied. I have seen those letters, and they moved me to tears. They and Sanderson's poem are the only poetry of FSM in existence. With one exception in all that I read, they were gently but staunchly unrepentant. But more: they were a voice I'd never heard from my contemporaries (or elders), the voice of intellect welded to passion, the perfect counterpoise to these books.

Perhaps someone will do a gentle editing job on them before the next rush of FSM books; probably not. I'd like to end by quoting the only one handy:

> We conducted a long struggle, assuming responsibilities we should not have been made to assume, heartbreakingly alone until the end, taking time out from our studies and our lives to do a job that should not have needed to be done. And we comported ourselves with dignity and grace, on the whole unexpectedly so, and with good hearts and trust and kindness for each other.
>
> Confronting an institution apparently and frustratingly designed to depersonalize and block communication, neither humane nor graceful nor responsive, we found flowering in ourselves the presence whose absence we were at heart protesting.

October 1965

Our consciousness intertwines with our media, and what was written about the FSM was an integral part of that experience. Those books soured what little regard I still held for the mind of the Academy and led to my leaving school for good that summer, to discover my own thought in looser circles. I wasn't alone in my intellectual alienation. By that time the colleges were at some kind of worst as homes for the free life of the mind—more retrograde with respect to the awareness and needs of the people they "served" even than in the McCarthy years. In these highly organized graveyards of thought, as in national social inaction, the bankruptcy of Liberal consciousness was revealing itself fully.

Right after the first FSM books were written, we began an active counter-movement with the first teach-ins. Soon those who guard the Academy's borders against live social thought were forced to fight it on their own turf. Now one progress of the struggle is marked by the beachheads insurgent radical scholars have established in the pro-

*fessional academic societies. But the institution of higher
education is still basically hostile to the evolution of
even the* thought *we now need. A broad purging of anti-
Establishment faculty began in 1967 across Amerika, defining one front of the thought-control war. Some are
being fired for overtly political reasons, but most get axed
for practicing more general kinds of unacceptable thought.*

• • • •

*A gut-recognition of the schools as a system of totali-
tarian control and personal impoverishment began spreading among students after the McCarthy numbness lifted.
By the early Sixties it was well advanced, though still
voiced only by a few in contact with the freer educations
of political action and beatnikism. In the FSM this gathering discontent exploded. Everyone—except students—was
astounded to find that the "quality of our education" was
an issue equal with political rights at the heart of our
action. They called our feeling "educational alienation,"
but I think it broods to revolution.*

*This poem came later, when the President of the State
University system was finally fired, for the wrong reasons.
An arch Liberal and the leading managerial theoretician
of the Multiversity, Clark Kerr was also a brilliant manip-
ulator of power. In the hardening political climate he finally lost his grasp and fell to Reagan's displeasure. The
media made a big obnoxious deal out of Mario's com-
mentary on the firing. Mario later amended it with some
kind words about Kerr being a human being and so on.
But his first spontaneous, incautious reaction spoke for
many. We were so weary of all the pretense.*

On The Firing Of Dr. Clark Kerr,
President Of The University of California,
As Seen From The Berkeley Campus

"Good riddance
to bad rubbish . . ."
—Mario Savio

1

Should I crow, say
told you so, thrown
in your own game,
you All-American?
Don't blow my mind
with your newspaper
wonders, I've been there
down under your laureate
trees, learning
to learn to breathe.
It was bad magic
you helped spell
and articulate, in concrete
numbers, numbed us

to answer your own
ice chill, unwilled
and unfelt, efficient,
with all its accomplishments
measured in numbers
and biggers, averted
encounters, degrees.

II

About your Minerva. We put our selves
on the shelves of her locker,
and entered the lotus trance
of class and classification.
She promised them back as soon
as we left, to greet with delight
and a bit of awkwardness, drape
like discovered winter coats
over finely-tuned four-barrel Vitamine muscles
that would work like an academic's prescription
to carry us charmed through the cold
Out There. She lied, she stole
something while we turned our backs in calisthenics.
In the dark, the connection we had with the world
sublimed, like a fugitive untended hue,
and we shaved facing our mirror names
each morning as if that face were ours.

But sometimes, spun over the rail far out
at sea, from the ship you captain
of doom, we recover, shake off
the drugged weary closure, and find

our other still in touch, remember,
respond, rejoin, rejoyce.

III

Hey there then Coach, I'm hip
to your style, and know what we lost
when we took your rulebook words
with what they said of play
to define our game's boundaries
of maybe and warmth. Your language
was legal and disciplined, all
you could offer us, proffer, profess,
answered only the questions
you knew how to ask.

So we learned at your heels,
read the inverse terminologies
of hierarchical order, stamped
on our earth like a trademark
or the signature on a decree
seen from below. Under your offices
wanting a word, ranked and attentive
we watched you and your playmates
playing at power in elaborate
silence, recorded pavlovian notes
in our muscles, responded.

And how you did chide us
for our earnest sport, whose shrillness
was metal still flesh
in dimensions of longing
that escaped your control!

IV

So what if those walls
come tumbling down
that still wear your face,
that your sojourn raised
with rational grace
and speed, and your exit
leaves unchanged? Will you be
surprised, who laid it out
to our critical student selves
in dispassionate ideology
how "the Knowledge Industry now accounts
for 29% of the G.N.P.,"
how by your most excellent instrument
the Mind is bent benevolent
to service of the State?

That's stark and crude, like the first stains
of our lost and unseen blood
now turned visible
on the steps of your Multiversity,
which will call us back
for another lesson, in that place
where we learned to spell *our minds
are not property*, and shook the State
whose backlash sweeps you on.

There was nothing personal, as you
would be the first to admit, leaving us
with our lives. Goodbye.

1967

The Movement and Educational Reform

We quite surprised ourselves, in the FSM, by saying so loudly that the broad process and basic premises of our education, as well as its political face, were for shit. How perfect that this feeling was first voiced at what was then the leading Multiversity of its time! But nothing was special about our perception. Soon college students everywhere began turning their energy to changing their education, in innocuous and radical ways. Almost instantly, the impulse spread down through the high schools and out into the beginning of a movement of free elementary schools.

Free Universities and kindred work began and spread with sit-ins, as the Movement turned on the campuses. By summer 1966, organized student action for ed reform was well begun, involving maybe 60,000, when I wrote some notes trying to sort out where it was taking us. I thought we could tell by examining the nature of the white Movement—not its momentary political goals, but its process, *which was beginning to become clearer as the post-FSM confusion lifted and our motion went on.*

A year later, in jail, I tidied the notes for The American Scholar. *Grad school still was strong in me, I could never write that straight now. From my jail introduction you can see what more could be seen by then. It did not change my mind, and educational reform continues to develop along the lines implicit in the Movement as it was by 1966.*

But these notes have a special relevance for re-tracing how we got to wherever we are. From now we can see clearly what I barely grasped in that introduction. Change only the names, in this description of the Movement's nature, and it becomes an inventory of most of the basic aspects of the hippie/commune movement which was then developing. Our nature has been steadily emerging all along, though the media mythologies have made us imagine false discontinuities.

Given that students are becoming the main source of initiative and energy for the reform of higher education, then the present style and concerns of the Student Movement should indicate the nature of future reforms. I have tried to sketch here some aspects of the Movement more basic than its political surface, and to connect these (rather stiffly, I'm afraid) with some general directions of reform.

Since these notes—originally written at the request of the National Student Association for a workshop on educational reform—were set down well over a year ago, there have been two important developments. The Vietnam War, monstrously swollen, has become the Movement's main focus (sapping much energy from its reform efforts). The increasingly anguished and desperate tone of antiwar activity has begun to color all of the Movement's works; and its character, which I try to sketch below, seems less clear in the stress of the present. With a provident symmetry connected with the War, however, this character shows more clearly in the second development: the appearance of what we temporarily call "the hippie movement," which is spread more widely and deeply than the media can recognize. There are certainly more hippies than antiwar marchers among the young. But these categories are not distinct: more and more young activists are drifting into "the hippie thing." What is becoming clearer is that among America's young a change in life-style is evolving that runs much more deeply than the political skin that first rendered it visible. This change carries important consequences for the nature of mass education.

But that these consequences will be felt within the present system is not at all clear. Current returns from reform efforts suggest that the investment in their present identities of our institutions—and of those who fill roles within them—is too great to permit real change. This neat tautology—that the system cannot change significantly while remaining itself—has an obvious, although inadequate, counter-argument: real change takes time, generations. But the progress of both the War and the "hippie thing" suggests that there will not be such time. For, in their respective ways, they cause and reflect a rapid, profound estrangement of the young from the forms and content of the culture that has produced them.

The young are leaving; they will not return. It is too early to see the shape of where they are going, but some of the colors are already clear. It is about this that I was writing a year ago, in the context of thoughts about the potential flexibility of the American college system which now seem to me naïve. The prospects for radical reform *within* the system seem dim indeed. But, with these afterthoughts as foreword, what I wrote then still seems to make sense; and I have left it virtually unchanged.

Some Aspects of the Movement (1966)

No one is quite sure where the Movement begins or ends. Its heart is SNCC and Students for a Democratic Society; and the NAACP and Democratic reform groups seem out-of-bounds. But how do we divide the spectrum within these limits? If the Peace Corps is out, the coincidence of its popularity in Movement centers needs explaining. Cooperation with the Establishment may disqualify; but the student-run Experimental College integrated into the formal structure of San Francisco State College speaks with the Movement's voice. To separate sharply pacifist living experiments from groups of hippies playing with psychedelic utopias in rambling old buildings seems difficult and foolish; and even the hippies seem more Movement than, say, the Young Socialist Alliance does.

It may seem that I understand the Movement too broadly. But there is an understanding of it that is certainly too narrow: to view it as being defined in any significant way by its occasional semi-stable organizational manifestations. For were the Movement the political phenomenon most commentators take it to be, we'd expect to have a clearer grasp than we do of its location and identity. But the kinds of concerns that seem to be the characteristic marks of its presence are not "political" in any familiar sense of the term. Indeed, most writers take the Movement's trademarks to be crippling flaws in its political potential. Within their frame of reference, they may be right; but I do not think we are talking about the same Movement.

For there is understanding to be gained by treating my generation's involvement in social action as if it were composed of two distinct phenomena. (The division is not entirely artificial.) One of these is a series of political engagements—over the War, Civil Rights, and so on—that do not seem to differ fundamentally from their counterparts of thirty years ago. The other, which I'll call the Movement because it is new, is a matter of *style*. Not all of our political actions are Movement; and only the iceberg tip of the Movement can be seen. For political involvement is a dye, which renders only a part of the Movement visible.

Of what does this *style* consist? First, there is a concern for the caliber of interpersonal relationships: for qualities like tolerance, openness and honesty, which are thought of in their positive, rather than neutral, senses. This concern springs from a feeling that the relationships among people working (or learning) together must constantly be dealt with in dimensions other than the narrowly functional. The Movement is increasingly sensitive to the delicate inseparability of means and ends and, as well, to the flimsiness of the line dividing the public and the private. "The price of the liberation of the white people," says James Baldwin, "is the liberation of the blacks," and, Black Power or not, the SNCCniks are deeply aware of how immune to legislation the need to hate is. Our slavery is to our condition and needs—but not simply to the economic or political versions of these. And so the bumperstickers read "Make Love Not War," rather than "Make Peace . . ." or "Make Plows . . ." Similarly, there is a feeling that much that has been characterized as the confrontation of public roles can and must be made interpersonal on some level. Part of the Berkeley Free Speech Movement's demand was for face-to-face meetings with administrators. And members of the War Resisters'

League, in earnest one-to-one dialogue, attempt to persuade small manufacturers to refuse war contracts.

A second characteristic of the Movement's style is the level of social organization on which it works. In this, the Movement is most clearly distinct from its political allele. For the present Old Left among us (not to mention the old Old Left) aims at the mass: at the racial, economic or occupational population. But the unit in terms of which the Movement conceives change tends to be the small group. And the mechanism of change is often thought of as the creation of a climate of self-propelled, autonomous groups engaged in satisfying activity, whose presence inspires not so much imitation as exploration. The way to influence large groups is by local example, rather than by global persuasion.

In a culture of the hard and soft sell, of too many words with too little substance, the Movement's alienation from rhetoric runs deep: when it does not proceed by example, it uses force (if it can). This pragmatism is not simply a reflection of the feeling that bare moral and intellectual suasion is an inadequate tool. Rather, *direct personal involvement* is the Movement's human backbone and colors all of its thoughts. "Lay your bodies on the line" is less a battle cry than a testament to the conviction that commitment and reward cannot be accomplished by proxy. In saying that people must be involved in the decisions that shape their lives, the emphasis is on *involved*.

There are two ways in which this essential "existential" component of the Movement's identity manifests itself. One may be seen by comparison with the extreme hangovers of the Old Left, like the Young Socialist Alliance and the Progressive Labor Party. These see themselves as tightly disciplined cadres enacting change on a mass level: the workers are a class to whom an appeal is made in History's name. In consequence, there is a remarkable distance between them as political actors and the subject(s) of their acts. But there is less distance generally between the callers and the called with the Movement. And it is at its best when this distance is least: when it comes not to tell but to listen and share, in the slums of the city and the academy.

The way in which the Movement tends to merge with the landscape is rarely noticed, and accounts for some of the difficulty in trying to establish its location and identity. This lessened distance and the small-group form are intimately related. They mean also that political dialogue must be cast in a different vocabulary than that possible with the comfortable separation of Changer and Changed. These close quarters, and the ambiguity of the Movement's outline—no one holds a membership card—mean that it must take seriously the qualities of the relationships that exist between people wherever it operates.

The Movement's "existential" orientation is expressed directly in the way its groups are structured and operate. "Participatory democracy" shows up as an operating principle in one or another variant, and there is constant debate over how to render the concept workable. As a result, many groups have explicit mechanisms designed to discourage leadership. The most balanced view seems to be that it provides less than it inhibits. (Concern about leadership can be subtle: at present SDS is conversing internally about the way the questionable coin of speechmaking ability by itself makes their conferences elitist, and encourages passivity and alienation.) Again, the Movement's groups tend to be sized and operated so as to avoid dependence on fixed and hierarchical roles for their members to play. The lack of structure that generally characterizes Movement groups is the result of *choice* rather than inability and is meant to create a climate that fosters responsibility and initiative.

Not only the structures, but the very identities of the Movement's organizations are fluid. To a considerable extent the Movement shows up in *ad hoc* groupings, and its less-evanescent bodies still engage in constant redefinitions of their natures and goals. This again is not from inability to create stable groups. In part, it is a reflection of the Movement's being alive and in a process of growth (indeed, perhaps the Movement *is* a process of growth): for groups no less than for individuals, a fixed identity is a death. But also, this is a consequence of the problem orientation—rather than theory/ideology orientation—of the Movement. Each problem, or each stage in a problem, demands its own group, unique as a key tried in a lock. At any rate, the continuity of even SNCC and SDS is more skeletal than real; and the Movement seems to depend on temporary group involvements as its basic modality of work and emotional sustenance.

Such disposable organizations—and a growing Movement indifference to marriage, put briefly as "People change, why tie them down?"—would seem to require that those involved have little fear and a high competence in freedom. "If anything, what we're trying to do . . . is to see how you can move even though you're afraid," said SNCC's Bob Moses. And people in many areas of the Movement speak often of the central necessity of conquering the fear that holds you static and afraid to change.

This brings up the essential and difficult question of freedom. To the Movement, freedom, like democracy, is less a political state than a psychological condition. The chanting of "Freedom Now" in university sit-ins is not incongruous, for in every area of its attention the Movement is concerned with the problem of ensuring or creating the ability to make real choices, real decisions. Clearly, the Movement's concentration on creating viable concepts of freedom is connected with other characteristics of its style.

One element in the Movement's notion of freedom is the concept of *non-coercive concern*. Whether the example be L.B.J. and the Negroes, parent and child, or teacher and student, our culture interprets "care" or "concern" to mean telling the recipients what to do "for your own good." The Movement seems quite consistent in its response to the notion of decisions being made for other people—whether in Vietnam or graduate school or the ghetto. Again, narrow notions of "efficiency"—whether in the procurement of jobs for the poor or graduates for industry—seem inimical to the Movement's idea of freedom. In evaluating social processes, it seeks indices of "efficiency" that are compatible with and include this idea.

There are other relevant aspects of the Movement: its interest in creating non-coercive modes of authority, a notion foreign to this culture; its gropings toward non-destructive community; and its developing notion of a group as a collection of autonomous individuals come together to tackle a problem of common interest, which is paradoxical in this culture, in which to belong to a group is to submerge your own identity. But these fall beyond the scope of these notes.

One last element of the Movement's style is of critical importance. The Movement is a collection of young intellectuals; and this indelibly marks the activism that is usually taken as its distinguishing feature. Draft board sit-ins are accompanied by teach-ins. CORE and Women for Peace conduct economic studies. SNCC and the War

Resisters' League use sociodrama as a sophisticated train-ing device. SDS and university reform groups analyze power structures. The Movement's intrauniversity disputes are often subtle and learned.

It is most fruitful, I think, to view this eclectic intel-lectualism as the product of the Movement's basic iden-tity as a loose assemblage of experimental social scientists. This picture is suggested by the Movement's constant pre-occupation with methodology, its facility at making and discarding models, its keen sensitivity as to how observer and observed interact, and, of course, by the way it views almost all its acts mainly as experiments to be studied and learned from. Also, throughout the Movement there is the sense that the end of research should be insight.

Insight into what? Into the question of human nourish-ment. The problems to which the Movement's style are addressed are tomorrow's problems, although they are here today. If we take politics to be in essence the lan-guage of men contending with a world of too little bread, then the Movement is indeed beyond politics, in a sense that is not at all incompatible with its very real political identity. For the Movement is a collection of young in-tellectuals concerned with the quality of interpersonal relations, who work on a small-group level in unstruc-tured temporary groups in which the dominant themes are existential involvement and effective (potent) freedom. This Movement springs, by no coincidence, from a mono-culture whose most obvious characteristic is the lack of social forms and institutions that foster or permit the engagement of men with themselves and with their work.

The suburb, the TV set and the bureaucracy—as we now know them—are three of many tangents to a circle, toward whose center not only our white middle class, but also the USSR, the Common Market, and the Negro are converging in their separate ways; and the rest of the World lags behind by less than our lives. However one conceives of the Movement, one must explain its motive power; and I see no other explanation than a reaction, direct or not, to this convergence. There are certain values that seem essential to our emerging and different idea of human nature, and that seem unable to survive in that center. The Movement may well be our search for viable forms and processes in which to embody these values—it is in this sense that I mean the description of it as a group of experimental social scientists as more than just a metaphor—and may itself be the process that creates them.

Some General Directions of Radical Reform

At the close of a conference held to evaluate the first semester of the Experimental College at San Francisco State College, a professor complained that all the discussion of experimental education was intertwined with talk about the Movement. He went on to suggest that the Movement was a limited audience with narrow interests and goals, and that its relevance to the question of educational reform had been blown up all out of proportion. But there are two reasons for supposing him wrong.

First, the society and the university are so intimately intertwined that their ills do not differ significantly. If the needs of either—formally recognized or not—dictate radical reform, some segment of the population will be most sensitive to these needs, and will indicate which way the wind of change is blowing. Surely the young adults of college age are this weather vane, having less of an inertial

investment in the status quo. We call the motion already
in progress in this group, the Movement.

Second, the Movement is a force as well as a direction. Our culture has created the juggernaut of mass
higher education, with no understanding of its function,
nature or potential. In this vacuum the faculty, performing
after their fashion, have shaped the institution in their
own image. That they can lift themselves by their boot-
straps to achieve radical reform seems unlikely. Granted
this, we are left with students as the only major source
of initiative and energy for reform. There is never much
free energy available for radical social change; we live
on a narrow margin. But what there is among us is embodied in the Movement. The disgruntled professor may
propose a whole conference of clever reforms; but reforms depend on response, and if they are not in tune
with the Movement's interests and nature, they will re-
main unaccomplished.

The sketch given above of the Movement's character
suggests some directions that Movement-centered radical
educational reform will take (whether or not it is possible *within* the system, which is a separate matter). The
primary drive will be toward expanding individual freedom, and creating engagement in the learning process.
Presently the role of the student is a dependent one. His
being placed in an autonomous situation—with regard to
either the subject or the method of his learning—is an
infrequent privilege, usually laboriously achieved. But if
education is to be a process that enables individuals to
recognize and meet their own needs, autonomy is a central necessity.

A drive toward educational autonomy is not, however,
a simple matter. Our college lives are cut from a single
piece of cloth, and the warp threads are all manifestations

of the Big Daddy Complex. There is little basic difference between dorm mother checking permissible hours, administrators checking permissible political activity, advisers checking permissible programs, and professors checking permissible readings and approaches: the motto is "for your own good," the effect is to inhibit autonomous adulthood. And so the subject of reform will be no single one of these examples, but the *attitude* itself: it must be, for the examples are tied inseparably to one another.

A consequence of the drive for autonomy will be a rethinking of the traditional teacher/student roles. (It is here, probably, that the stiffest resistance will be encountered from Those Who Have the Students' Best Interests at Heart.) The present role of teacher as leader generates passivity. This role will constantly be attacked, and attempts made to replace it with basic group-learning situations that involve minimal, nominal or no leadership. The permissible kinds of interaction between student and teacher will have to be broadened, in the context of a growing understanding of the learning process which sees these two as being involved in more than their narrowly functional roles. In consequence, the line between teacher and student will blur, despite its present sanctity.

Emphasis will shift from the teaching process to the learning process; this will produce new applied models of human nature and learning and further alter the traditional roles. The notion that learning must be embedded in a coercive framework—with threats of poor grades and no passport degree—will be increasingly challenged. Learning energy must be generated by the importance of the work itself to the individual or group; and mechanisms will be sought to make this more possible. Again, if we conceive of "getting an education" as the acquiring of an attitude rather than an object, the role of the teacher as the transmitter of a fixed body of knowledge will undergo a radical change. The way to teach students to learn may be by example rather than bombardment: by learning in various ways and publicly; and lecturing, disguised or overt, may be replaced by the displaying of raw chunks of developing understanding, with all their sloppy edges dangling, and all the ego-danger this involves.

The shift to the notion of teacher as learner-and-sharer will have other consequences. The way in which the teacher now doubles as a cop will be attacked as untenable. The "each one teach one" philosophy behind community tutorial programs will be taken up in the academy; and attention will shift from the faculty to the student body itself as the main source of (newly conceived) teaching resources. There will be a drive to shift the learning experience along the dimension of what Roger Harrison, now with National Training Laboratories, calls *encounter:* the extent to which emotions, values and deeper aspects of the self are actively involved, touched and changed. This will perforce involve the "teacher" in a new fashion: he must join or be left behind, and either choice means that his relation to the student (and conversely) must be newly conceived.

Along this line, our sense of how intimately we impinge upon each other will begin to deformalize all small-group learning situations, and make their occasional resemblance to encounter groups both more noticeable and more deliberate. Indeed, the single most persistent phenomenon now found in experiments in higher education—within or without university walls—is their turning inward upon themselves to become conversations about the nature of the learning process and of group interaction. Surely this is a barometer to our sense of our needs.

There will be several kinds of change aimed directly at increasing engagement in the learning process. There will be pressure to structure theoretical learning—especially in the social sciences and to some exent in the humanities—around problems in which the individual (or group) is already involved. This will mean a renewed attack on the artificial barriers that disciplines and time-divisions of study present to learning. Engagement with real problems will necessitate decentralization of the learning setting, with a consequent further de-emphasis of the classroom. The curriculum will be forced to become directly relevant to the immediate social (or artistic) concerns of those who will be applying pressure. For example, cross-disciplinary courses in rapid transit problems or election campaigns will be requested, not as fringe enjoyments, but as central academic concerns. There will be an increasing realization that the individual in a standard classroom is neither fully himself nor a member of a real group; and thus there will be demand for an ambience that permits groups or individuals, whose educational interests are purely their own, to be accepted as having valid educational identities. In particular, there will be pressure to allow the *ad hoc* group to become the normal form in which non-solitary learning occurs.

It is clear that there will be demand not only for the abandonment of grades with their attendant coercive and standardizing influence, but also for a broader revision of the kinds of indices by which educational achievement is measured. Some way must be found to evaluate (or simply recognize?) the degree to which a student has undergone a personal process, rather than become a processed person.

There are other kinds of reform, more or less radical, that appear as plausible targets, given the present energies and interests of students. Perhaps the most important, and certainly the most discussed at present, is the radical redistribution of power within the academic community. In many ways, freedom and power are inseparable. So student attempts to gain control of curriculum, degree requirements, the hiring, firing and tenure of faculty, and all the other broad aspects of their academic lives, are natural and essential consequences of the drive toward autonomy that characterizes the Movement. The possession of such power will deeply change the nature of student relationships with faculty, other students, and their own work.

I have tried to indicate broad kinds of reform that are both radical (have non-trivial consequences for the nature of the educational process) and currently plausible. My perspective has been specialized, although I think there are solid grounds for accepting this narrowness as realistic, and I am under no illusion of having sketched a complete catalogue, even in such general terms. There is a danger, however, in confusing those radical reforms that are attractive to the Movement as it now exists, and hence are possible, with those radical reforms that are needed. There are kinds of reforms that current interests and energies seem blind to. The need for a deep synthesis of the Two Cultures (to put a very complex matter briefly) grows daily; one can only conjecture how critical the need is, but surely the project will entail a complete revolution in the nature of our knowledge. Less broadly and more immediately, the current structuring of knowledge and research into disciplines appears more and more restrictive and untenable; yet our interest in the problem is piecemeal and peripheral.

In our time, knowledge—or data, at least—proliferates unbearably; we have no viable mechanisms for coping with its present qualities, let alone with those soon to come. And there is a clear need for a revision of the place higher education occupies in our life space, from a localized to a continuously distributed activity. Matters like these should also be our concern but seem not to be. It is hard to tell if we will turn to them once significant progress is made in the areas of our immediate interests sketched above.

August 1966

When We Sighted the Yellow Submarine

On campus one day during the FSM I was handed an invitation to a CORE picket, done in ornate curlicues and advertising "an elegant cast of imported performing bigots." It was the first political leaflet with a sense of humor that I'd ever seen. As our aspects emerge, a slow and difficult wedding of them goes on. That leaflet marked one stage; this one commemorates another.

In December 1966 the Administration sent their police to evict an antiwar table from our Student Union. The scene blew, and by midnight a crowd of 3,000 voted to call the school out for its second major strike. As usual, our action gained us nothing tangible except reprisals— for the rest of the Sixties, after FSM, there was no significant institutional change, political or educational, at Berkeley.

But also as usual, our action gave us something of ourselves. Flesh in a granite canyon, we held one last meeting, to call off the strike and seek another way. A thousand crowded into a lecture hall, we set up an open microphone, and for hours people rose to testify. At the end all that was clear was that something had come together in us. We stood up, some weak scrap of the Internationale *began and stumbled, and then suddenly the whole room burst*

*into singing "We all live in a yellow submarine . . . ,"
chorus after chorus.*

*What we were celebrating was quite precise. The myth
of flower-child innocence had been ours at first too. Even
without the media to confuse us, while we were digesting
the first major effects of grass and acid almost all believed these divorced the will from political action. In
this strike for the first time we saw hippies and activists
join together in action. And in this meeting, we made our
first mass public call for a broader community of our own
in Berkeley, beyond the campus. (It was already coming
together.)*

*This leaflet was Strike Committee's last formal com-
munique. We decided upon the mask because throughout
the affair we'd been accused of bringing "mass coercion"
to bear upon the University. Of all the leaflets I wrote
or helped with in a decade of Berkeley politics, I signed
only this one, because it was such a joy. (The submarine,
of course, was yellow.)*

MASSKOERCION

RESOLUTION OF THE STRIKERS' MEETING

IN 2000 LSB ON DECEMBER 6, 1966

This body reaffirms its commitment both to the basic principles of the strike and to the five specific demands;

Declares a temporary recess to the strike;

Empowers the Strike Committee to continue negotiations with the Administration;

Will organize and prepare for the resumption of the strike, or for other appropriate activity, if our demands are not met;

Encourages all who supported the strike to wear the mask of their choice to class on Wednesday, and urges the Strike Committee to make such provision for this as is possible.

A REMARK

From this past week, and the quarter in which it was embedded, we have drawn four lessons:

* The faculty cannot solve our problems. They did not choose to implement their 1964 FSM Resolution, and the Muscatine Report demonstrated their inability to deal collectively and constructively with the educational ills of the University. Their Monday response and resolution complete the lesson.

* Direct action against the Administration can only create us the space we need for freedom, as it has done. But the Administration cannot be forced to build for us what we need in that space. That task is ours.

* We can defend that space. In the Regents' resolution, retribution was not retroactive. We read this to indicate that they respect our strength and recognize that if they took direct action against us the University would be destroyed. On the other hand, their resolution shows that in the future they are ready to force this destruction rather than accede to our just demands.

* A community which had seemed submerged has revealed itself again, discoverable and developing. What is needed now is the building of institutions fit for this community's expression and growth.

Let us now, with this learned, begin to build.

- The Strike Committee   (mr)

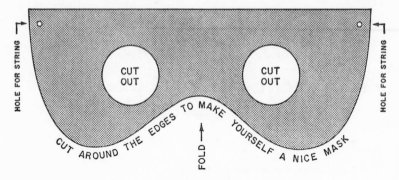

HOLE FOR STRING

CUT OUT

CUT OUT

HOLE FOR STRING

CUT AROUND THE EDGES TO MAKE YOURSELF A NICE MASK

FOLD

AN EXPLANATION

The Yellow Submarine was first proposed by the Beatles, who taught us a new style of song. It was launched by hip pacifists in a New York harbor, and then led a peace parade of 10,000 down a New York street. Last night we celebrated the growing fusion of head, heart and hands; of hippies and activists; and our joy and confidence in our ability to care for and take care of ourselves and what is ours. And so we made a resolution which broke into song; and we adopt for today this unexpected symbol of our trust in our future, and of our longing for a place fit for us all to live in. Please post, especially where prohibited. We love you.

NO CONFIDENCE

1967
Cooling It:
The Adventures of Garbageman

My last year in school, I taught in a system-sponsored experimental undergrad program. It choked off its promises of freedom and participation and convinced me that if I wanted to work on re-creating education, inside-the-system wasn't the place to do it. I left school in 1966, hung out at the Experimental College at S.F. State for a few months, and then went East to visit campuses. In spring 1967 I came back, to play around in the Haight while I was waiting to go to jail for the FSM. The Supreme Court finally rejected our appeal, and I spent nine summer weeks in the Santa Rita Rehabilitation Center.

Ah, young political prisoners! especially when they're trying to learn how to be writers! Who can resist a traditional experience, a rite of passage? Not me (though I drew the line at the whorehouse door). I marched into Santa Rita proudly—and reality snuck up and overwhelmed me from behind.

Jail was a stunning experience, in the quietest of ways. Three years of turbulent action had left me weary, and I

*would not find another nine weeks of such calm detach-
ment for years to come. Into that place, peaceful as a
campus that had never known disruption,* I went to think
about all our changes—like, to write articles. I adapted,
found my niche in the jail ecology, started writing—and
then found my attention turning inward, to observe my
own behavior and what I was feeling, to ponder the details
and startling ease of my co-option into that cold context.*

*All my ten years of training as a super-student at the
World's Greatest Multiversity had prepared me perfectly
to be a model prisoner in the county jail! It was a tremendous flash, though it didn't come fully clear for a year.
I mean, it's one thing to know stuff like this with your
mind, and quite another to be forced to live it through in
unmistakeable theater.*

*Naturally, these notes from jail were smuggled out by
the traditional trivial methods, and then mimeographed as
a letter to my friends.*

---

* At that time and place, there were not yet significant stirrings
of revolt from within against the penal system.

The Adventures of Garbageman
Under the Gentle Thumb of the Authority Complex

They locked us in mess hall again, to wait through a recount and a recount and a recount outside. Shadowboxing, the black kids singing. "Hey, sport, you're kinda crazy," said my new sidekick on the garbage crew. A Mexican kid with a sour expression, he pulled his toothbrush out and combed his moustache. You see it on most of them, that bent-over plastic handle hooked over their shirt pocket. Sideburns and beards are verboten, a moustache is all one can nurse. "Grows out all kinky if you don't keep after it," explained the kid who married a virgin. It really gave me a start, the first time I saw someone pull out their toothbrush and use it, casual as a comb through greaser hair.

"You're kinda crazy, sport," said my partner—he does the kitchen head, I keep after the cans. "I know," I said, idly. "No . . . you act kinda crazy most of the time." "Yeah, I know." "No, I really mean it, you do." "Man, I *know*," I said, "it's cool." "You like acid, dontcha," he stated. I cracked up and eyed him for a moment, doing that little widening motion so the pupil floats like a blue yolk in its innocent white. "Man, I was crazy *before* I took acid," I said, "but yeah, I do." He was the fourth one to tell me I liked acid; they all say that with the positive relief of a bird watcher hitting the right page in his manual. No one asks about grass. It's taken for granted: everyone here smokes shit on the outside (which adds to the notion that grass, at least, has no direction intrinsic in its properties and use; and that its middle-class connection with interpersonal openness, etc., is simply a product of where we are). But—even though a number of the spades have tried acid and dug it, and some of us haven't—LSD is taken as a kind of dividing line. We are the hippies. Even though we stalk around with books in our hands all the time, that's our identification: not college kids, or "professor" (as it was when I used to dig ditches, that traditional tag), but hippies. No question about it. The other inmates are friendly, curious, josh us. There's a goodly amount of respect for us as a group: we have status, an identity. Hippies.

"They don't understand you guys," said the wiseacre kid who tools the mess hall truck around and jokes with the guards. "Whaddya mean?" I asked him. "Like, what went on between you'n the officer inside, it really put him uptight. He was about ready to roll you up and send you off to Greystone, thought you were some kinda fruit." We were sitting behind the mess hall, waiting for the count-clear siren. Earlier I'd walked into the little glassed-off office in the kitchen, to get the duty officer to clear my work so I could go. Four of the mess crew were clustered around his desk. "Whaddaya want?" An antic impulse, I answered, "Love." "What?" "Love, man, and I'm happy. Also you might check out my work." He gave me a very odd look, and said to wait a bit; cleared me later without mentioning the incident, which I thought no more about till the kid brought it up.

He went on. "A lot of the officers, they don't like you guys. I mean, they're cops, you know, and you guys fought City Hall, and got away with it. Now with us, that's cool, we understand and dig you, know what I mean? But they feel you made the cops look foolish then, and a lot still have it in for you even if it was a couple years ago. They look for you to be troublemakers. And when you aren't, well, that bugs 'em too. You gotta be careful with them, they don't understand you."

But aside from not letting our books through, there's been remarkably little hard-timing. Partly this is because, almost to a man, we're easy with being here. (Today at lunch I remembered how bristling with hostility we'd been on our first visit, the night of the arrest, and we all had a good laugh at the contrast. "But," said Mario, "there were reasons then, you know, like getting dragged down stairs and all that.") But also it's because we've violated their expectations. We're open and friendly and curious. And we work hard; that counts for a lot. Garson, Lustig and Salaff are on Bakery crew, up at 4:00 in the morning; now Mario has joined them. At first the ex-service guy who runs the show was down on them, riding them. Now he treats them with open friendliness, so much so that it's getting to be a bit of a distraction. "He keeps trying to father me," says Mario. Word has leaked back from the Booking Office, Santa Rita's nerve center: he keeps talking about us. "Get me nine more like them, hell, I'll have this place so changed . . ." There has been a bit of trouble: a couple of kids have wound up in the Hole for four days for refusing to work. But the work was painting Army barracks, the objection moral, rather than lazy. All in all, our stock is sound and rising. But still no books.

• • • •

Movie again. "Boy's Night Out," starring Kim Novak and her angora ass. The big attraction though is the woman prisoners: herded into the balcony, they peeked at us behind the curtain: a chorus of enthusiastic catcalls, conducted by their waves. Our girls did most of the waving.

Tonight was incredible. On the left, three Scarsdale commuters and their bachelor fourth for bridge. He's tied to his mom; they, to American Suburban Wives and lives etched in the most vulgar terms. *"What will the neighbors think if they see you fixing the garage door?"* *"They'd think we were trying to live within our income."* *"That's exactly what I'm trying to avoid."* And, facing them, Kim Novak, post-grad researcher in sociology, doing her thesis on "Adolescent Sexual Fantasies in the Suburban Male." They meet her complete with *Playboy* dream apartment when they decide to pump for a joint mistress. She tapes them spilling their guts, plays Kinsey with the three shrewish wives, adroitly sidesteps fucking (*"That's what a nice girl is trained to do best, Professor"*) and winds up snagging the fourth after a plot sequence you can imagine. *"Hey, she didn't mention money. There must be something wrong with her if she doesn't want money."* In the middle of the film—with the noise from the seats and loges crescendoing antiphonally in response to the suggestive dialogue—they cut off the angora cleavage and wiggling stretchpants to lecture the men on what *gentlemen* the other part of the compound had been the previous night, seeing the film. The air was electric.

"Rehabilitation" is the word. "It blows my mind," said Al, "the kind of flicks I go to see are *The Pawnbroker*, *La Strada*, like that . . ." And here we all are, straight from Berkeley, having our noses rubbed in the middle classes' crude and deadly satires upon itself. Last Sunday night, when the girl learned her Texan was drawl veneer over Boston brass, her roommate sketched a plot for revenge, and held out the thigh-high blue-mist nightie. She reached for it as for a rifle. Annie Get Your Gun. I have seen that look in my lover's eye. We sit around on the barracks porch at night, talking delicately about Vietnam with the eighteen-year-old Mexican kids who blow their bread customizing cars and want to marry virgins. And on that magic screen—which has brought the refrigerator behind Missy Novak to stir aspirations and revolution in heathen lands—flash these artful images of the constant damage we inflict upon ourselves and endure.

I have seen the scars of napalm or atomic war only in photographs; my political friends and past find in them the image of us as destroyer. But these are far away, a level of abstraction distant. Though all my conventional conscience cries out against this, I am more struck with pity and terror at the little I let myself see with different eyes of the scars on the selves I know. The napalm falls like occasional mad thunder, but our machines of self-violence are the most cunning, constant as hunger. The child in the bed is unwilling at first to believe his foot gone. I see only enough of how I am crippled to guess at how much I will not let myself see. "Movies"—extensions of the eye and the imagination—"are better than ever."

• • • •

Everyone's curious about Mario. "Which one he, where he, he you leader? Say man, point him out to me." Sitting around behind mess hall, waiting for the count siren to sound all-clear: a dozen of us, all but two black. They talk about Mohammed Ali, about the fighters he admires, about us. "Mario, he the leader of them hippies." "Shit, he had a million people following him, that dude. And why? Man, because he spoke *freely* what he thought, that's why."

• • • •

A bird flew into the garbage compound. Some wanted to kill it; three of us went in after it. One heaved a brush at it as it flew, missed. I climbed the mountain of boxed empty tins, retrieved it, jumped down. Outside someone took it gently from my hand. "Look here"—to no one— "here's how you hold it, see, so he free in your hand." Then chucked it into the sky, underhand and up. *Away*. The tension broke, and suddenly a tall black kid did a spot routine. "Ho, when he get home . . ." The circle acted it out: the girl birds hanging around twittering, testing his muscles. "There they was, hundreds of em, two of em had me by the wings and one by the legs, oh, but I faked em all out. Shit they was *all* over me, man, they was gonna roast me . . . you got any idea what they smell like?" "Tell it, man, tell it . . ."

● ● ● ●

Syllogism

Suppose the sun
were a ball of wax, a marble
to look through, your kneecap
detachable and comforting. What
would the officer say, trying to avoid
the slight smile on your lips?
He takes out his notebook, enters
your name with a tiny check
like the English teacher who waited to catch
you closing your eyes to hear: *have*
some respect, swallow that butterfly. You invented names
behind her back too, she took them away
with an extra assignment. Then
or therefore, who can guess why your nonchalant finger

pauses from writing 500 times
to trace the warmth that still lingers
like morning candy or egg
in the turn of your smile?

• • • •

Rehabilitation? With a vengeance. This place is so middle class I can't believe it. Dig: we get up at 6:15 every
morning; our lights are out by 9:30, though we get till
ten on Saturday, our big day. Make your bed, sweep up,
keep your area clean. Or Else. I shave and shower every
other day, and change clothes on the day in between.
Three square meals a day perforce, nutritionally adequate
and sometimes even good (with respect to regularity, bulk
and nutrition, I eat better than I do at home; Karen's mad
at my spreading that about). We work five or seven days
a week. No beards permitted, hair to be kept neatly
trimmed. My mother would love it.

Me, I'm the Garbageman. Three times a day I keep after
the mess in the mess hall, so to speak, cleaning and jerking
150-pound cans full of slop, again so to speak. "You gonna
have some muscles when you get out of there, I bet,
man." (The slop goes to the hog farm, where Jack is
working.) "How long you in for?" asked the mess guard
when I reported for assignment. "Ninety days." "What
for?" "Sit-in." "*Garbage.*" I don't know if he was for or
against me: I dig the job. My hidden advantage, of course,
is that I can't smell; but if I keep after the stuff, even that
doesn't make much of a difference.

My day is chopped up by counts, meals at the odd hours
of Messman's schedule, and slinging garbage (which gives
me two or three hours of welcome work). I am left with
seven clear segments of an hour or two. Morning and
afternoons I read or write; evenings now, volleyball, or

an occasional game of chess or dominos. That's an idyllic picture, actually; unless I go off and hide to write, people are constantly falling on to me, and I into conversation with them—or more often, listening and watching. I've begun mild calisthenics morning and evening (many of us and some few of the regulars go through some such counting ritual). All in all, there's much more usable freedom than I'd expected.

Taking a page from Cassius Clay, when he still used that name, I cultivate a somewhat antic air: careening down the tile corridors with an endlessly varied wail of *"Gaaaaarbage, ake way for de gaaaahbudge . . ."* like a London street-cry. And at other times, endlessly with a book and writing pad in my hand. "I'm conditioning the guards," I told the kid who asked why. If they think you slightly mad, you can get away with a lot.

• • • •

Many of us are looking on this imprisonment as our only possible live rehearsal for what draft-resistance might bring. A county jail isn't much like a federal prison, nor is a month or two like three to five years, but it's the best we can do. I have been cheered both because I adapt easily to the life and people here, and also because I've had no trouble launching and sustaining a mind-project: the essay I'm working on, about the generation gap. For the month before I came in, I was working my ass off on another manuscript: I expected to need an involuntary vacation. Instead, my desires to talk with people and to plug away on the essay are constantly fighting with each other.

Paradoxically, even as maintaining an independent mental and emotional life here is much more practical than I'd expected, the idea of spending a long time in jail becomes even less appealing. I'm not sure why. Weinberg points out that Santa Rita is more oppressive than the S.F. county jail, where he did time for Civil Rights, precisely because it's more humane, a model county jail (he likens it to the ideal socialist state). I dig what he means; it confuses me even more about doing federal time behind bars. S——, W——, a couple of others have already decided to split for Canada, though their stay here has had little impact on the decision. I have begun thinking about it, for the first time. Barely.

Visiting days are a mixed blessing, mail call also. "You have to be where you are to make it," points out Steve, "and news or touch of the outside pulls you back, between two worlds." There are other reminders, besides the papers, to keep our thoughts ambivalent. Last Sunday's flick was a WWII romance, set in Southeast Asia: jungle warfare, the whole bit. We have been well-conditioned: we cheered when Sinatra and his faithful handful of natives wiped out the Jap jungle airstrip with its planes near the end, in a sneak attack, and then penetrated the Chinese border and executed a couple of hundred captives taken there, in retaliation for their attack on the supply convoy that was supposed to support our boys. Back in the barracks, the papers describe Westmoreland's request for 140,000 more men. How many of us lay awake that night, trying to pick apart that snarl of feelings generated by the flick: exhilaration, regret, detachment, anger, and fear?

● ● ● ●

Some word from the women's quarters filters in through the lawyers—mostly about Tina, who besides being the only one with a long sentence has a belly big as a watermelon. She went in cracking jokes about the kid getting a discount on his first sit-in sentence, for time already served. "She gets protein three times a day," said Alex to David and me, "and milk with every meal." We just sighed.

When Tina went in, the lady sergeant was shaking. Why? Rosemary and Patty had gone in a week earlier, and somehow word had sprouted that they were preparing a sit-down strike, to be triggered by Tina's arrival. She capitalized on the situation, if that's an acceptable word for a Communist, telling them coyly, in effect, treat us right and there'll be no trouble. Notwithstanding, they put her to work in the supply room, where she sees the new women as they come in. "We felt you'd be good at organizing things," the matron explained to her.

Tina gets an immense volume of mail. They let her have one letter a night, on weekdays. Yesterday her daily missive was an anonymous hate letter. She protested: that was going a bit too far. They let her trade it in on real words. Mario got a hate letter too, from New Jersey. But the censor returned it to the sender because it was written on both sides of the page, against prison rules.

• • • •

Saslow has built a microscope—an improvement on the Leeuwenhoek model, with a carefully formed drop of Karo syrup held in a thin pierced metal plate for its optics. A rock base, string, twig structure, glue, paper, pencil pulleys for focusing, tongue-depressor slide platforms, the chrome blade from a fingernail clippers as reflector. The prisoners have been very attentive and helpful, scrounging things he needs. They all agree on the one ground rule: no contraband material to be used in its construction. His first slide is onion-skin tissue, stained with beet juice to bring out cell walls and nucleii. I overheard some of them discussing it—they use "telescope," "micro-scope," and "mangifying glass" indiscriminately, but no confusion results. "Mario showed him how," one said. "He smart, that dude, he the Leader."

• • • •

College kids in jail. We learn quickly the patient shuffle that the random cloddy shoes enforce, the perfect comple-ment to the floppy prison blues we wear. "Too fast to be standing still," as the regulars say, or to be yelled at by the Man; slow enough not to raise a sweat in the sky-covered roaster of Valley summer (105° yesterday). For those of us who have lived in dormitories, this *en loco parentis* scene is basically familiar, and—save for the fre-quent recall-to-barracks-and-count, which I imagine the girls recognize—is scarcely exaggerated. The food is better than at most college dorms. The barracks may look like Army, but the pace of our lives and the general atmos-phere are much closer to the Academy.

At night, after lights out, we visit other bunks and swap stories about backgrounds and travels, and (again like a dorm) talk a great deal about our past sexual exploits, in boastful detail, and how we wish we were getting some pussy, and what we'll do when we get it. Under the con-stant glare of the blue bulbs in the tall ceiling, the young spades in their corner chatter like jaybirds for hours, punc-tuating it with horseplay yelps. The studious long-timer sits on the john, where there's still a dim light, fighting a compound interest problem. The old drunk blows silent insomnia smoke, as Al and I crouch at the foot of Dennis' bunk listening to him tell of burglaries in Berkeley: a life of smashed windows, snatched TV sets and suits, and ca-reening 3 A.M. chases down the quiet streets of the town we know so differently.

Still slightly sweaty from push-ups—the silent spade across the way looked up from Richard Wright, said not to do them just before bed, didn't do no good—we listen to the lanky kid from Tennessee dissect the lives and loves of the small California town where he was sent up for moonshining. Al knows the town and some of its people —*yeah, I remember her, tall skinny girl well-hung, she was half Piyute Indian and half Scandinavian*—and is particularly tickled. "So there they was, going at it on the mountain, and him sitting down there with this fifty-power sniper scope, everyone in town come have a looksee. Whoo-*eee!*" Vern, the gentle old alky who taught me to tap out the mop deftly in the morning, allowed as how if they legalized pot it would be the salvation of him and a lot of others. But Tennessee's never touched grass, "No, nor bennies nor H nor none of that stuff." We try to straighten him out on drug categories, tell him of hiking on acid at 11,000 feet and swimming on grass, balling on both; invite him to Berkeley. The door to the barracks slams open, an officer lurches through, waving his flashlight. "Bull session, huh?" We swallow our start of guilt and fear. He's only looking for someone to butcher a deer just brought in, and leaves for another barracks. The meat will grace Officers' Mess; we'll never see it.

• • • •

Bananas for lunch. The fragments will reappear tomorrow, encased in jello. Similarly the beans will turn to soup: the principles of cooking here are few and predictable. They saunter out of the mess hall, sly pockets full of peels. "Mellow-yellow," they whisper, with a knowing wink, and later that afternoon: "Hey, hippie, what you guys know about how to fix these? There a special way or sumpin?" We are in demand for certain minor specialized functions. "Hey, what kind of complex you call it, when a guy keeps coming on like he knows everything?" Since we haven't been singled out for any special treatment—good or bad—by either guards or inmates, we are left to define our own identity as a group. We aren't overly clannish, though a few stick to their own devices, and with most the book or writing pad in hand has become a trade mark. Except among ourselves, we listen much more than we talk. But sometimes art or politics will flare in a tight knot for an hour on the street in front of the library, and some of our new friends or strangers will hang around the edges, curious to hear us at our own game.

• • • •

The dormitory atmosphere is partly due to the age-distribution: a good half of the inmates are twenty-five or under. Many of the rest are old alkies, their numbers rise after the weekend—you can tell them in mess-line Monday morn by their shaking hands. Most all are here for trivia: driving with a suspended license, dodging child support, burglary. A few for heavier things: slugging a cop, manslaughter. And so on: the county jail. "Shit, most of them are just kids, nothing serious," said the officer who confessed to having read *Walden* five times, after I complained to him that we were disappointed because we'd expected to be locked up with criminals.

There's very little sense of being among evil doers here. The kids in the kitchen constantly mimic the "crank" (methedrine) rituals, going through the motions of tying up and shooting—but with the same good humor with which we noisily inhale the last drag on a hand-rolled cigarette ("square"), holding the roach delicately between thumb and forefinger, and our breath by reflex. To have a candy bar and a pack disappear from my drawer came as a surprise. "Hide your stuff in your pillow," advised the queen trustee, "remember, you among thieves here."

It's hard to believe, as I lie here stripped to the waist on the beach of the volleyball court (five days in the Hole for stripping to shorts), remembering college. Sounds of argument drift from the open doors of the barracks. There are always arguments going; most discussions get there quickly, from any subject. But they seldom flare into open anger—there's been only one fight in our first three weeks, plus a few punches quickly concealed at a flick. Al points out the high aggressive quotient, the many overlapping pecking orders: everything becomes a vehicle for proof, in this arena of constant enforced contact. Yet there's a strange lack of pressure: you are in the pecking order only if you choose to be. (None of us do.) To opt out is simple, and nobody bugs you to get back in. As in the Haight, there is much tolerance for deviant behavior. Nobody comes on—or, rather, coming on is so clearly that, that it makes no difference.

Low-key and easy is the word. Almost everyone's out to do easy time. Those who aren't soon get on the guards' wrong side and wind up in Greystone, so overt hostility to the guards is almost completely absent.

Such action as takes place occurs as games, with the eternal humor of men-against-the-System. Two kids come furtive, zip! out of mess hall, with a twenty-pound tin of coffee under an army blanket. They post a guard at the door, split it up in the john to stash it, crush the can's carcass, hide it in the garbage. They boosted it on commission, for packs plus grass if any came through. (It *is* here, but pretty far under the surface.) Needles zip out of Mess hall Clothing, to be embedded in toothbrush handles and wound with black thread, as tattooing devices.

Born to lose. Slippers disappear from Little Greystone, to be hidden under mattresses, worn at night, and turned up among protestations of innocence in occasional shake-downs. All things considered, the atmosphere is pretty familiar. As Mario points out, this place is no great shucks as a deterrent. If they'd let our women in on the weekend (as they do in Mexico and Russia), pass through our books, and make a decent cup of coffee now and then, I'd be nearly contented.

• • • •

Most of the people here are black; most who aren't are Mexican. Beyond this, discrimination is not active, though colors have a way of hanging together to chatter. The reading room, with its stock of tattered journals, has no black magazines like *Ebony* or *Jet*, nor any in Spanish. The library has a handful of books in Spanish and a double handful of black books—Malcolm X's autobiography be-ing conspicuously absent—balanced by a magnificent col-lection of mysteries, a fair one of science-fiction and westerns, a lot of old novels, and little else. (We are rediscovering the classics, Zola, Dostoievsky, Flaubert—mainly because these books are old and worn enough to have found their way here.)

• • • •

A week ago, a dozen of our thirty clustered to rap after every meal. Now more than four is unusual. One by one they are leaving; after this weekend, almost all the short-timers will be gone, and soon we'll be down to five, two of whom I don't dig. It'll be lonely. Partly for this reason, I've kept more to myself than I usually would, not wanting to build a dependence. Aside from talking with Mario—we fall into instant intricate dialogue on any trivial or major detail—I've spent time only with

Steve and Al, neither of whom I knew before, both of whom I dig immensely. (Within a few months both will probably be out of the country to begin the long exile.) Today the mess officers offered me a new job, Leaderman of the mop crew. I blew their minds by refusing. They kept coming back to make sure I understood. "No, man, I'm comfortable at it," I told them—not sure that *they* understood how one programs even days full of life into a mechanical pattern, so as to make time pass quickly and unnoticed, without disturbance.

• • • •

Behind mess hall, gathered, waiting for the all-clear, a scene. Dennis is jiving, and somehow this other kid brings in pimping, and they build a contrast. You got to have a hustle, says Dennis. Don't got one, the kid says, I can shoot a little pool, but got beat out of $20 last time I tried so can't really do that; but you really gotta work at a hustle like pimping. Big money in it, says Dennis. I pimp too, says the kid, for Ford, brings me $127 a week, she do; I drive to work and back with the heater on, don't have to get out in the rain and make them broads work. Same thing every day, says Dennis, today and tomorrow, you get home and go to bed, too tired to do anything; have a hustle, you work when you choose. Got a car but not one of them fine, fine Caddies, says the kid, and a little in the bank, about to get married, save up for a down payment on the house. A stoniness invades Dennis' face. The kid goes on, sure would like some of that money though, but I'm too strung out behind my woman to put her on the street. Get home too tired to do anything, repeats Dennis. Tha's right; this here's my vacation, two weeks, that 127 keep coming in; if I had the kinda money you make hustling I'd sure use it to bail out. "How much?" I asked. $59 or nine days he gave me, tickets, didn't have the money so here I am; I'd say to one of them broads, hey, go out and get me some money. I c'n dig it, Dennis keeps repeating, meaning I understand or you're right or I'm cool with what I'm doing or I'm hurting, depending on how you read the look in his voice.

And against this background the kid goes on. "Where I made my mistake, I learned to do something!" He's a welder, for Ford. "Got stuck in it, went in the Army, took two years at college, got an Associate of Arts degree in Criminology. Sure wish I had a hustle, still owe $33 on five suits that're almost wore out now. But when I want I can go down to the bank and say, give me some bread . . ." "And they'll suck your blood," chime in Al and me, enthusiastically. We've been totally absorbed, providing a third voice about not digging work or the things money can buy; fill in the antiphony yourself. Abruptly Dennis gets up without a word, takes his milk box, moves it twenty feet away into the sun, sits down on it. The circle reforms, talk shifts to unfaithful lovers (wives). "I didn't know whether to cry or beat the shit out of the dude or beat the shit out of her." "So he asked him for $5." "Cheap." "Wait, you ain't heard what he did. He nailed the bill over the doorway. Whenever anyone came over he'd take out his .38 and say: 'Honey, tell em what that five dollars for.' And she knew he meant it, and she'd say, 'My husband caught me fucking with another man.'" They can't believe I feel the way I do about Karen seeing Denny while I'm in.

• • • •

Scarlatti this morning, over the barracks radio that shakes us from sleep each 6:15. Like fresh water, that crystal streamflow of melody. I have forgotten what real water tastes like, I no longer notice the flat mineral-thick taste of the hydrant and bathroom streams. Only the coffee reminds me. Once a week I try a sip, recoil. And the Beatles and the Stones tonight, just before lights out. Real music: what a treat!

Usually the mornings are breakfast-club chatter and song, bright and false as yellow formica in an L.A. motel; and at evening either talk-back programs or cocktail music, denatured mush to drown us to sleep. All too loud, you never quite get used to it. Even when the radio's silent the speaker is still live, so that the Morse machine-gun of the mad telegraphist, frantically punching his key somewhere beyond the hills of Pleasanton, for the SAC, can catch your soul at any moment: unaware, floating free of your body.

For a time it was KJAZ—good jazz—twice a week, rock once, some rhythm and blues. The spades and everyone else dug it. Then mush. No explanation. Eventually they got up a petition: Can we have our music back? No—the answer came down from the office—because the petition was a *demand*, an attempt to pressure.

Well. Mood control, that's the secret to making it here. At first I was genuinely, perpetually cheerful, because I'd imagined a constant boot-camp attempt to grind us down that didn't materialize. So I made the mistake of relaxing, of letting my guard down. All of a sudden it looks like a jail with cops, and I feel somehow reassured, vigilant again. Like the food: initial hosannahs because it was edible; but now that the menu begins to repeat its weekly cycle for the fourth time, we realize that you don't need any teeth for it; that everything is full of pepper for a reason; that . . .

A chorus of groans goes up from the dark main room. The radio has just snapped off for the night, after the first bars of a good song. An inflexible rule: if the last song is slop it plays through to the end; good songs get cut in the middle. That's how this place is, no kidding. Seeing that I wasn't dismayed by the garbage detail, the mess officer started also putting me on the short line to serve in the mornings. Innocent, I asked why. "Standard practice." And suddenly I found myself promoted to long line: an hour and a half sometimes serving food before I can eat. I got the message. Then, gratuitously or to make sure, he sent me to get my second haircut in three weeks, at the butcher-barber. I now have the shortest hair of any Anglo or Mex in the whole mess barracks. That was the guard who'd read *Walden* five times; I don't smile at him any more.

The blond, sallow one with the big ears and the hard voice did the pre-mail-call count last night. (Our main recreation's getting counted, at least six times a day.) He caught me with a book in my hand, Dennis with a paper, Fast Black slouching; pulled us outside; gave us what-for, with words that slapped like dominos. You will stand up *straight*, have *nothing* in your *hands*, five *days* in the *Hole*. I wanted to kill him. We blew it off inside, horseplay, yelling. Dennis slugged the wall, hurt his hand. Most of the guards just whiz through counting, but you can never tell when one will play ego-games like that, or get the bakery men up at 4 A.M. for the early shift by standing in the middle of the barracks and yelling their names until they dress (though their names and bunk numbers hang together on the wall by the door).

So mood control is the word. The cheap bit with the second haircut cost me two days of rage: my head was sheerly scrambled, I couldn't write a word, all those intricate lovely thoughts scattered like trout when the wind rises. I read science-fiction furiously, five books, a drug.

(I remember when I was a kid, used to read that way for weeks; me and the Authority Complex have had a thing going for a long time.) Finally I pulled up to a real smile, thinking what a joke it was, to have let the *Walden* bit shape my expectations so deeply. The sallow-faced guard only cost me three hours; I'm learning. Mood control.

And you've got to make *genuine* changes. There's no burying anger, not here: it builds up and blows at any unforeseen stupid order, the place is full of them. Those who can't work the magic of transmutation on their emotions wind up in the Hole, almost to a man—maybe that's why there's so few fights in the yard.

All yesterday the Beatles were singing, "All you need is love." I think maybe we also need less cops, no cops. I am not sure if it comes to the same thing. But people who enjoy having power over others are a stone drag, and the matter is worse when it is cloaked in a social sanction. They offered me Leaderman of the mop crew, the guards who still seem sympathetic, or at least not harassing, did. "No," I said, "I'm cool with being Garbage-man"—no one knows I can't smell—"and besides, I don't like to be nobody's boss." Nor, but this silent, to have nobody boss over me. Benevolent or not. Not even the Beatles.

• • • •

Reading this last rap, Mario is worried lest I give an unbalanced view of the guards. I don't mean to: the place is not actively vicious, just erratically petty. Yesterday I actually got some books, after three weeks trying. There's one compound officer who's overtly friendly to us—and hides out most of the time, seems completely ineffectual in the officer pecking order. He has a good reputation with the inmates. Such is the fate of good guys here, his goodness is become an ego crutch in a losing battle: how lovely, how common, how sad. He felt guilty because I'd searched all over for him six days running, asked him each time to get an article from my box so I could revise it; took my name each time, forgot. So when I bumped into him with a note from the history teacher that okayed my getting books, he escorted me up to the front office, glaring around with a bluff protectiveness made safe by the note, and let me take out Kenniston's *The Uncommitted*, Friedenberg's *Coming of Age in America*, and *Ulysses*. "*Ulysses*," he mused, "I flunked that book once . . ." His voice trailed off, lost a couple decades away. "Yeah, tough book," I responded glibly, "my chick's flippy about Joyce, been after me three years to read it, promised her I'd get through it while I was in. You know . . . Gee, thanksamillion for helping me get these," enthusiastically, scrammed. Not daring to meet his eyes, or ask through the excuse of literature what lies beneath his lonely and passionless decency.

The history et cetera teacher was most obliging when I showed him my book list, even though he didn't understand quite why I wanted them. He wrote me a note only the second time I saw him. "Hey, Mac," he called over to the accounting et cetera teacher, in his high piping voice, "how do you spell 'taking'? T-a-k-e-i-n-g or . . . ?" Mac told him, while I stood respectfully by, and as he finished the note in his childish scrawl I looked down on his bald head, worn as the once-linen backing on the ancient texts, and thanked him very much and honestly; left him to his two occasional students; wandered toward the Front Office thinking of model jails. "It's a model jail," said the guard in the office, "known all over the state." "It's a model jail," said the old-timer in the mess hall, "why, at San Bruno you can get a steak out of Officers' Mess for a pack, and pussy now and then. And they don't hardly have no commissary."

Commissary here is run by an old codger named Dyke, who is subject to unpredictable fits of temper in which he imagines he hears talking in the line and closes it down for the day, those still on the outside being out of luck— for he's an officer and can do what he wants to, right? A staunch free enterpriser, he uses his store's privileged position to get merchandise discounts; there is endless speculation about into whose pockets the take goes. But he has his kind side. The twenty-seven-sheet tablet I'm writing on says 25¢ on its cover, but he lets the prisoners have it for 20¢ (and carries no larger size). All in all, it seems to be a much straighter operation than the one the old junkie doctor runs.

• • • •

Episode N: Garbageman Meets the Authority Complex

I was thinking about the haircut incident, which happened well over a week ago, while shoving garbage after dinner today. It was probably not malicious, I decided, but was meant as a sort of benign amusement. So my account of my reactions probably says a lot about my hair-trigger feelings about authority.

That being so, and me being in jail, I've decided there's a decided advantage to my college background, despite the way the high school dropouts in Officers' Mess tease me with their oranges and corned beef. For what is jail but a primitive form of the Authority Complex, cast in locks, alarums, and barbed wire? And what sort of problem does *that* present to a young man trained for nine years in the most Prestigious Multiversity in the land? Despite my touchiness about personal integrity, my dislike of stupid orders, and so on, I'm getting along just fine: doing easy time, an exemplary prisoner. *My* suntan will never pale from days spent in the Hole, and if they gave Extra-Good Time I'd get that too and be out of here the sooner. For if there's anything being in college teaches you, it's how to relate to authority—even more than being black does, though the techniques are similar.

For here I am, the friendly Garbageman. With an antic smile and an off-key wail of "Gaaarbaage . . ." (Establish a distinct but non-threatening identity.) My cleaned cans upside-down on the cart, so the imprisoned steam can *puff!* impressively as I upend them back in their places. (Pick a symbol of excellence in your subject; accentuate its display.) Clanging the cans with honest though unnecessary zeal, risking an occasional caution about too much noise when the officers are eating. (Be passionately dedicated to the pursuit of Truth, venture a daring hypothesis whose subtle flaw the instructor can point out.) Candidly confessing—when nothing could be proved—that the carbon paper found among the empty cans was mine, thrust there because I didn't know what else to do when someone I'd asked idly for a sheet brought me a sheaf, swiped from the Office. (Admit an evident mistake gracefully; show yourself open to instruction and able to profit by it.) Wheeling the cart down the hall like a madman, past others leaning indolently on their mops; cleaning up someone else's mess silently—but in public—every now and then. (Invite favorable comparison, but let others provide it.) Changing clothes at best every other day, and not trying too hard to keep clean—it goes with the role. (Be a bit of an eccentric—you *must* be bright.) Hosing

the whole garbage-room down on Mondays; asking innocently if this wasn't standard practice before. (Establish
a minor but admirable innovation to better the System's
procedures; undervalue it.) Catching the attention of the
mess officer before leaving, each time, though I know his
response will be a routine "Yes" which no one else bothers
to get. (Let them know you care and are proud.)

I could go on, but fuck it. The truth of the matter is
that I *do* hustle—partly because I simply dig hustling
and doing a good job, partly because being a political
prisoner is or seems to be like what being a Jew and short
was for my old man *in situ* thirty years ago. "You've got
to be twice as good as anyone else to come out even," he
reasoned or felt, and he may have been right, who knows?
But over all this, as a surface gilding long since learned
into instinct (Woodrow Wilson Fellowship, '63) is the
complex of little actions, attitudes, and details that constitute my way of relating to—"of handling"—the Authority Complex. They are as involuntary as the deep anger,
whose possible consequences they so nicely avert, even
as they disguise and are fueled by that anger. I learned
my lesson well, in a thorough school.

● ● ● ●

Garbage from Above

Someone up there doesn't like us. The rules say "business
correspondence" may be of any length. So already late
for a deadline, I mail out an article. Two weeks later
Karen tells me, at our unreal weekly half-hour visit, that
the magazine has called, mildly frantic: no manuscript.
Despair, Righteous Anger, and the relieved delight of the

persecuted mingle to keep me high all the next day, until at evening I'm summoned to the main office. I distribute the contraband carbon paper, paranoid copies of articles, and the segments of this not yet smuggled out (prison rules prohibit writing about the inside): clean and curious, I trot down to the office.

As I'd figured, that manuscript and the next one had been placed in my property box—without notifying me, of course, which is against the rules, but so what? What prompts my being told now is a call from our lawyer. And so Sergeant Parker calls me in: to show me, stapled to the manuscripts, the note written that day by the Captain Himself, stating that nothing like this by me was allowed to be mailed out. Enjoying himself, Parker accuses me of having tried to smuggle the article out (!); tells me the Captain has His reasons, which are none of my business; and warns me that if I try to drop it or anything similar in the mailbox again, he will see that I get, not just time in the Hole, but an extra jail sentence to boot: Penal Code Section Blahblah.

Well. I wander out stiff-faced and silent, not wanting to give him the pleasure, and back to mess hall in time to shove dinner garbage. Why, I ask my favorite officer, Santa Cop, is Sergeant Parker such a prick, such a . . . ? Sadist? he supplies. All he knows is that the Sergeant took his daughter out of Berkeley right after the "riots." I tell him the fate of the manuscript; he lays a steak sandwich on me and asks what I'm going to do. My lawyer's gung-ho to pry it out with a court order, I tell him; what do you think that would cost me? They'll put you in the Hole, he suggests, and you'll lose all your Good Time (i.e., the twenty days off my sentence which being a nice cog "earns" me). They can do that? They can do that.

It's nice to belong to a community with a unifying principle. "That's *cold*, man," says Frank, when I get back to barracks; and within an hour I'm offered six different routes out for the manuscript. This place is like a sieve, and all the holes open in sympathy. The guys whose stash of potato brew I arrange not to notice in its garbage incubation are delighted to do me a good turn, since, non-drinker that I am, I refused a cut of the lush. The whole incident could be set to a light opera score—even one of the two guys I'm feuding with comes up to offer help. My paranoid carbons come in handy. The manuscript is on its way the next day, well in time for a new final deadline; and an insurance-and-insult copy follows a few days later.

The anticlimax is fitting. A week later, talking with Santa Cop about the incident, Mario and I realize that the bureaucracy may be defeatable with its own rules. For one of them states that anything *in* one's property box can be released to any visitor simply by filling out a Form. Sure enough, that very night I get both manuscripts released to Alex, who has dropped by to lawyer us. Parker will shit when he finds out.

Number Lesson

Count me to sleep, blue lights like four angels
guarding my bed in the doublebunk barracks
all night till the siren arrives to cry *count,*
recount, countdown the days, repeat after me
fiftyfour, fiftythree; remember your number,
the changes you see are your own, it endures,
they descend, like a line marching single file
to the barracks or chow, in orderly sequence
of domino peg or handball score
that mounts, rehearsing a circular menu
(too much pepper in your serve today),
collapses, returns in an endless lesson
to teach you not to step out of line
while you wait to be counted or count your waiting
by visiting Sundays at endless tables
as narrow as barracks and empty from touching.
Do you touch the pictures that promised touching
in letters you count at the compound gate
and compare before count comes, answer like serves
in a far competition whose rules are suspended
or made endless and simple, like the blind permutations
two and one, three and two, of the baseball game
that insists on instructing the sweating night,
three and one, two and you, while the blankets pulse
under watchful blue lights in imitation
of the touch you're surprised to forget so soon
like the proof of an absent geometry
that you counted on learning, never quite mastered,
recall, recount in the womb of the gym
where sweat remembers another motion

in your arch to push the numbered iron,
to atone with a ton on the calendar wall
in weights rising by fives, four sets of ten presses,
a month of Sundays, while sweat tickles down
like a missing touch or the blood that trickles
to earn you five days in a plastic bag
that they stamp with a number you won't remember
when you shape yourself into geometry
to be counted by fours before filing to chow
in the world of tin cup, big spoon, stamped platter
where you deal in packs for nothing that matters
and can find your own way back to the barracks
and an empty nap on your numberbunk
in the blue afternoon. Last of the seventh,
a letter sealed with the kiss of your number
flies like a bird to the volleyball court
where a nest of hands raised to answer or punish
marks time like worn clothing regathered on Thursdays
and endlessly circled in a game of losers
of no account and never quite clean.
Are you losing your touch? By twos and by sevens
the dayballs swish through the hoop of your patience
with slight variations, leaving you nothing
but a mattress of numbers that bring no more ease
or relief than a pad of answered assignments
that no one will count, though you count your fragments
like insomnia hours, and learn to forget
what is missing, what was it? Numbernumb to the moon
which is sliced into diamonds by impassible windows
but escapes like the ghost of a recess ball,
you accept the lights and their integral blue,
the seven and four, the three, the two.

• • • •

Garbageman Reflects on the Emotions Appropriate to His Incarceration

Strolling through the litter of porkchop bones that graces the barracks yard on the rare morning after something decent and portable appears for dinner, a puzzle came clear to me. I phoned all over the country to get quotes for an article before I came here. It gave me a chance to hear some dear voices again and apologize for my absence and silence. But there was an awkward air about some of the conversations, which I only now understand.

One friend confessed shyly—to my complete surprise, though I knew him for a long and ardent student and admirer of Gandhi and King—that he envied me deeply and would take my place if he could: that he felt keenly as a lack in his own life never having gone to jail for his beliefs. Another friend was terribly agitated because no one was making a fuss over our finally going in, or seemed even to remember why. Somehow a proper response was absent: we, and what we meant, were unheralded, unsung. "Surely someone must say something publicly," he cried to me over the phone.

I was taken off-balance and touched by their real concern, and responded to both with the embarrassed careless callousness I so often face emotion with: toss it off, downplay it, trying badly to be gentle. My own closure is so familiar that I didn't realize till now that something else confused my response—and what it was. One of these men is a college president; the other, usually one of the two most perceptive observers of my generation I know, was offered a presidency and refused it. I love them both; but neither can afford such romantic innocence about the contemporary young. For it is dangerous to lose track of which revolution you're watching—especially if you'd like to help it—or you'll find yourself responding inappropriately.

My grandfather, whose eyes were also blue, was a Bolshevik: prison and exile. And I too had certain time-honored feelings when my friends and unknown beloved peers were beaten and bailless in Southern jails. But we are freedom *trippers*, not riders. And there is nothing romantic, nor inspiring, nor unduly grubby, about being this kind of a political prisoner. It is a dull and practical necessity, and should not be emulated or repeated. For FSM was a signal beacon which started much, both locally and nationally; but its message was sounded and heard, and 800 kids should never again need to choose arrest to spite an administration that doesn't deserve so much respect. The small price of our current jailing (and the $100,000 in fines) is not even a symbol, merely the tangible mark of a learning experience, a necessary experiment, to show that we should not put ourselves in the hands of the Authority Complex and its legal system, at least not in this way. We'll save our energies for ourselves. And so our own know better than to waste inappropriate or sloppy sentiment on us. Being here accrues no capital save the (considerable) writing I'm doing and insight. Grandfather or not, if I could buy out, I would.

The spades who are going to jail for the flaming cities are quite a different story, as it will be if—no, when—they try to frame Stokely and Rap Brown for that. And those brave kids who are choosing, quietly, calmly and without hope, four years in a federal pen rather than play the System's death-games or run out on what they know of their souls—they are also a different story, partly because Vietnam and the spades are slices off the same overdue hunk of my grandfather's flesh. But the steadily growing pool of kids in jail across the country for grass and acid and "street-blocking" are political prisoners just as surely as we are—I think of beautiful Michael Solomon with his black flame halo, busted in the Haight on a trumped-up charge, forty-five days, light compared to kids here doing six or nine months—and, because they are movers in the same other revolution as we, as little deserve to be romanticized. Though this is not meant against feeling or action for the human cost involved in their imprisonment, which is considerable.

No, a new trip demands new guideposts; and jail simply is not our thing. Not that we too are not romantic—though I think we will ultimately prove less so than our elders, because we are more willing to abandon our foothold on what we have known. But the voices on the telephone wished me well with the expectations of my own past, which will no longer serve. We cannot inherit the form of our symbols now: which leaves us nothing but trial and error to find or build them.

• • • •

Granted, I too had those nice warm feelings when we were busted, as much as did anyone; and the martyr's pride did not entirely evaporate in the disgusting tedium of that hot spring's trial. I have traded on it since, for which I somewhat dislike myself, and will again; and a residue accompanies me here, probably making jail a bit more bearable, spice in the stew of my feelings. But by far my main emotion on coming here was simple and sheer iritation: *What a drag!* I have better things to do with my time—not only making love, but building what

I went into Sproul Hall for and have pursued since, in forms that have changed with my understanding.

In 1960 no one could have suggested that America was beginning not one but two revolutions. Even after four years of thinking about their visible intersection, it took FSM to begin to make me see this clearly. We lived in the shadow of the Civil Rights Movement (and an old politics) for a long time, and coming out from under it is hard—especially when the place to which we are coming is in motion. The old visions, the familiar forms of martyrdom, are not enough to lead us on.

But though I struggle uncertainly with their residue, I don't mean to put down the feelings I once had. They are simply inappropriate now. That is something I had to *learn*, for myself, by passing through them. My problem now, and ours is this: to learn, by doing, what feelings and actions are appropriate to being observers and shapers of this other revolution, of which we have no choice but to be a part even as it outdistances our understanding of it.

July–September 1967

*My meeting with the Authority Complex left me strug-
gling with the gut recognition that all the conditioning of
my education had prepared me to perpetuate the coupled
roles of Cop/Prisoner. From here I went several ways. I began looking into the question of authority and learning. I
became more aware of the outer aspects of the violence
of our lives in Amerika. And I turned further inward,
to cope with the sources of violence in myself—not to
deny them.*

1967–68
In Violent Amerika

From the FSM till the Haight, as the edge of our political action was moving "from Protest to Resistance," we revealed in public theater our rejection of Amerika's institutions and ways and our first experiments with new ones. The message got across to the whole nation through the media, variously distorted. Complex responses began in every class of people at these inescapable signals of impending death and birth—not simply of one nation's social and political order, but of an entire human culture. Everyone is still caught up in the surge of first reaction; its rich conflicts have barely begun to sort themselves out.

But this much was clear instantly: the reaction of Amerika's established order would be violent. When we started behaving weirdly around the San Francisco Bay, the first skirmishes began. After two years of local rehearsal, in 1967 the conflict began to be acted out across the whole country. Amerika began turning openly violent against the young of her dominant class. First the Vietnamese; then the blacks. Now her favored children.

The War was coming home in truth—though only after it was openly declared at the 1968 Democratic Convention, where Amerika's Liberal mask slipped off completely, did the Weatherpeople spring up to say so.

On the Road

In 1967 I began a schizy life. For three years I spent half my time living in Berkeley, and half traveling around the country, trying to see what was going on, learning how to help it along where I could. Mostly I worked on campuses with students, for our new communities were just beginning to form. Mostly my work was organizing and training in the political action of education, with a little general agitating thrown in here and there. Many were at work in similar ways. I moved with some and crossed the wakes of others. Our work developed and changed as quickly as did our lives and the times.

Here are some notes from this period. They bear only vaguely on the work I was doing. What they have in common is a climate of consciousness, mark of the violence weather on one who was watchful and active. You will notice, I seem paranoid. Why not? (You will also find many examples of male sexism. In this my consciousness was typical of most who were called "leaders" then, before Women's Lib arose to develop the language and basic analysis for us to begin dealing with sexism.)

A Violence Sequence

1. Flashbacks

Two years after we acted our anger out in a social form in the FSM, I left the protected environment of the West for the first time. I began 1967 in New York, working with Harold Taylor, studying the interface between the Movement and educational change. The work freed me and focused me; I thrived on it. But life in that city was something else.

For years I'd been building up an image of New York as the showcase for all the human bruising of our great cities. My friends went and returned. I watched them like a scientist sending projectiles to study some strange inaccessible moonscape. They came back crumpled, corroded, bent out of shape. Often it took a year or more before their fright unthawed in the relative warmth of Berkeley.

My pre-image of New York was shaped by this, and by the pieces of jagged heartmetal that Lorca left in *Poeta en Nueva York*, written during the early thirties when he was a student in strange Columbia, wandering alone with his duskflower face through Harlem:

o black men black men black men black men . . .
there is no anguish to match
your downtrodden scarlet . . .
it is blood that comes, that will come
on the roofs and sheds, everywhere,
to burn the chlorophyll of the blondes,
to sob at the foot of the beds before the washbowls' insomnia
and explode in a dawn of tobacco and vile yellow . . .

So when I went there, I went to live as a stranger and
alone, in a bare cockroachy room, not to wrap myself
in the warm familiar blanket of friends. I wanted to expose
myself more directly, to try to sense what imprint the
social architecture of the city left upon its people. I tried
to make myself sensitive; and New York really put a dent
in my head. I had never before been in a city with such
constant inhuman scales of space and speed, pressing its
inhabitants to harried smallness; nor in a place where almost
all human encounters were received essentially as blows;
nor in a place of such constant random violence. For the
first time, I started to understand what it is like, to live in
physical fear.

When I got back West, I spent the next three months
in and out of the Haight. These were the months before
summer, and the Haight was trembling in anticipation of
the stellar grubby agony it was about to undergo, victim
of America's first full Media Blitz. What had been a
healthy and creative community, growing slowly and
naturally, was about to be violently strained and broken,
all its real brotherly *caritas* given, hopelessly frail and
inadequate.

All spring the Haight shook with premonition; the

airways of gossip were incessant with flashes of apocalypse, constant rumors of angry black invasion. The immediate hostile reaction of the city government—Health, Fire, Police, Building Inspection—to any humane planning for the summer's influx of kids gave fuel to visions of police invasions and minipogroms. The visions were real. In April the cops began their darting sweeps down the Street, snatching up juveniles and "drug suspects," appearing on corners like cluster grenades, exploding fear everywhere.

Deep fear throbbed in the Haight. I found it had been growing in me for months. For two things struck me about having long hair and traveling young across this country in the spring of 1967, in a breaking culture whose atmosphere was charging up with rage, hate, despair, frustration, and pain; energies seeking focii by which to discharge themselves.

One was my own inward reaction to the way the flag of my hair waved in the social wind. I struggled constantly against letting myself eat and internalize the negative self-image, the cry *you're bad you're bad* that I constantly saw, reflected expected or projected, in the eyes of those I passed as a stranger, an impersonal image in hair. I mean, I was really of two impulses, part of me *wanted* to eat that bad apple and suffer—the part that my culture hooked up to my death-force, to warn me when I was getting out of bounds.

The other was the obverse of this. I began to see into the roots of the coiled emotions that sometimes were triggered into striking by the signal of my hair: how they were rooted in a deep fearing of the sexual/sensualness of all life. And I saw beyond this, that the energies locked up in that fearing could some day swell and burst into a real cross-cultural pogrom.

This is the feeling I got, as I wandered alone around

Eastern America, watching the constant violence of the Lower East Side in New York define the tone of America's third major youth ghetto even before its identity had become established: before the sensational murders, before their Free Store collapsed in beatings and bikers, before the cops began planting, beating, tear-gassing there, and the bottles started flying.

And everything I saw in the Haight reinforced these premonitions. It was only a few months since the Haight had been exposed by the media. The System's reaction was unmistakeable, and already people were clear about its ultimate killing intent. By that fall, it was said that everyone into public life in the Haight had a gun; and next spring Free City people made a beautiful silent film of Kerouac-mythical heroes and heroines at target practice, and were showing it around, organizing.

During this time, most of my writing was going into an article trying to sum up what the War—the foreign and open projection of America's violence—was doing to the Movement: how it was absorbing the available energies of our beginnings and focusing us away from building and into desperation. We made many responses to the pressure of the War upon us—the massive organizing effort of Vietnam Summer (1967), for one. But our only effort that seemed to me really to have a chance of binding a part of our energies into work that would leave a permanent imprint, and perhaps catch the cutting-edge of our changing spirit, was the Resistance. Within a year, it had more than gathered its goal: 3,000 young men committed to jail, and to developing and acting out in their own lives a changed relationship to authority and government which would form a basis later for community and a new Way of living.

So one way and another, I'd been pretty well into violence when I went to spend my summer in jail for FSM.

Jail is the cast concrete house of our social violence. I expected to find it somewhat like New York, always lighted and steadily twinkling with flashes of brutality, unexpected and understandable. But as a system, jail works better than New York does, and I felt safer there. It was more like college, and I found myself disturbingly at home.

The big event of fall 1967, after I got out of jail, was our attempt to close down the Oakland Induction Center for our October Days of Protest. At the height of the week-long demonstrations, 8,000 of us paralyzed forty blocks of downtown Oakland. But first several hundred kids had gotten the shit clubbed out of them. It really messed my head, to see this cop who was running after me veer, knock down a girl who ran slower, and beat on her with his buddies in frantic enjoyment, moaning, *Hippie hippie dirty hippie*.

Six months earlier the Haight's first street closing was busted up by the cops. I was caught in their rush, taking pictures, and crammed into a paddy wagon with this Mex kid tripping on acid. He kicked up a fuss, yelling; the cops proceeded to jump into the wagon and beat him bloody and almost unconscious. He went into convulsions in our arms, we didn't know what to do; they came in and beat him some more.

I caught one remarkable picture of that, before they broke my camera. I kept a big blowup perched by my desk, trying to understand where it put me. At first all you can decipher is the hand and the club, gleaming and descending; not even the white curve of the helmet makes sense. Then slowly details begin to emerge from the paddy wagon gloom—Tri X, f3.5 at 1/15 with a 35 mm lens, overdeveloped like crazy in UFG and then intensified twice with mercury, and printed on hardest paper— and sort themselves out: the kid's vulnerable shoulder, the black leather geometry, the cop's face, eyes hidden under his helmet brim.

Pretty heavy. I had been there, helpless. In Oakland, running too fast to take pictures, I was helpless again, though there were eight thousand of us. Later I wrote in my notebook:

> They've really got me conditioned: I look at a uniform, any uniform, and I see Cop: with no reference to the person underneath. Now, that conditioning's a neutral tool: I might feel, say, trust toward the abstract personage Cop. But given the context of the time, I don't: that figure serves as the focus for an immense and growing charge of anger-frustration-hate-despair. And I get stoned a lot to defuse that anger, man, I mean I really want to kill someone.

Earlier that year cops had descended on a peace parade at Century Plaza in Los Angeles, sending scores to the hospital. And around then all the trouble on Sunset Strip was coming down—teenyboppers entering cultural politics, and in their midst one hip SDS organizer trying to learn to work with them. The Buffalo Springfield were singing about paranoia, how it invades our lives, wells from the fear of the Man catching us out of line; and warning us to stop, look, and listen to the rumble of something coming down.*

So one way and another, it was becoming pretty clear that violence was in the offing for me and us in particular,

---

Stephen Stills and Cotillion Music, Inc. demanded $250 for permission to quote the chorus of "For What It's Worth."— What have we come to, when our poets cling jealous to the words born through them, which now belong to many people's lives and will outlive their private fortunes?

let alone more largely in America: black and white caught in the cities that grind the human bean for a dynamite brew of pain. And I had only a blind sense of how to respond.

It was time for me to stop admiring people like Burt Kanegson, of the War Resisters' League, and gentle flaming Dave Harris, who started the Resistance, for the ways they had approached the problem of their own violence, trying both to get near it and to act out its resolution in a social form, moving toward a world in which violence was not used to resolve conflicts. Why had I only watched and loved them, and not sought to learn their thing from them? It was time to get moving on myself—for the club was aimed and descending.

II. Minnesota

NSA threw the "first" National Student Power Conference in Minneapolis in November 1967. They brought in a couple of hundred student government people from all over, and me among a bunch of speakers and resource people. There was no bread, but the deal included going on to Washington to consult on ed reform, and I wanted to see what was happening in the East.

I got there a bit early and fell in with the people running the conference. They were a bit uptight. The local SDS, small but rhetorically militant, was rumored ready to crash the conference, take over the platform and try to call the delegates out, or something like that. Well, some of us had been having thoughts about how conferences should run, about what accounted for the times when people learned in them. We were in a mood for experiment. In cheerful subversion, we argued for a radical destructuring of the conference. Instead of the speeches and panels slated for opening night, we left the platform open, as a free stage, a place of improvised theater, so that even the SDS kids, if they came, would find themselves part of a natural process. Make Open Space For Things To Happen In, that's the motto for now.

It worked pretty well, though the first couple of hours were pure open chaos, as expected. The current president of NSA greeted everyone and told them no one knew what was supposed to happen next, did they have anything in mind? Panic ensued. "We demand to be Speeched to!" "What's the plot?" After a while some SDS kid grabbed the mike and made what was supposed to be an inflammatory pitch. It was pretty timid, but then this was Minnesota. Within twenty minutes, delegates were standing on chairs demanding to be heard, delegations were rallying and declaring their exits for regional caucuses and purposeful work, chicks were crying, and some stilted Southern cat was yelling in his best male manner *You cahn't speak like that in front of ouah women* over and over.

So much anger, my my, popping up the minute you lift the lid! It was some show. I found myself tripping on its dynamic, waited for a lull in the floor mikes and took over with a hard rap on learning, really asking them to stretch and integrate their experience right there on the spot. How we react to open structures, what fear and anger in us they tap into, why educating for freedom must involve the skills we lack for dealing with them, what we as planners of the conference had been about, and how to start bringing the lessons home to their campuses, where pressure for freely structured growth—in politics, culture, learning—was gathering rapidly; could they respond to its needs?

All fun comes to an end. The NSA officials were getting edgy as the affair continued, still seemingly out of hand.

A bit later they took the mike and stuffed the happening into the parliamentary bag of Passing a Resolution. As well as being a bit panicky, this was cruddy manipulative politics, given the resolution and how it was being pushed. But, though I was mad at the time and didn't see this, the maneuver supplied just what was needed: a chance to let the group settle out its anxiety and disband, absorbing the experience, after rejecting the resolution.

Two of the three main poles of thought about Student Power (1967) were under the tent of that conference. Over here, some of us were trying to prepare kids to deal with the textures and emotions of environments of conflict and change as they move toward power. Over there, the NSA center was leaning heavily toward society and Law, presenting the *Joint Statement on Student Rights and Freedoms* they had articulated with handsome, aging Prince AAUP, and arguing its virtues and relevance. A thousand miles east of us, the Columbia SDS kids I'd met at a party after the Princeton Radical Education Project Conference were planning for their spring 1968 action . . .

Later that night we checked out our experiment. The electric field of the earlier drama had opened everyone up. We moved between the triangle of motels that housed the conference. All were buzzing with open conversation, kids getting into what mattered with them, horseplay and love and talk about law and spontaneous groups deciding to T-group or microlab through the night in endless offering and probing, winding up with their legs entangled and the milk gone sour and morning sun making rainbows in their sandy lashes.

We were in our room at midnight, busy with analysis. The corridor outside was jam-full of kids; we heard speakers arguing dimly through the door. Their discuss-in was almost a sit-in, they were even considering whether to block people from their rooms. That sort of caught my fancy and gave me an idea. All day, from the planning meeting to the height of the evening's chaos, I'd been rapping about how real experiment means real unknowns and real risks. And I'd been feeling accurate but hollow, for I was performing experiments but not risking my self in them.

So I was ripe for a bit of guerrilla psychodrama. Half an hour later, after some sociable talk, our door bursts open. Trench coat, boots, helmet, club, a cop arrives to bust up the sit-in. *"All right, you've got thirty seconds to clear the hall!"* he yells, and strides into the throng laying about him with the club, *whop whop whop.* When he grinds to a halt, he scatters the club into a shower of Yellow Submarine posters. They flutter down, with their message about non-violent disruption, while he scurries for the door and disappears.

Well, I almost got murdered. The group dynamic in the corridor had peaked half an hour or more before. Instead of a crowd centered on a shifting drama of speeches, which could respond naturally to the entrance of Violent Authority and generate a group reaction, I erupted into a warm mosaic of small groups turned softly into themselves. All into the role, and flashing on how naturally it came to me, I dug this all helplessly, and the action ended before I could sort myself out.

Luckily, the kid I chose to wind up whopping on while he slowed me to a stop was this cool blond Resistance type, who wound up on his back with his feet in my stomach, totally startled, totally furious, totally gentle. His buddy was beside himself, came bounding into our room later staring wildly: "You tell that guy, he coulda got killed! He coulda got killed!" It was an hour till he could let himself recognize me, and he never got around to saying quite that what he meant was, "I wanted to kill you."

The guy I beat on and I were about equally shaken up by the experience. We wound up talking for hours, about violence and how to move around it, about America and what we were into. His buddy sat in, and a few others; it was a heavy conversation. But what a way to begin to make friends!

III. Paranoia Waltz

By then, even a rational man would have been a bit paranoid. In October already I'd felt nervous, a known non-student standing and rapping to an illegal campus meeting about how we should go and shut down downtown Oakland with guerrilla street theater, which we did. Two weeks later, I moved to photograph a plainclothes agent, a friend wanted to do a poster of him. He turned and greeted me by name. How nice, to clear out of Berkeley for a while, into the peaceful hinterlands of Minnesota.

Where, between threats to dynamite the President's house, a pending SDS sit-in, and thirty-five busts for grass in the previous fortnight, the campus was simply crawling with feds and narks. They turned out en masse for our opening night: after all, it was a Student Power conference, right? And everyone knows what that implies. I had the longest hair in the place, though the kids in the Haight take me for a straight. And so the dour gents with the credentials of impossible Southern splinter sects—Anabaptist Evangelical Congregation—kept sneaking around taking my picture and bumping into each other, especially when I was doing my bit on the platform. (We stopped and unmasked a couple, but what was the use?)

So innocent me on a work vacation, I wander into this with my tool kit: blue cords, hair, flute, a hundred *Yellow Submarine* posters, camera full of Tri-X, and six lids of grass, meant more or less for friends in the East, though I wasn't adverse to dealing off a couple for fair Western prices, as I mentioned to this local kid I dug there the first afternoon. But that was before I picked up on the paranoid lie of the land. After that I kept my mouth shut to strangers and sweated slightly thinking of the dope in its nice plastic baggies in my unmarked luggage—left in the Student Union instead of my own motel room; it seemed safer.

There'd been no hint of trouble, it was late in the third afternoon, an hour before cab-to-the-airport time. I was with Tony, black fox with an eloquent pen, sharing a joint in a third floor office to start floating down from the lovely frantic turn-on I get when I'm working with people; it had been a good conference. Outside the door: "Rossman?" A guilty start. I ditch the joint to the roof. "Yeah?" It's Pennsylvania Bob of the merry laugh. "Someone said you guys were on this floor, Christ, all down the hall you c'n . . . ," he wrinkled his nose appreciatively.

So the three of us are traveling to Tony's office to smoke, when this kid comes up and onto me; he wants to score. I don't know how he found out I was carrying. But I remember him giving me this long rap about morality that first night, and making a big deal of his belonging to SDS.

He comes up in the corridor. "Hey, there's the man I been lookin for, c'n you lemme have a lid?" "Yeah," I tell him, gesturing vaguely, "it's back in my suitcase, we'll get it later; come on, we're going to smoke." Suddenly these two young fellows show up, dressed in shades in the Minnesota winter and meek precise two-week unshaves. The joint and my stash go *whisk!* out of sight, as paranoia mercury soars in the sphygmomanometer. Tony leads us outside, casually. "Yeah, let's get some air," I boyishly chime, "take a walk across the bridge." We walk ahead. Some chick joins them, she doesn't say anything. Tony doesn't know her either: only the kid, and him by vague sight alone. Higher, mercury! We compare notes on the state of our intestines, decide coolly to split. Yes, but how? We turn and stand. Tony shrugs: "You tell 'em, little bro'."

I come up front with it. "Look, where we are is painful, gotta say it to clear the air: no offense meant, but please let's part company, we're freaked." "Well," says the kid, "glad you came out front with it"—I'm thinking, is he trading me for some leverage on a trap his leg's in or what?—"and it's good to try to work with it now. If we can't deal with that here, what chance of movement, I mean it starts with us, right?" "I c'n dig it, brother," I say, "and ordinarily I'd make it first priority to pick at the knot. But neither my heart nor the circumstance nor the short-time-to-flight make room to do it properly. And I wouldn't want to botch it. You understand."

An invisible conference takes place apart from us, their concealed antennae agitate the air with vibrations. The two fellows and the girl beat discreet withdrawal. Why not earlier, when it became clear we were freaking? The kid says, "Look, can I still . . . can I?" "Sure," I say expansively. "Need a ride there?" Then the flash hits me: he thinks I haven't checked out yet, he expects my luggage and dope are still at the motel. "Crazy," I say, "I got a ride wanna play some bridge meet you there ten to five?" "Sure."

We wander off, toward the bridge tables. Inside the Union, Pennsylvania Bob rejoins us; he had lagged behind innocently probing the three strangers. He is shaking his head. "Like ripe fish," he says. "Do you have any reason to risk it, or not to split straight for the airport?" We caucus, make contingency plans—inside spinning and panic flashes, outward calm decisions—and then move through clock-work melodrama. Bob goes to hustle a chick with a car, we go to clean out my luggage. Hand off: her car takes Tony, my suitcase, and me; Bob takes the film canister and the black executive-length sock, full of Christmas cheer. But he has to leave from the same airport. "Look man, I can ditch it, it's only weed . . ." His smile, again: "I can pass it back in New York. Shame to waste it." I have no words. We embrace tightly while the unheard music does something slushy about brotherhood and shared danger. The second hand begins another minute; we spin away in our choreographed steps. Across town crouching out of sight in the fastback, two stoplights, drop the motel key in the mailbox, then to the airport.

I'm walking up to the check-in stand oh so casually, I look back, these four immense identical plainclothesmen are catching up, in formation. The attendant scrawls on my ticket, turns his ear to them. As I pass out of earshot into the plane I hear them saying, "He's supposed to be on this flight, we have orders . . ." I buckle my seat belt, *whoosh* with relief, I'm half-hoping they'll come on the plane and arrest me, with half of NSA officialdom right across the aisle: sweet fantasies of an airtight damage suit.

Oh, it would have served me right. The film can I handed to Bob had high-speed Ektachrome in it, the one with the hash was still in a side pocket of my suitcase, as I found out when I reached New York and collected the dope, leaving a couple of lids with him, over his embarrassed protests. It was meant for friends anyway, not to be sold.

IV. New York: The War Is Over

And so I came to New York again, running scared, to tramp through the filthy snow of despair, see magazine people, find an agent, settle the deal on the book and meet my editor. And touch with my friends, to find how they were faring, and whether this harsh pain I felt growing were mine alone.

Was there an objective reality in winter 1967? I'm afraid so; I wish it were my madness only. Spock, Coffin, and the rest were already committed, and one thousand of the Resistance. Articles in the *New York Review* were busy defining and explaining the draft "from Protest to Resistance," and calling on the left-liberal intellectual Establishment to sympathize and maybe follow. All in the most noble Academic-Man-Enters-the-World terms, of course.

Meanwhile, everywhere I went I kept bumping into kids who'd been at the Pentagon. The national media pretty much blanked it out, till Mailer's monumental piece. But our people had come from everywhere, and everywhere were hip to what it meant, that the wheel of our change was advancing a hard notch. A girl from Iowa told me how eager hands tossed cartons of cigarettes and sandwiches over the wall (it sounded like the Cop Car scene). "They charged up the steps," said Bill in Washington, "swinging flags and singing *Hey! Hey! Viva! Che!*" "My fantasies are getting really violent now," said the NYU grad who transferred from Berkeley after FSM, in which he'd been afraid to risk arrest, "I find myself trying to remember what I can of my chemistry course . . ."

Before I left for Minnesota, I spent a week in Santa Barbara at the Center for the Study of Democratic Institutions, rapping with the resident intellectuals about youth culture and beginning a long study of the evolution of mass political behavior in Berkeley. When I got to New York, the Center's branch there asked me to speak in a panel about Youth for a select dinner of their monied benefactors. There Ira Einhorn, Taurus guru from Philadelphia, and I began a friendship, as we took turns freaking the customers with dawning apocalyptic projections and masques, our anguish in a game. For a small fee. Shit, what a mess that causes in the heart.

Anyway, my head was really into this evolution-of-political-behavior business. And I was anxious to pick up on some mass demonstrations in New York, to see how nearly correct was my notion of a basic evolutionary track, on which the West preceded the East by about a year or so. Luck was with me, for right at the start I hit upon one of the nicest. The demonstration was named "The War Is Over," after the song by Phil Ochs.

It was organized by him, Paul Krassner of the *Realist*, Digger Abbie Hoffman, and I don't know who all else: that crowd. When I got there three thousand kids were clustered in and around the stone bowl in Washington Square, digging singers and children and costumes and each other and themselves, color us Affirmation. I heard a blues guitar, saw a thin kid with a fringe of beard sitting on the rim, center of a knot. To hell with Observation, the vibes were so good that I wasn't embarrassed—as I usually am, not for my music but for myself—to play in public. Among friends, I sheathed my camera eye and my I, knelt down, unslung and assembled the flute, joined him. Swaying in the darkness of closed eyes and the brightness of reaching human rustle around us, our sounds moved toward each other, played and built. Oh, it was a singing: I had been so hungry to play well with someone, even so briefly.

When we came out of it, an agitprop musical had started in the bowl. Audience-in-the-round, so firmly packed. The guerrilla actors were lively and well-practiced, really into their thing, a long hippy string of anti-war, anti-draft skits and songs; and the audience was really with them. It was all so classical. But its obvious imitation of NLF peasant agitprop didn't keep it from being effective.

Suddenly it was over. I turned to look for the guitarist. By the time I turned back, a handful of fifteen-year-olds had surged over the bowl's rim and through the great stone arch, shouting *On to Grand Central!* and were headed up an avenue with almost everyone following.

God, that was a pell-mell chase, a linear shout of defiant useless joy circling like an anagogic metaphor through a City of Death! All the way to Grand Central Station, blocked off well in advance by the cops; then over to Times Square, cops again; back to Grand Central, back down to Washington Square, and crosstown to Tompkins Park before it petered out, miles and miles, running and running, like some forming Word split up to human rain spattering frantic with excitement and longing, filtering through concrete and steel, finally to fade.

"The War Is Over!!" they cried to startled matrons, stalled angry Marines, the young lovers standing under the marquee of *La Guerre Est Fini*. The cops controlled the destinations and damped the festivities by keeping the kids off the streets. But our life was in motion, not in place;

and the free surface of the demonstration splintered into a thousand tiny beats of street theater: hunting down a Viet-cong by the cashier's window of *How I Won the War*, turning manhole covers to peace symbols, blowing bubbles at cops, standing in paralyzed microdrama with the woman whose son died in yesterday's helicopter.

"I declare the end of the War," said Allen Ginsberg to two hundred straight student body officials attending an NSA Congress at midnight somewhere in summer Illinois, 1966. He was ending the most beautiful reading I'd heard in years with *Wicheta Vortex Sutra:* the flat heart of America, broker of killing abstractions, the delicate sallow flesh of far children. Never had most of them seen anything like him before, and he broke through to them, true voice that speaks from our plight and warmth.

And here, fifteen months later, that flash of understanding was translated to flesh, sweeping like a deviant ephemeral emotion loose in the streets, vanishing. O, there is something common happening in America! In the Bay Area, that flavor of public behavior had appeared conclusively in April, seven months before the East. Don't let me bore you with indices of similarity. But the critical index was the leaderlessness of the street demonstration, its flowering into a multitude of little centers of independent drama. Not even group songs along a portion of sidewalk could be maintained. The only instant of uniform response I saw came when my block sighted a car full of pressmen from the *Post*, and burst into a synchonrized chant: "*The* Post *sucks!! The* Post *sucks!!*"

In so many ways, that demonstration reminded me of the joyful spread of our action in October, trying to close down the Oakland Induction Center. (Our percentage of active actors is much greater, however.) Except for one

critical thing: these brothers in New York were still basically playing it safe. They weren't trying to close anything down.

I do think that kind of theater is a potent political
technology: I wish the subways and department stores
were full of it. But events since have shown how inevitable
was our next experiment: resistance carried to active,
though still non-violent, opposition. For "The War Is
Over" to mean anything, we had to be saying it while
trying directly to stop the War.

V. New York: Whitehall

That test was coming. It was so important to me to
watch that I hung over an endless extra week in New
York. I was aching with the harshness of gathering city
winter, wanting blindly painfully to get back to Karen.
But I got to see New York's radicals stage their version
of what we did in Oakland in October. They tried to
close down the Induction Center at Whitehall, on the
lower canyon-towered tip of Manhattan, on December
4. The affair was gruesome.

It began dismally enough. As with our Western stint,
the first day was given over to pacifist-type people: symbolic resistance. The high point came when Dr. Spock
crossed through the police line to sit on the ground at the
entrance and get arrested. Only they wouldn't let him
through, see? All around are these barricades behind
which are cops. And he's too old and unlimber to climb
over them, so he goes around trying to crawl under them,
and the cops keep blocking him with their legs, oh grand
fun, until finally a ranking cop sort of orders them to make
him a place to crawl through because everybody and
maybe even the Media are beginning to pick up on how

shabbily this old human being who is still on the edge of retaining his dignity is being treated.

Ode to Benny Spock

I met you crawling down Whitehall Street, trying to get to the door of the place where they take the young men in to war,

bony old man turned child in a playpen of uniformed legs, cruel blue bars laughingly blocking your tantrum of Justice!

Did they finally let you pass, embarrassed before the cameras still blind to your knocked-off glasses, the dust on your ass,

the rip in the knee of your rusty and dignified cutaway, torn like blue jeans in the run and stumble of some game of war?

In the name of my Mother, who tattered the bindings on three of your book's 21,000,000 copies, raising us four!

In the name of yourself, the only lone man to whom history credits a visible share of our strangeness and change,

who with so few loved so clearly our selves and your own, to move in true harmony of spirit and danger!

O lovely common working example of the old culture's cream dream in Liberal flower:

tireless paternal cornucopia of articles in *Family Circle*, two bits at the supermart checkout stand,

telling still-pretty girls whose only dances were learned from their Kansas mothers not to freak when their children touch themselves lovingly!

popularizer of technical reports on abnormal Roentgen levels in infant cartilege!

patron of clinics! correspondent of Russell! reassuring proud
   name at the head of each earnest SANE sponsors' list!!
O Daddy! Daddy! when will you learn??? those men won't
   even mimic your dear symbols of grace and respect!
O Teacher Thespian, now you are on the Street your children inhabit! you act out the ritual of defiant honor to
   Law, offer yourself up in ram sacrifice!
Can't you see profane magic has touched the altar and turned
   the wine: furnace and meatgrinder, acid and hemlock?!
Don't drink it! Too late! I love you! Anyway! Because of it!
   Don't call me to follow you!
O Daddy! Daddy! your cock grows abundantly, endlessly!
   they cut it off piece by piece, there is never enough to do
   the deed! I stand cupping my figsweight in codpiece hand,
   watching your martyrdom!
O Daddy, Daddy, living out your grace, can't you see it's too
   late? your electric example draws no sentient response
   from Leviathan in whose soft tongue you're floundering,
   only a swallow!
O beautiful Daddy, can you still learn that to spring a world
   entire from ourselves not just beauty's the key, but we
   must survive?
O Daddy! I cry from my street to your cell, this time they
   will eat you alive for only a few years, ignoring your
   radiant warmth in their bowels,
while through your slow newspaper window you'll watch
   and learn how they'll come to treat your children!!

• • • •

Hmmm. Writing this is such a heavy trip. I didn't feel
a thing when I watched it happen: I was stunned, closed,
aching, only my cold notebook eye was open on that

next-to-last day in New York. Nothing in the months
since then, either, forgot all about it. And now at this
morning typewriter, punch-drunk from going for fifteen
hours, it comes all up in a lump. I wonder what the
original feeling would be like, if I could stand to dig it
directly?

• • • •

Anyway, about Whitehall, which I'm avoiding because
I can't bear to write about it. It was the most inept,
self-endangering demonstration I've ever seen. But it didn't
get smashed up hardly at all, because it was so impotent
the cops couldn't even begin to respect or fear it. These
several thousand people were going *to close down the Induction Center*, remember? So at 6 A.M. they start stream-
ing cold and disorganized out of the subways.

And meet thousands of cops who won't let them near
the place. There are also a thousand plainclothesmen, off-
duty cops in beef and green lapel buttons, who infiltrate
and lead groups around in circles. So do the demonstrators
take this lying down? Quite. They don't split up like we
did in Oakland and saturate the downtown, because the
whole area's filled with hostile toughs, and small groups
might get brutally handled. (They have no idea of tight
small self-defense/tactical units, ready to fight and defend;
though to be fair, these are only now developing in the
West.)

Instead, they straggle together in three or four large
disheartened groups; and march behind their elaborate array of monitors, up streets and down, flanked led and followed by cops. My group walks right down a quarter-
mile exitless cul-de-sac by the sea, into a wall of mounted
policemen. My, they have it soft here so far! Since October 1965, it's been clear that any similar maneuver in the

Bay Area would result in several hundred people smashed, and maybe a few dead in the trample. But here we just turn around, all the time in the world; and then proceed to get so fouled up and lost behind police lines that we have to ask them for a police escort to guide us through their lines and back to the park where we are supposed to rally.

Big joke. Whitehall made it clear that, in New York at least, and likely all big Eastern cities, the authorities have everything perfectly under control in this area (if no other). Any demonstration on that plan, and with that style of leadership, can be at best symbolic. If it tries to get substantive, it'll be helpless bloody in an instant.

I wandered around the dispirited crowd so down I couldn't even take pictures. And suddenly came on this scene: scruffy cat with lots of hair standing atop a Volkswagen yelling, bunch of people gathered around yelling back with bitter grins. He reached and ripped off his monitor armband, held it aloft, people cheered, he set fire to it, crying, "Follow me!" Armbands thawed off like snow from mountains that had forgotten spring. And I felt suddenly one fragment redeemed. For here sprung to view, full-bloomed already in many hearts, was the belated spirit of revolt against our own adoption of the old culture's forms of leadership, which betray us in our action.

The symptoms of that spirit are long familiar in the West. But I think the New York-style brutalization of Western cities will have to proceed quite rapidly (as it may be doing) if the spirits are to take parallel tracks in their expressions East and West. New York is too stone hostile even for that flash of light; I mean, I can't see anyone staying in N.Y. to try to work with it. San Francisco maybe: there if anywhere.

Walking away after this Volkswagen drama, I bumped

into Jerry Rubin, bulky in woolens and moustache, and his slender lady Nancy. We hadn't seen each other since he went East after his 1965 Vietnam Day Committee work, summoned by HUAC to testify in his American Revolution uniform, oh lovely burlesque! We had been equally turned off by Whitehall, turned on by the arm-band-burning; and we repaired to long coffee, rapping excitedly about what new flavors of action were rising in our stew, and how to move next with them. Finally they had to run; we promised to keep in touch. I drifted cross-town to my suitcase, uptown to the plane. Six hours later, I was a continent away from New York's grey violence defeat.

• • • •

Need I say: in body but not in spirit? Lifeheat on the left pan, deathcold on the right: each mounted up, as I went around trying to bring together what was happening to us. New York, the Haight, jail, Oakland October, Minnesota, New York. At each new stop I took on another burden of despairing premonition, heavy cover for the catalogue of new beauty I wanted to compile.

Too much, already I was breaking with it. In those last days in New York, I went to see Harris and Hiram. Harris heads an experimental campus of SUNY: he's forty-five, charming, magnetic, an upwardly mobile, Kennedy-King exemplary liberal, slick rhetorical exponent of educational freedom. His love for MLK and JFK was fierce, blind, and genuine. I care for him terribly, and think his politics will kill us. At some three A.M. I poured it all out, glibly, brokenly, my gathering sense of what was coming down on us. All he could say was: no, no, I'm sure it can't be so, it won't come to that, I can't believe it will happen, things will get better. I wanted to fall into his arms sobbing and have him hold me; I wanted to smash him in the face for his blind stunned reassurance, ir-responsible and convictionless.

Can I bring nothing but my pain to my friends? I laid all that on Hiram too, the first time I saw him in eight months. "The doctor permits me half-an-hour visit with people I care for," he says, "no more than that, the excitement . . ." A tableau. Big grey editor of scholarly journal, bluff and avid and gentle and sixty, wrapped around the heart that has lately played him deathly false. Nutty breathless kid from the West, who for some reason Hiram took a shine to, patiently coaxing out his first Eastern piece. I wanted to hear where he was, and of his children. But he waved that aside. No, he says, what's on your heart? And I spilled it in a gush of cruel love, hardly daring to watch the weather wrinkles on his face. I respected his response much more: he did not try to reassure me.

July 1968

Notes from an Eastern Trip

for W.S.

1

They were half an hour late picking me up. I stood on the corner in Manhattan warm smog wearing a suit and feeling foolish. Not my thing, that, nor talking to adults, a convention of Unitarians. I hadn't prepared a speech. I tried to reassure myself that was because I owed them no less respect than I do my juniors and peers, even if they *were* paying me and whatever they expected.

"We're learning to place our faith and training, not in plans made in advance and maybe inappropriate, but in the ability of our people to respond appropriately whatever the context," said my loved friend Annie, once my "student," as she was switching over from campus ed-reform organizing to community-building among Berkeley's young hippy population, setting up Switchboard. I dig it, and I'm learning to work hangloose and effectively with kids who are into making change, in their various ways.

But adults looking on, wondering how to perceive and *cope* with what's happening with us, are a different matter. What to say to them? I drove up with Lynn, the District Manager, and his wife. I pumped them about Unitarians, they pumped me about where it is with young kids and drugs, what I thought the ethics of it were. "They're going to encounter grass anyway, likely try it—especially if they're where most Unitarian kids are, fairly flexible and inquisitive, and hip that it's harmless and subversive. Can you unbend enough to make home a free and receptive place for their experiments? Because if you can't . . ." They listened; I couldn't tell if they bought it. But I dug on the way they talked about their kids: a bit over-protective, but solid. They should make out fairly well. So unlike the run of the delegates there.

When I got there a bunch of kids were setting up a lightshow, and we fell into an easy chatter amid glistening watchglasses and incense. They all looked so much younger than they are (twenty-three, twenty-six, thirty), and so pretty, in a way I'm now familiar with from pockets of kids trying to build things all over the country. What can I say about it that isn't soppy? They all reminded me of my brother and lover; I wanted to hug them, hold them.

This was their first paying gig away from home. They've been working cooperatively, trying to live communally: seven of them, in Long Island, sometimes in one house, sometimes in two. "It's hard, man, takes a long time to begin to come together . . . you know how it is." We traded news: grass is scarce and twiggy on the Island, the cops tore up Haight Street last month with tear gas and clubs. "I was there in '66," said the kid with the dark ringlets of beard delicately framing his face in the warm backglow of the projectors, "I saw my first lightshow at the benefit for Tim Leary; I wanted to do one." He talked about how clubs, businesses, advertising were begin-ning to pick up on lightshows. They make enough to keep their show going, exploring, growing. "That's enough, right?"

It was raining in Westport, Connecticut, long way from New York. Inside the laminated wood belly of this church-whale we met in a workshop of tools of light, in a quiet and warm recognition. I wished for some dope to lay on them, they were clean. Instead we talked about Chicago, almost casually.

"How long you staying on the coast here?"

"Gotta be home by late April, Stop the Draft Week; it may be bloody, October was; my woman, friends, community are there. Be in and out of New York till then, doing gigs, seeing friends."

"Chicago?"

"Oh sure. We'll take a vacation, travel slow to get there."

"See you there. I'm not sure why, but I know I have to go, to be there."

"The lightshow too?"

"Yeah."

He grinned, and I wondered on what dark wall their images would flash, and all that delicate glass—remembering how the lightshow at the Straight Theatre had gotten shattered when the cops filled the place with tear gas.

"What are you going to say to them, how?" I didn't know. We talked about that, the problem of reaching adults (no better term): most of the Unitarians were full middle age; the kids didn't expect any of them to turn on to the show. "They're used to words," said my sociologist, "which they usually treat as if they understand and whose impact they can control." Later I wondered: loud noises and bright lights frighten them?

Behind our talk, after I indicated how I travel and what kinds of scenes I touch, I seemed to feel them asking what so many of ours do, in so many ways: say something to *us*, something that makes sense, help us learn what we know and what we're learning, and that we're not alone.

"I'm going to step out there and let them poke at me, let them find something strange, but only if they choose to," I said, thinking I would do that. And I laid a copy of *Violence Poem* on them, the nice green edition our people in Urbana printed up, and stepped out of their protecting screen as the show began.

Beautiful. They played images and noises in the style of the classical raga: wandering first in a largo of genesis through sunburst colors, fronds and liquid shifting forms with alluvial sound; evolving; ascending the changes to a cascade of hammering, beckoning images of despair and glad tambourines and Rusk and pornie and soldiers advancing and childlike celebration; and then a coda slow down to darkness. Their beginning didn't hold. I learned from playing Purcell: slow stuff is hardest to sustain, takes peaceful strength. But their thing came together midway when they took to working with the present images and concerns of their hearts. Soon the vibrations of something real being created began to pulse in the room; I surrendered happily to the pull.

But where was the audience? Impossible to tell; their bodies and faces didn't betray them. How was it hitting them? Were they trying to understand its *meaning*, make the images *make sense?* All that seemed clear was the delicate trance of people under unaccustomed bombardment—so different from the state of people actively digging that intimate sensory sauna.

I gave up wondering, stood by the big speaker, arching my ears to the fireplace warmth of its volume, vibrations through my body, digging the images. Six people came in late, sat down nearby, slowly realized the uncomforting intensity of where they were, moved away from the speakers, as if at a picnic avoiding the discovered wasps' nest.

De gustibus non est disputandum. I went outside to turn on, where I could still see the show through the terrace glass door. Getting pretty good at that, scraping off little flakes of hash and putting them on the cigarette-coal, by touch in the dark yet; swiffing in that sweet acrid smoke. Enough for one Marlboro, a seven-minute turn-on. Safer to carry this way.

Why grass, the images were turning me on? I talked twelve hours with the chicks at Manhattanville the day before; it was gentle and very natural, very trusting, especially when we came to how to raise children free. I got stoned from digging them almost immediately, also about half of them were grace to my eyes, and I wanted to ball them all. No need to smoke. But these convention people were mostly stone distant unknown, not like my hosts. And by then I'd decided what I was going to do. I needed an amplifier, I couldn't count on drawing feedback energy from an "audience."

Blow their minds. The lightshow kids were giving them a sensory and cultural overload thing that was clearly penetrating them. I decided to continue the overload, shifting the medium: words and drama and desperation. No conversation, no letting them probe me, not this time. Try to break through, to make an impact that cannot be translated into words and the familiar, with whose troubling unnamable echoes inside their world they will have to contend. Hefting the proud lance of a Theory, I scarfed the last drag, regretting there'd been too little to share, popped a mint to ritually satisfy my paranoia, and wandered back in.

I stood behind them, the last part of the show. "They told us thirty minutes," said the kid with the sideburns, "but it didn't make sense if we cut in under forty-five." My body danced to their tape, echoing the way they moved with quiet growing grace and efficiency tending their machines, embracing moments of relaxation tucked between changes. When the blonde bird handling the delicate watchglasses and their cleaning was free, I asked her if they could throw a soft spot on the screen when they ended, so I could go on without pause.

"Violence gathers in America," I began, and laid out the heaviest and most heartfelt chunk of words in my artillery, went into what should have been an evoking performance. It wasn't. Every so often I'd lift myself out of the poem to check for response: but there was no feedback, mostly only a stony attention I didn't recognize. Here I was, trying to sing what it's like to see the vectors of the war, the breaking black thing, the incipient hippy pogrom focus on our heads, and us on the streets of Oakland and at *Bonnie and Clyde* for the third time, trying to learn what to do next while the culture decides to eat its young. And absolutely no sense coming back to me, save from a few mavericks, that the people there made any connection of this with their own lives or spirits. Nowhere the welcoming signal *you speak for me speak on*. So I'd plunge back into the poem's ten-minute eternity, willing it alive for me and trying to project, with nobody hardly helping on the other end, oppressed by the blankness.

"Give them something to think about," Lynn said earlier, after I told him how I dug it, that he'd set up this thing, the lightshow and me, to keynote the convention and its business meetings. It's his last set-up as a bureaucrat, a rump affair; soon he's off to become a freelance ethical traveler. "I wanted to try to give them an experience that would shake them, that would let them know they'd been reached, before I left."

I tried, coming out of the poem without letup, talking about the deep anger that throbs in America, about the classrooms as factories of despair where new life is being strangled by behaviors that don't change fast enough to permit life for the newness they control, of a unique culture whose prime product is change in its own human stuff, and of beginning to learn to build in the face of the death this impends.

I tried to put all the love and despair I feel into my rap. It was heavy going, I blessed the grass that helped me tune to the string of strength within me, as long as it lasted without fueling from outside. I wound up my half-hour by talking about the lightshow, how it had reached me and touched me, and about the kids who did it: my sense of their beauty, and the sketch of their bare brave beginnings. "It's all there, in the images; but if you can read them, you don't need these words, and if you can't, these words won't help you . . ." And my throat went dry, and I went for water. I could have come back, but we'd done our thing, the lightpeople and I.

Out in the corridor Lynn and I agreed: break them into workshops, see if they could deal with however they'd been reached, don't allow the impact to settle with a question/answer bit. An experiment, right? It didn't work so good. There was indeed a busy buzz in the lobby, but less of substance than relief. Me, I just heard it as background because I was feeling uncomfortable and confused, silently fending off this dame who told me three times with lengthy slight variations how she had been like that too and she wanted to understand and she wasn't guilty and of course I was making sense but she couldn't be expected to respond to those other hippies, the lazy ones, who don't work or articulate with university polish. Every place I talk to olders, I tap into that stream of confused guilt.

Anyway, about the experiment. Most people didn't meet with their groups and most who did didn't expose even in that small public much of where they were with themselves and what they'd experienced. Most disliked both the lightshow and me, being put off by the noise of each. Most also thought that I was "another of those high school kids doing the lightshow" when I stepped out to do the poem. Several had been quite upset until, after rapping for twenty minutes, I identified myself in passing mock as Your Keynote Speaker. Strange habits, these natives.

I talked with the kids, packing their show: they had to travel, had a gig tomorrow at a club. "What are you doing after this? Come to our place on the Island, stay a couple of days, smoke some tea, clear your head out. And thanks for the words, man." "I've only got two days to see friends in the city," I said with real regret. We went out into the dark, said soft casual words with each other, drove off. "See you in Chicago," said the oldest one. Yeah.

Then I went downstairs to sit with Lynn and his wife in the moist nightlight till 4 A.M., talking quietly of lives and change. That was good, I really needed to talk with him, it fucks my head around when I can't come on straight with the authority figure in a scene, but he's cool. And I dig talking with people warm and loose in bed together, it's cozy.

I had groggy breakfast with the people who got me this gig by showing around a mimeographed letter I sent to friends; they'd gotten some second-generation Xerox. We nourished each other with news of friends and good changes growing. "We didn't come to hear what you had to say," said Caroline, mother of an SDS/Peace Corps daughter and a son doing the intentional community bit at Morningstar back home, as they dropped me back at the motel and prepared to split for Cape Cod's sunwaters, ducking the afternoon session. "We just wanted to meet you, see who you are. Come by if you have time, we have plenty of room."

I watched them drive off, feeling somewhat more alone. Vern came to pick me up, and as we drive out to the church for the second round I tried to tell his wife Dottie about why so many kids are into magic and similar vocabularies these days, discovering energies they have no names for and must name. I don't get it, everybody keeps telling me how optimistic and warm I seem, nobody's hip that I think we're all going to die, I mean I say it but they don't believe me.

What to do for this second round, given what had happened in the first? "They will not talk about what concerns them," Caroline said, and Dotty embroidered that text with gruesome details, as we sat talking, digging the air, waiting for the business meeting still going on inside.

Soon these two kids, Bill and Jackie, came wandering by and joined us. They'd stayed around last night to try to help a discussion group, they wanted to tell me they really dug on what I said, and told me how they saw the others: "they don't want to hear." We came on with each other in a gentle upfront manner, buoyed by that same sense of recognition. It was worth it, that conference, to meet them. Deep sideburns, pure bloom; direct luminous eyes; they look like nineteen or twenty. Curious, I asked. "Twenty-five, twenty-six. But we're not our age." "Smoke a lot of dope?" "Yeah. What can we do to make something happen here?" "I don't know. You know these people better'n I do anyway: what should we do for them?" "Just sit and talk, maybe?"

I went off to check the meeting. It was still going and my despair became complete as I basked in the sun in the church's plaza, watching the three pink-frocked serving lasses in their artless chatterdance: alike as $15\frac{1}{2} \times 3$, as different as snowflakes. I relaxed enough to take out the camera, pick up on their chatter . . . ouch! what could I say to the adults inside, if they couldn't hear it from these their own kids, so knowing, so unknown?

They spotted the camera, posed poised in grave effortless grace. "For a magazine or for you?" "Me mostly, I dig pictures. It's like stationary lightshow. But writing's my thing; I'm supposed to say something to them inside about changes, can you talk with them?" One shrugged, they all smiled small and secret. "Smoke grass?" I asked. They counted each other with eyeflicks; looked up, nodded. Parents know? (Of course not) What percentage of upperclassmates? (30%) What changes has it put you through? (. . .) Maybe the massy purplechord necklace Karen made me is a talisman: they were absolutely easy and open with me and my klutzy sociologist probing.

And then they just started talking, and I stood there awed by their analytic song. They talked about conferences, the ones they threw: what made for their being learning-events and what didn't. (They run their own, like on Zen and on the War, and have a much more sophisticated sense of structure than their elders do.) And then about schools: comparing them with conferences as environments, describing with precise candor the games that adults play and impose, and their disfunctionalities. The chick who was laying out the most straight words about

learning is a bobbin with bands on her teeth, her parents
are down on her because her grades come back C+. Yet
Friedenberg's perceptive analysis of the social system of
high schools is a hippopotamus beside her deft sketch.

Learning might be possible without those games, I suggested; there are people who're trying to make it so,
here and there. You know it all already; but it might be
possible to put that knowledge to use. They absorbed
that, however they did. Birds. They need to know inside
what you've said to me, you know, I said. They nodded.
Will you come help make a conversation about it? Wise
slight shakes of their heads. I laid copies of *Violence Poem*
on them from my portfolio/knapsack. *Sorry to give thee
such grim coin in trade for thy grace. But you need to
be clear on this.*

I found Bill and Jackie again. After quick coffee we
slipped off down the hill, to sit on sunwarmed concrete
over spring water laced with leaves and share a joint in
the lazy light, talking quietly about community and recognition and how to keep cool and keep moving on. And
about the conference, deciding reluctantly to go back to
the church early, to pre-empt its open space and try to
build.

We decided simply to sit and talk in the center of the
rows of seats, pulling a few around for a first circle: to
talk about our lives, their process and form. Lynn came
along and stood listening. I was worried: this meant twice
we'd pre-empted his program. But he was easy with it,
open and curious: just by being himself and asking his
questions he was helping build the conversation about
learning and change that we wanted: and we went on,
with him, open for others to join.

But it was absolutely impossible, no human tone of

voice could survive in that place. The acoustics of the church's architecture were impermeable to anything except Speeches, only a bellow could be heard beyond four rows. Any sensible conversation would lie on the warm lawn anyhow. But almost everybody was determined to play Audience, their expectations frozen into Speeches, and medium hostile. So Bill and Jackie and Lynn and a few others sat back, receded from me, as the geometry reshaped from circle to Totalitarian Platform. Trying not to look into their eyes only, I spilled myself to that Audience of mostly older uptight Annual Unitarian Conventioneers, stone trying to make them recognize a difference. I tried to lay out some of my fragments. What I'd seen in the Haight, of our acting out the dreamed lip-liberal values of freeness and touching. Where Karen and I are, with not being sexual property. How the graceful intellects of their children may move when mature, and of my own incapacity already to quite follow them. What their kids know about learning that they don't, and how the Birchers were right about Rock undermining Respect For Authority. And about where it is with drugs now; 10,000,000 smoking and scorning a stupid hurtful law, and 10,000 in jail.

It went better than I'd feared; some nice action got going toward the end. This teacher stands up to read a beautiful letter from some seventeen-year-old chick that says what I've said but in clean talk of her own. A young black teacher in quiet excitement begins to lay out for us from his new classrooms these luminous snapshot experiences, saying scornfully painfully openly "Why can't you believe us, believe in us?" And this older black maverick from some congregation, two front teeth missing—we'd met and dug each other at a glance before—

stands up and says, "Hey now, waitaminute there, man. Lemme hear you straight on this, you dodging. Is you saying we can do maybe a little reform here and a little there? I mean tell me where you are, about working within the System as they say. Or does it all hafta come down?" "Down, down, it all hasta come down," I yelled in glad answer and exposure, "we gotta clear it all aside and start up from scratch, that's where it's at, brother." "Just wanted to getcha to say it aloud, 'sall, glad to hear it, brother." And we slapped hands and cracked up together, and some few laughed with us. There was a nice warmth in the room when we split up, many intricate and genuine goodbyes. But those who hadn't been near being reached or opened had been long gone since early afternoon, most of them.

Before, when we'd first gone into the church, in a silence I had blown on the flute a bit, the blocky bamboo tones ringing oddly off the laminated curves of this place hostile to talk. My fingers itch for music whenever I get stoned, slide into it easily; I played for Bill and Jackie from their warmth. Later, Bill said, "That music, it makes me think of: a sparrow, flying over the ocean, just on and on"—his hands fluttered on and on—"and he knows he's going to make it . . ."

The image rang me like a bell. Ten years ago, when I first dimly sensed the change we've since entered into with such totalness, I was onto Maxim Gorky a lot. Partly it was spiritual kinship with my exiled Bolshevik grandfather, partly I was turned onto him at fifteen by an old C.P.'er who'd fled the McCarthy purge to become a chicken farmer in Petaluma. Anyway, his *Stormy Petrel*, waterbird harbinger of revolution, symbol of the Baltic sailors and their brief, brave Kronstadt revolt, fluttered through my romantic fantasies, my prosepoems: "But someday our wings shall be free of this night . . . And what a wind shall blow, when first our wings spread free!" Ouch, brother: you catch me right in my adolescence, still alive and kicking, like a corporeal homunculus, perhaps in my right cerebral hemisphere (I am right-handed).

I rode back down from Westport with Bill and Jackie, sweet swift afternoon. He works driving heavy construction machinery, cranes and cats. They both finished high school, live in a working-class neighborhood, try to work inside a congregation but find it just archetypically hard; no one wants to learn. The isolation has made them almost self-sufficient. They looked blank when I asked, Do you have your community yet?

And they talked about learning and love and the freedom of balance and being able to move: in deft simple words, economical as lichen. I ached for a tape recorder, all my cumbergrand theories translated into human language, escaping. Their children are two and four; they're raising them freely. "Our kids aren't destructive, you know. Though they like to draw on things. Our friends come over, they can't understand, they ask us, 'What do you do? Do you hit 'em a lot?'" Soon the oldest will be in school. Jackie said, "School will kill them. I'm afraid."

Bill pulls $250 a week, when and where he chooses; they own their own house and are easy with the idea of chucking it and splitting. "If you travel, try West," I suggested, "there may be more people to cooperate with, we need to learn to work together." I promised to put them in touch with people who might know about existing free schools, and to connect them with a college that might be able to shelter one. Harris's College really needs to know that people like this exist, and to meet their needs, even give them degrees in some humane way should they happen to want them. For they're about set up to learn whatever they choose to learn next, balanced and free. So nice to be able to connect, even maybe. "Look, if you can ever make it to Long Island, we have an extra bed, and a friend who grows his own . . ." From the back seat I leaned over them in their easy Detroit buckets, drinking warmth from their nearness to that center we so inadequately call peacefulness. Whirl is king; will I see them again?

II

Night, Cambridge. I go walking with my brother; he is moody and bothered. His trial is going slowly, not well. The cops gave money to children, told them to buy the paper: but this is not—legally—entrapment. And his conviction for "selling obscenity to minors" may stand even if the paper itself is judged not obscene; stupid law. Scholarship freshman at Harvard; felon-to-be. My strong paperboy brother is learning about America.

But something other troubles Jared's face as we stride in the dark through the wind off the Charles, talking about change. He hasn't seen Andy in months, her place in him is locked away, unmeasured. Last week his two ardent California correspondences turned up the same message in chorus: I dig you're confused, but don't fuck my head around with it; I'll deal with you as you are, but don't dance your blind whirl to play me unfairly with my longing and expectations. "I had expectations," Jared said, "I got every course I wanted, what more could I ask for, right? But it's the same scene with them all, papers, schedule, it's not what I need. I got into Lorca in one course, just when we were doing Nietzsche in another, and something clicked; I want to do a long thing on Lorca, Nietzsche and Dostoevsky, together. But already I'm two poets behind in the Spanish course, I'm supposed to be doing an assigned Nietzsche paper tonight, I keep getting whirled off in a million directions . . ." Are your grades good enough to get you any leverage? "I dunno. I made Dean's list, found that out 'cause they wrote the folks; I didn't go pick up my grades, I'd worked so little, it was meaningless. I think I'd, I'd go to Europe or somewhere, next year, if I were free. But there's the Army . . ." "I think he would have done it," said Leisa to me the day before, "I was with him on Resistance Day, you could just see how he was suffering, watching each of the kids walk up and turn in his card." I flashed on how totally involved he'd been last summer back home, working as a key organizer for the Vietnam Summer Project. "Once he even started to move up with them, but he stopped. If it wasn't for being in that trial, he would have done it."

Do nine years divide us? I remember that spring of 1960. Bruised and jagged from a year of tease and denial with Tina, I wrote Kathy long letters of my confused heart across a continent. Longdistance love: it had its advantages; it kept that paralyzing ribbon of need confined to quarters, and so freed enough of my inner space for me to go through the changes that were upon and within me. And plop! out of school, starting to realize for the first time that my need was to know myself, rather than to train willingly for an elite role in this mad technological culture. In that spring when politics—Chessman, HUAC, the Bomb—first deeply engaged and jolted our lives: my senior year. His time comes so much more quickly.

I say him a poem written during that season:

All things come to their change:
some come under come slow
like deep moles tunneling dark
and painful to surface a mound
of earth foreign to flower bed
and in it a hole from somewhere
not to, you hold your hand back

and others come on come fast
a boat waking a lake
aimed and certain the from
is clear, no need to ask

and others come down are here
without time or passage were there
are here not through but from
like bombs or headlines or memories
or memories they take you unaware
suddenly you turn see that hill
it's burning you can't go back it's gone
smoke on the summer air
and you are here, not there

Walking like weary camels on cobblestones, holding hands, for the moment the constant tug-and-play of young strength between us lapses. We talk about grass, as a clarifier and facilitator of changes underway. A passing cop gives us a queer glance. We drop hands. I tell him about Kuhn's *The Structure of Scientific Revolution*, about the wrenching shifts of world-view that companion scientific change, which is not at all the patient grain-on-grain-of-continuous-knowledge-accretion business portrayed by our official propaganda. And I leave him with my concerns. Why do we lie, why does our cultural mythology proclaim that scientific and social change are (and must be) continous rather than abrupt and disruptive? How is this mythology rooted at the level from which ideas are nourished, in the way we perceive our own individual lives and the problem of change within them? Is there a deep connection between our notion of a rigid adulthood tolerating no serious change or discontinuity, and our rigid America, now beginning to crack with pain? And how do we learn to break free, to turn and step off the cliff of the Known, fall into change without breaking with fear?

Exhausted, we rest on his co-op's steps for five minutes, before going off to late dinner with Leisa, siblings reuniting. Six hours of walking, scant opener on months of distance; tomorrow I leave. Face to your fear, I say, look at it clearly and measure it. How do you feel? Do me a metaphor. "A bundle of pickup sticks, not thrown for the game. Racked billiard balls, before the break shot." Another. "Separating an egg yolk, using the shell to do it. Blowing up a balloon, stopping short of popping it." Another. "Waking up at 7:59 and reaching over to turn off the alarm clock set for 8:00. Watching the guy with the cymbals raise them above his head and draw his arms back. After the lightning flash, waiting for the thunder." You'll make it through to summer, man, I say, let's go eat.

April 1968

III

At the Dartmouth conference on Experimental Education, the older Establishment of this frontier met those of us who were fast becoming the new Establishment. It was our first mass public encounter, and was just too heavy for words. But after, I rode down to Boston in the back seat of a Falcon with Libby and Ronnie, these two girls from Simmons, and we had this fantastic conversation.

In the conference's terrific tides of opening energies, sprung from polar conflict, they suddenly turned on to whole strange spectra of interaction and ways-of-knowing. When I touched Ronnie at that late night party she cried out *Oh! he has electrical vibrations coming through his fingers!* But since there'd been so many people trading flashes of that new contact with them, they couldn't lay the strangeness off on anyone in particular and were forced to take it objectively, struggled to deal with their own participation in it.

We talked a lot about that, how kids all over are getting tuned in to the fact that our culture has repressed whole categories of experience so thoroughly that our language has lost its words and power to describe them. Their real experiences cry out for naming, and so they rummage in the closet of discarded languages and metaphors, checking out Tarot or astrology; or go to the kids in the culture next door, asking, "Can I borrow your Ching, your Tao?" Or, in a few places, try from scratch to construct new words to name the new.

Anyway, I was trying to help them help reassure each other that they'd experienced what they'd experienced, that it was real; and I told them some vocabularies shared by others tuned in to the same phenomena. My recipe bag! Ronnie, stone felt strips opaque over flashes of pure desperate joyful energy; Libby, a slow and deepening glow. (Was I crying to them *love me love me?*) Libby has decided to drop out of school. That gentle kid Fran got to her; he was the only one in the whole conference who up front said to turn our feelings to a ritual of action on the second night, when King was assassinated, and did. The rest of us were all locked into the hypnotizing terms of the conversation we'd created, which absorbed all power and death, yet somehow shocked into life.

You are each very beautiful, I said to them, as I drew their shoulders tight to me above their clasped hands and we formed a triangle of touching, and I'd like to make love with you both, and you must learn to help each other, to survive. And I watched with a sadness only my eyes betrayed, while their faces changed as the car and its uptight blonde driver sped us toward Boston, the stone set of fear invading their features, working its ugly changes even in the bone structure—I've just learned to see that— as they struggled to invent or recreate a protective buffer of disbelief against the openness they'd experienced. For they knew what was coming, as we sped toward one of the eighty cities where that night fire engines ranged through streets of shadow smoke and broken glass.

I walked Ronnie into the dorm. Hard yellow walls, bright and harsh with the familiar timbres of cop and trivial anger and despair. She stopped for a long listening moment. Then the impact caught her and she actually crumpled, acting it out in her body. She spun to me with this stricken look, and said desperately: *Then it was real, wasn't it, all that?* I nodded yes. What could I say? I grimaced. I wanted to hold her, but I have a touch that kills. Libby came back with her roommate, the student president, who was all a-chatter about the post-assassination festivities. Come on, said Ronnie, let's go out for coffee, we can't stay in here. "If you're dying," I said to them, wondering how many times in the last wandering month I'd said it to people, "get out. Let's find something to eat."

IV

I stayed with dear friends in New York; it was really dismal and only compounded my heavy trip. Tom I met three years ago when he was special assistant to a Peace Corps director. Now he was a special systems analyst for New York's Bureau of Budget, no shit, a Lindsay Bright Young Man. But I love him anyway, skinny gentle nexus of people and information.

Tom was hurting and recuperating a year earlier, when he descended with a bunch of us on a Southern campus to do a two-day crash educational reform shot. He had just split with his wife and radiant daughter—his giving of himself to his work kept him absent, they grew in different directions—and he was taking it hard.

And there was Judy, deft chirpy girl, Southern chick bred to the charming art. When we got there, she was a pert industrious senior, friend of the girl student body president who'd invited us, and affianced to staid somber lawyer Derrick, to be married that summer. Our manic entourage hit her nest of girls like a whirlwind breath from another culture of possibility. Educational organizing goes on on all levels: after the seminars we demolished their virginities with fine grass, news from the outside about what was really coming down in America, and the Airplane's new album, *Surrealistic Pillow*.

Once when he was out West on Peace Corps errands, I turned Tom on to the Airplane, I took him to the Fillmore in its live youth. He learned to dance there, during his first total immersion in our high culture. Converted, he returned East spreading the word, moved by a vision only whose memory he could remember. It burned in him, his legs echoed motion whenever rock stained the air, he dared to sing with the music, and inflamed his contradictions.

He danced that night with Judy after the seminars, and touched us into dance on the intricate bright carpet of sound. And he and she made elegant hand patterns of play in the candle air. And then were gone, smiling.

Early morning, bound for the bathroom, I watched her lying casually rumpled in the tender sheets, breathing unaware somewhere away. Wondered where her changes would bring her, wanted to write her a poem. Found a paper towel, did, rejoined Tom and the others rapping in the kitchen.

Hey, bright birdsprite—
we worry on you, though
or because we hardly know
you, how you'll fare or fly
in the dubious joining you face
which turned your face tears
of alone when that song echoed
in each of our private night courtyards
of sorrow, reaching us reaching
out and alone, together. Go
where you want to go do what
you want to do, will you
will will you will you be able
to fly, to draw the clever cat grin
of my sister your sudden and deft
delight, discover your own worlds
of touching open in passing

like a quick vulnerable wing, committed
to motion and flight? Uncertain bird-frail
your bedded body remembers
passed sleep in dreams of dancing answer,
rising progressions of unresolved chords
that are lost in the soft of your hair, disheveled
as your pillow soul, hesitant light
on water. Do go, do good, be free
as you were and might be: don't be
afraid of the fall from the not-enough tree:
your brothers and sisters inhabit the air,
are waiting for you to make flight,
meet them there.

(2 March 67)

Three months later Judy was alone in New York with
her roommate—a college friend—and Tom. Bye-bye Derrick. Completely unprepared she opted for change and
away from a life whose predictable closure suddenly terrified her into motion. Tom had taken the Lindsay job,
and was struggling with alimony and debts and guilt
and the ponderous social catastrophe of New York City.
The two of them huddled in a small apartment on the
West Side, trying to armor its walls with color, to survive
in that stone hostile environment.

When I came East last fall, Tom and I bundled would
walk snow streets, pulling the endless taffy question of
where and how one works for change. I was merciless:
genuine beginnings were *being made* in the West, our
strong young talent was needed there, to invent and fill
new tasks: why drain life trying "to shore/the wreckage
up that made an age before"? I was the stout post against

which he sharpened the catclaws of his self-doubt. And I was sort of a shit; I gave him long air time but didn't really listen with an open self to what he was saying of his roots and how they fed, guided and constrained him. Something drove me to lay my trip on him. But his real pain at this was willing: it served some cruel psychic function or balance.

At night, when Tom, wizard connector, was away connecting—we need that talent—Judy and I would talk, with stark tender tears, of being uprooted in our floating time. The only comfort I could offer her was clear recognition and description of the simple desperation of her position, irreversibly detached from the culture of her nurture, with all its training that had not prepared her to *connect* with anything (she was "earning a living," as our society expresses the matter, as a design firm secretary).

What can you say to another human being in this time, except that you recognize and share their struggle for life? Each new event, major or minor—an assassination, our campus visit—tears more of us loose, to learn, change, and build, or die. I told her I was sorry I lied in the poem: our brothers and sisters flutter helplessly too in the air of change; there is no easy habitation of flight. We held each other wordlessly for a long moment while soot blew in the open midnight window, then went out for a doughnut.

After they were alseep, I lay on a rug in the other room, reading *The World of the Formerly Married*. This work of unconscious pop sociology, intended as an introduction for the newly divorced, lacks only a self-conscious framework to constitute a study of an emerging new cultural institution: a different modality of sexual liaison, whose social and cultural ramifications are already well developed. We are moving, blindly and painfully, toward some group or floating arrangement, beyond the couple: there are many linked indications of the trend.

And I lay comforted against the rain by late radio, reading this book about people coping with their reaching and pain, thinking of my far life with Karen, and of how much of the unrooted future of this century I already felt named and calling in my bones, and of the merciless desperate way I learn from my friends.

Now it was spring come round again, and my spin had brought me to New York, vibrating like a clapper in the sounding bell of my life. I was open to all pain, resonant in sympathy, and to be with Tom and Judy almost tore my head apart. In that barren city Judy had sunk no even temporary roots, clung to Tom as only source of warmth and other-to-her-self. Her only comfort was to comfort his pain, but her comforting was pain to him.

He was desperate for distance, too tied up in his sense of failure as husband-and-father to soothe her unsoothable sorrows. He held her and armored himself; they went through the stormy tender rituals of touching, and the silence between them was deafening, they could say no simple word about their pain.

To top it off, Tom was utterly downcast at what he felt was his impotence in the job, at which he'd worked his bright ass off. I had made a long apology about not listening openly before and how it had preyed on my conscience in the months between. And I started off willing to grant him his due: that such semifreestyle working within the System as he was attempting was a coherent and maybe even viable option, for people whose roots and heads were in the appropriate place.

But when he spun out to me the intricate tale of his motions between the Bureau's bureaucratic maze and a despairing suffocating citizenry, and when I saw how his

sense of energy dissipated and impotent closed the crush-
ing ring of failure upon him, and saw their trivial agony
together, his face sallow and weary, hers dulled, all bird
gone, I simply cried out with grief and anger; I took it
all back, all my liberal reasonableness about where to lay
the tender heart of man's work.

I said to him, fuck your plea for my understanding,
I have no patience with your roots, you've got your head
up the blind ass of history and you've got to pull out
fast or you'll die. How much pain does it take to con-
vince you? You're spending your precious karma and all
that rushing accomplishment in a System that *does not
work*. No matter how many Bright Young Men they give
how much freedom to run around with, that System will
not produce humane results: it mangles, and at best you
can rationalize—not even comfort—the processing of the
powerless. They gave you all the latitude you could ask
for, right? "Make better," they said, and no one stood
in your way, you could stretch preconceptions. (But it
is necessary to break them radically.) And you shouted
yourself, poured all of your beautiful energy into that
machine of despair: stand waiting for some echo of a
voice less alone. It's useless, the architecture machinery
damps all human sound. And you take the blame upon
yourself, call it your failure, that with all your love and
curiosity you can't, you can't, you can't. Impossible! It
tears me apart, I hate you for your reasonable self-
torture. All the evidence is long in, when will you look to
see what is written? it reads: *Up against the historical wall,
motherfucker; change or die*. All you know is ways that
won't do, and you long for work to be an affair of the
heart. It is the only choice possible: go with your newness and start new, though it promise you nothing but love

and sorrow. O leave the State of New York, which is
Death!

The old forms will no longer sustain life. As far as
couple-marriage goes, statistics already back up the premonition. And in the massing social debris of people for
whom that institution has crumbled or faded, new modes
of sociosexual interaction already begin to flourish, life
energy seeking new form.

Some directions are clearing. Tom and Judy can't hang
together as man-and-woman unless they're embedded in
a deeply supportive community (and more and more it's
looking like such group connections will be not only intense, but sexual). Isolation is *out* this season, in work
as well as love. They must also find or form a community
of work, or perish as social beings.

If that's the present imperative, they moved with it.
A month later they were gone from New York, to run
with the state-hopping McCarthy caravan, smoothly
tying together webs of communication in a mobile community of work, unrooted and rejuvenating as summer
love. When they reached Berkeley, after the California
primary and Robert Kennedy's assassination, their faces
were alive again, their psychic geometry recharged though
unchanged. Balanced on that moment of history, we lit
the candles and listened to the Airplane again, floating
on gold, and wondered with helpless youth and vigor
what to do next.

July 1968

And so we came to Chicago.

*Of all the accounts of our protest at the 1968 Demo-
cratic National Convention, mine well may be the mildest.
Violence was clearly to be expected, and I couldn't manage
to get hysterical in detail about it when it came. Even
in the streets, dodging with practiced skill and blind luck,
or in Grant Park, as we waited to get creamed, my mood
was mostly reflective—for me, Chicago was a kind of
action-meditation. Not that I wasn't fiercely concerned
with the violence coming down there, where Myth was
being forged. But my mind was on deeper aspects than
its familiar blow-by-blow—on how we were moving to
meet it, and of what it portended.*

*Outside of ingrown political groups, the counter-culture
has always been weak at responsible self-criticism. Though
we bite ourselves a lot, we still haven't developed common
standards to tell useful criticism from destructive, espe-*

cially when it focuses on personal cases. So I feel as awkward now in reprinting this letter as I did when I first made it public in the Berkeley Barb. *But we must learn to speak of these things.*

Letter to Jerry Rubin

16 March 1968

Dear Jerry, Brother:

I've put off for a long time writing you about this Yippie thing. I feel bad about that, because you asked a personal thing of me when you asked me to organize for it, and deserve a real response. I've delayed, because I've been trying to pin down my deep unease with the way Yippie's coming about; and because I've been trying to find a way to talk about it that wouldn't play any of my warring fragments false, or be untrue to the perceptions and dreams we share.

Let me tell you what I see happening. A scant handful of guys—centering around you, Abbie, Krassner, etc.—are pouring charismatic energy into an unprecedented style of organizing. In the first stage you people run up and down the Coasts, turning on rock groups, head shops, happeners, underground mediamen: "Come to Chicago to do your thing, be the Festival of Life confronting the Convention of Death; and spread the word." Many are coming, from Ginsberg and Country Joe and the Fish on down. And then you click on the second stage, the freaky amplified Media Stage, to amplify your offer. Through this promised convocation of singers and seers you evoke potent symbols, pitched directly to the unexplored mythic consciousness of the young. We talked about this in New York last December, about making an experiment; and it's a genuine one, for its results are impossible to predict. Will a great swarm of kids lemming upon Chicago? Or will it turn out to be a Media Event, a Media Shuck, like last year's flowers-in-yr-hair invitation to come visit the Haight? As you do, that predicted 200,000 pilgrims; but only a tenth that many showed.

However many go, the ground condition they will find there seems clear. There will likely be blood. The black thing there is near blowing, black radicals are warning white organizer friends, "Stay off the street, we won't be able to protect you." Chicago has more cops per capita than a nightmare, Daley's preparing the sewers for mass arrests. Chicago in August will harbor the nation's richest pool of uptight bad vibes, set to flash. Pack 200,000 kids in there, with where we are with America these days when not even our inner millennium has come, and it's sure to blow.

Even 20,000 makes it likely. Remember how that number—spread over three months—left the Haight exhausted, closed, her hospitality broken; and left themselves bitter, wanting and pained? Here there is not even a fictional brotherly community: no guide, no protection, no refuge in this flat hostile landscape, which offers not even a space to sleep. Shit, what makes you think they'll give us the parks (or that we'd be safe there)? You credit them with being rational. But they're not, they're *stupid*. Why should they change their behavior to avert a human catastrophe which any fool can see coming? They run by the Law. And also, they'd *like* to see us go down. You know that, you've been writing about what the revolution means: "Is America going to let us humanize her without a bloody fight?"

So given that there's probably going to be violence despite what any of us want—and maybe in part because of what some of us want, yes, those are our boys too, Jerry, just as it's part of myself that's standing there with a brick in his hand aching to smash a cop—how do we act responsibly, or well, or in tune with that which we would like to build and be? That's what's been puzzling me. And I don't know much that's new, but I think I recognize some old mistakes being made: one by the Yippie group, one by you.

The Yippie thing really troubles me, man, because it's deeply and dangerously irresponsible. So are the politicos working around Davis and Hayden, projecting their clockwork peaceful vision of multicentered independent demonstrations around and at the Convention. For both streams of organizing are raising serious false expectations. The brilliant formless Yippie publicity, in waving the magical beckoning symbol of our Music, projects grooving and warmth, and does not warn that joy there must be won from within—not absorbed from others—in a landscape of total hostility whose ground condition may well be the terror and death of one's brothers. "I don't think anyone will come to Chicago innocently," you tell me. Perhaps. Do you understand the seventeen-year-olds in Des Moines? I don't. All I know about organizing, as opposed to Leadership, is that you have to help people see clearly all that is of importance to them. Can Yippie's mythy publicity be modified to include an accurate portrayal of the landscape's dangers? I doubt it. Can it be damped, defused? Maybe.

It's dangerous to bandy about a figure like "200,000," especially coupled with sugarplum visions of a freebies post-Monterey rock festival and all kinds of fun games, which you so lovingly articulate. For the expectation becomes that the Event is *organized* and can be *attended*, that it's set up to process great drifts of people. Such events mostly draw our young as spectators, not participants. That might be cool: somewhere else, some other time. But if we're mythmaking, let's build our symbols with deliberate care. The lasting radiance of a Festival of Affirmation would depend less on its immensity than on its quality. If it is to demonstrate a real alternative, be a celebration of glad freedom, then let those come who are able to move freely, fed by what they value, choosing the possible risk of their skins: not the passive kids. Let those come who have genuine reason to be present—feeling the need to be there is enough—and let their free joy build what it will, creating in the unpredictable open space that confrontation affords. But a multitude of kids loaded with false expectations will at best dilute the symbol, and may render it unworkable, or, at worst, help tramsmute it helplessly into quite a different symbol, dark with despair and pain. And if a lot of our people come away from Chicago feeling tricked, endangered beyond their consent, their expectations and more betrayed, then whatever is growing within us of public trust will be seriously set back.

This kid Dennis, your advance man, came by a month ago, and I tried to talk about these puzzles with him. I tried to tell him my sense of it, that the Call to Chicago must be moral to be worth making; but he was wrapped up in visions and energy, and wasn't having any; he found my concerns a bit abstract. I was remembering FSM, when Mario and Bettina, especially, drove it home to us: if there's any ethical principle we can fix for our actions in this fractured time, it's that we must keep straight with our own, with those we speak for, lead and invite. That means telling it (and setting it up) straight and in public, with *Where We Are* spelled out explicitly and vividly enough to help people not enter the Event with false expectations. But I was speaking from my own experience, and not to his: a bit abstract.

You and I, we have common experience: the VDC, which despite its numerical glory was humorless, unimaginative, and unliberating. This was connected with its elite style of leadership, which escaped the control of the open meetings and twice brought the community into totally unexpected dangers: in the narrowly averted confrontation with the cops on the 15 October 1965 night march, and in coldly setting up the bloody April 1966 clash on Telegraph. We ought to learn from that, yes?

Here in Berkeley, after October in Oakland and the Rusk demonstration and whatnot, we have now a wiser population, no one needs to remind us: we expect to get beat on the head whenever we show up in public in a political context. It changes our consciousness, makes for apocalyptic visions maybe. But the kids in Cincinnati haven't had our luck; and what's more, they really wish they could've made it to Monterey for the Pops Festival last summer, see you in Chicago. They aren't the kids from the Haight, now familiar with tear gas and clubbings, who will go to Chicago wise and to express who they are, with their warm danger and cold joy, and who are the people you want there to fashion a symbol, the best of our own at joy. They would go without a YIPPIE symbol fashioned in the plastic media-air. Most of those whom Yippie itself will draw will be endangered and superfluous for the occasion. And this sort of organizing, however spectacular, is neither moral nor efficient, effective.

Enough of that. Let me switch to a different perspective, by talking about you yourself, and the mistake I think you're making.

I ran into you at Whitehall, after the most inept and endangering demonstration I'd ever seen. The East Coast has more Authority Complexes than the West—come back, it's warping your head!—and the N.Y. version of "mobile tactics" let itself be Led, hopelessly so. We both were delighted to see that kid climb a car after the fiasco, rip off his monitor armband, set fire to it, and cry "Follow me!" We went for coffee, rapped for the first time in years. I was amazed and gladdened to find us both so much on the same frequency about what was happening and how it projected. We talked about that burning armband and what it meant, of new styles of organizing and organization that had to be developed for a new population, of our need for myth to crystallize our consciousness, of how to begin creating myth.

Since then, I've been digging heavily on much that you've been writing. What I do as sort of pop sociology of youth culture, comes from you out in a useful political rhetoric, almost a poem or an incantation, and sometimes brilliantly; I mean sometimes your clarity really stuns me. You are saying important things well, even if most of them are already known in some way to those in the center of change. Singing informed by politics and acid, you are helping articulate a myth of central significance to us.

But when you come to the Yippie thing, you play it false. You're wearing a media armband. In our developing theology of organizing, you're into the Leadership Heresy; Yippie is a hippy bureaucracy that decrees. Look around you at the structure: already a central permanent office, regional chapter contacts, regular weekly meetings, press conferences, proclamations. It's starting to look like preparations for an SDS or NSA convention. So the resource people play drums instead of write grant-proposals.

So what? It still looks unpleasantly familiar. I don't care that the Yippie publicity announces proudly, "Activities and resources will be planned so that everyone who comes will become involved." I don't believe you can legislate participation any better than LBJ can.

"We teach by doing," you say. And you're right: at our best, we make change, not by calling for it rhetorically to a mass anonymous audience, but by creating real examples of what we want to build. Their presence blows people's minds, breaks expectations; and within this expanded sense of the possible, they move to make their own things. So act true to your understanding, man. Don't be a media pitchman busy *Organizing a Festival*; what is this shit? In your columns sing our changes and our dawning identity and our struggles. Proclaim the importance of Chicago, offer in public your reasons for going there, tell us about the quality of Life you dream to bring to that complex classroom with your presence. That's groovy, that's true. But don't *Organize a Festival*. Tell us your brothers whom you touch or encounter, one-by-one, what you see, what you're doing; write me a letter, as you did. But don't *Organize a Festival*. That's not Right Action.

Your perception of what's needed in Chicago is absolutely accurate: our being there should create a symbol embodying not only our opposition, but also a real alternative, born from our new dimensions. And you are right about the broader context: for us Chicago will be a theater and a school. It is *our* Convention too, gathering the most diverse delegation ever from our multiform Movement.

And that is the key: that the warring strands of our nature must come together. The politicos make no provision for the nurture of joy there. You are mirroring their mistake, seeking too easy an alternative. The joy and the politics must be fused, as they began to be in FSM, and in Oakland in October. To create a separate Festival, even in the same place, plays much of our nature false: those others who come to demonstrate at the Convention are ours too, and we must teach and learn from each other, together.

I think there are better ways of coming to Chicago, and working for the goals we share, than by making the Yippie Festival. Simply accept that Chicago will happen, that it will be a diverse learning group of our peers, operating in what well may be a spastic spectacular class-room. And come there to do your thing. That's all. Music is needed; let rock groups come of their own accord and play on sound trucks, or get their own permits. If you want to help them get bread for travel, you can do so just as well without all of this Official Festival bullshit. Let those who wish to, crown a pig; let guerrilla theater happen; run a free newspaper yourself. If our creators and free spirits recognize a need, and want to come and learn to work among their brothers—well then, they will, and will spread the idea and help each other; and if they don't they won't. The Festival isn't helping them learn how at all. Instead, it's setting up an us/them split within our own ranks that may prove quite costly to us.

What matters is *beyond* Chicago: how we will move next, with the learning we do there. Me, I'm going be-cause it's my Convention and my people, and I want to be with them and make my presence known. I'm going to go there with my fragments—my political man and my singer, my cop-killer and my lover—and try to do something whole. I think we share this complexity and this desire. And I wish I could find better words to tell you my sense that you are going about it wrong, in a way that plays it and yourself and us false.

Living in New York, you have forgotten San Francisco. I see you surrounded by Death, wanting to reach out in a gigantic gesture of Life. But you can't do it save by leaving the old behind. A redefinition of Leader in the new wilderness of the Media won't do, you can't reach out larger than yourself. Years ago I asked one of my students what she thought of Leary and his League of Spiritual Discovery, traveling pitchman selling the Way. "Leary," she said, "is a Harvard professor who dropped acid." Don't become known as a politico who dropped acid, Jerry. Step up on the car, rip off your armband, and burn it, yelling (if you wish) *Yippie!* as you do; and disappear into the crowd. Let what happened at White-hall, and your own words, teach you. As long as we wear armbands—no matter how gaudy, or if they're la-beled "This is not an armband"—we will never create the mobile tactics of the heart.

Love,
Michael

Chicago, First Day, Last Day

The First Day

First I drove by Lincoln Park at noon, to see what's
happening. Not much, just a loose cluster of kids pre-
tending to be grooving: maybe two thousand, faint per-
centile shadow of the quarter million promised and plausible all spring. Which suits me fine, to see so few: for,
though I've come here deliberate hot and cold myself to
help some ugliness reveal itself, I've still been warning
kids off for months, traveling, laying out the vision of
Convention Death Chicago, pure pool of danger.

At worst now, few will go down. And I can almost
pretend that the smiling young men in the autumngold
sun of the park farther south are some new healthy
version of Boy Scouts, with crisp tents and hand tools
of wood and oiled metal. So picturesque in their olive
uniforms, enjoying their encampment. Even old ladies smile
at them, snap their shots with Polaroid "Swingers."

I should Be Responsible, make the rounds of dim offices
where my brothers are working. But I can't stomach
another meeting, so I decide just to drive around and see
what vibes I pick up from this city which has, by its
preparations, already broadcast the message, and now waits

in blind calm, not knowing what to do next, unable to alter the course of its fears.

I weave in and out of the streets around the Amphitheater, center of the local beehive. Neighborhood's almost empty of people, but each corner hosts a small swarm in helmets and nightsticks, their uniforms glow bluer in the sun than a J. C. Penney work shirt. Enough of that, I know them from Berkeley the Haight New York Denver . . . *cop killa creep, pow pow pow.*

Likewise I already know about the people of North Lakeshore, where I'm staying on an umpteenth floor of wall-to-wall carpets and electrostatically precipitated air. I've read their romantic literature, I know what images my sideburns and moustache, shoulder-slung-weary leather camera bag, and all that send them flashing on. Romantic frosting on the cake of ice repugnance they're too polite to betray by more than a glance when we cross in the elevator. Not that I look much different from any other kid on the streets these days, maybe a little older.

So I spin away from the Amphitheater in a widening spiral of aimless search. I drive through the black flatlands. Board houses with asphalt torn shingles, must date from when this was country. Streets lined with slim black people, dour long young men, girls in bright ribbons, in an aimless Picasso silence (Blue Period). Until I drive through: *hippie, hippie,* they cry; not the little jump-roping girls who shrill it elsewhere, but the young men already long jobless, their voices dusky with anger.

I drive through the white flatlands. Dingy brick duplexes, isolated on tiny lawns like pathetic embattlements. Young men again, with the thick shoulders of Poles or some other rough ethnic. Not a sound, just stares. Except from those who sweep close in a muffler-blasting car, explode in derisive laughter. Enough, some food. BARBE-

CUE BEEF! yells the sign, and I stop on some border between black and white. Peppers and generous beef, I lie on the lawn watching a gang of kids playing baseball, deep and timeless in that dear corny drama. *"Here comes Easy-out, here comes Easy-out!"* and up to the plate walks this skinny little kid, his bat already heavy with defeat, to ground out to the pitcher. I take a few pictures, feeling nostalgic and a bit unreal: am I sure this isn't Dearborn, Mich.? Or maybe Manhattan, Kan.? And where does all the hate and killing come from anyway?

I'm walking back to the car, this Resistance kid just in from Minnesota appears to ask me questions, with his bedroll, two young girls from the block rush up to answer, they're in bell-bottoms, maybe fourteen, and so I'm a taxi dropping people off. He goes to the Resistance's central office, near the university, from which seventy-five of his brothers are doing their deliberate solid organizing. Finishing his Ph.D. in physics, he is quiet, polite, intense. Jail glitters in his spectacles. He doesn't smile at the girls alive and easy with chatter and giggles, but they ask him what he does and listen earnestly while he explains: . . . to build something new takes a total life commitment . . .

On me the girls turn serious as we drive away. "I can't *believe* you didn't get jumped," says the tall one with braces and thoughtful eyes, "they jumped even me . . . I mean even *me*." "Yeah, three days ago," says her blonde buddy, "I just couldn't *believe* my eyes seeing someone like you just standing *there*. We thought we'd never get a ride. But if a gang of them had seen you . . ."

I let them out at the Park, wander around for a while myself (they're amazed, too, that I leave my car unlocked). Kids are still doing mostly nothing. I decide to go home and read *Playboy*, sit with a Scotch (how quaint!) on the umteenth floor, look out over this city's intricate vista of black and white, and think about what it all means.

What it all means. Chicago is a Teaching Machine, and its lesson brings us—the hip and radical young, America's white niggers—almost up with the black people. For why have the ghettos been quiet this summer; has America changed? Scarcely. The black people now know it's for real, this matter of theirs, life and death. They have watched their local and national governments arm against them, and now ponder and organize what to do next.

Likewise with us. Chicago advertised its lesson: cops and troops, against a landscape of simple hostility. We got the message in advance, which is why we stayed mostly away; now the other America will eat this vision of violence borne by the Media. We know now, too, that our matter is for real, watching our governments arm. And the sparseness of our presence here, like the black summer silence, is not acquiescence. For while Humphrey's Convention plays out its charade, and after, while the country slides right toward the election, new styles of action will be debated, formed, and resolved among us. Perhaps they are already presaged in the industrial sabotage spreading through the San Francisco area for about the last year? Whatever. But that so few came to this war they've staged doesn't promise peace.

The Last Day

Tear gas isn't so bad, after you get used to it. By the third day no one panicked and ran, and few complained though it billowed in gusts for eight hours straight. It's a bummer, but you recover if you don't rub your eyes, and the only place really to fear it would be in a closed space, like inside a corridor.

It sure made an air pollution problem, though, and distinguished the general action. They gassed and beat kids out of Lincoln Park Tuesday night. The next night they broke up our planned march opposite the Hilton with massive clubbing and gassing, and on Thursday unloaded more soldiers than you can imagine in a dream of boot camp on the street to divide the Hilton, which they imagined we were going to storm, from us, four thousand raggedy pretty kids sitting on a compact mass of park we'd liberated, steeped in tear gas and waiting to get stormed and impounded in magnificent on-the-spot cages formed from their barbed-wire-enclosed jeeps. Like a movie set. Would you be surprised if they got a training film out of this affair?

The rest is familiar, from the streets of the Haight, Berkeley, Oakland, Sunset Strip, Century Plaza, Whitehall, the Pentagon, and so on, where now perhaps forty thousand kids have received this odd form of training. Seen one street action, seem 'em all (so far). Save for novelties like sustained tear gas and them soldiers, Chicago was simply more extensive than any other in its damage and drama.

After each time I tell myself: the next time I have to watch a cop clubbing and clubbing a fallen chick, or leaning down to squirt mace in the face of someone three others are kicking and beating, I'm simply going to crack, and pick up a brick and try to kill one. And the line of cops charged in screaming *Kill Kill Kill*, and I didn't, and nobody did, as usual. And split heads turn out to be an interesting if fairly predictable art form after you get used to them. And the medics were fearless and brave and totally magnificent, as always and even more so, constantly rushing with gauze and tape and squeeze-bottles of liquid to wash tear-gassed eyes.

There was visible evolution in the community and co-ordination of people on the street, who grew from a discontented bickering rabble to a group able to move together and begin to protect its own and keep coherence under stress. Granted, no one was actually rescued from the cops by battle, as far as I saw, though two stray cops were beaten joyously. But if the Thursday march, that was tear-gassed at 18th Street and regrouped opposite the Hilton to face the National Guard, had been allowed to proceed toward the Amphitheater, it might have held together well against the neighborhood gangs, who were waiting on street corners with piles of garbage and cans and stones, and signs reading DOWN WITH HIPPIES!

Anyway what I mean to report is that (a) we learned again that you can't fight the fuzz by massing in the streets, you get smashed; and (b) the way this group of strangers learned to move together under stress augers well for our survival adaptability in even quite more violent circumstances. Which may well be coming. For can you *believe* Nixon vs. Humphrey? Or not flash that they'll move to smash us? And meanwhile kids in their growing strangeness have all this energy that will out, and no place within the system to park it. Campuses will blow like popcorn this fall.

I should mention that I imagine the images over the telly, of what went on both within and without that Death Convention, will spin around many people's heads, in America and around the world. In the sense of a massive media-multiplication and -manipulation, our action in Chicago was a total success. It was too tremendous an exposure, all that could be hoped for. Or planned for. And my only gripe with the notorious YIPPIE! and National Mobilization organizers is that what happened was perfectly predictable; and that organizing for Chicago should have been carried out honestly on this basis, instead of with images of lollipop non-violent Festivals of Affirmation, or of clockwork controlled coordinated demonstrations, which were bullshit from the start.

I'm glad our people have more sense than their leaders. So many sensed the dangers well, so few showed, and these so well. We made our point at the cheapest possible price, a few hundred split skulls. Given the army of destruction they saw in our few thousands, can you imagine how they'd have over-reacted had even 50,000 of our brethren with their passions showed up, and how many dead we'd be mourning? The time for that's not yet. Pardon my sad fantasies. But everyone senses that Chicago is not over, that it's another in a series of beginnings. Something's going on, and it's getting clashy and turbulent.

One other thing I saw in Chicago has left me thoughtful. I've been seeing street people—activists, hippies, what have you—and picking up on their recent tone and gossip across the country. Moods sweep us, partly as a result of our training in the Fad Machine of America's technological economy. Our sound's been growing darker, harder. Guns. Up Against The Wall, Mafia threatening our friendly neighborhood dope dealers, sabotage, check the state of your stomach, hard rain's started falling.

But here we were, this brief community of a few thousand kids, huddled choking and weeping with tear gas, waiting to get creamed by this array of soldiers that just kept arriving and arriving. And nobody during the three days had really seriously flung stuff at the cops; and despite the surrounding social evidence, our mood was not one of killing. And every one was singing; and I could hardly believe my ears, pardon the cliché, but it was like dirt had been scrubbed off the apple-cheeked face of the calendar of some long-ago year when we were young in our hope and hadn't yet run around telling each other to go see *Battle of Algiers*.

We were singing "America the Beautiful" and "We shall not be moved" and "Lay down my sword and shield," all the same corny stuff kids waiting for the cops sang during the FSM in 1964, in S.F. City Hall during the 1960 HUAC demonstrations, in the South, at the Pentagon, and at peace marches, god knows where else. Also Dylan's "Blowing in the wind" and "The times they are a-changing"; and Phil Ochs in harmonic person. You can identify a people, a culture, by their music. And maybe tell a bit about them; draw your own conclusions. But I just wanted to say that, despite the grime of recent time, and the sad early knowledge we're beginning to accumulate, and our premonitions, the face we turned up in Chicago was the same face we've been working with and trying to will into social existence, all these long twelve wandering years of the Movement. We are still in some sort of touch with our selves.

August 1968

Reflections on the American Theater: the 1968 Elections

Both SDS and Wall Street completely ignored the elections this year, which makes sense to me. For within my lifetime, the elections have never involved any significant redistribution or reshaping of Power, despite their proud rhetoric. The history books say they used to, sometime before I was born (1939). But then, the books say this also about the elections I've lived through, so what should I believe? So, as a social organizer, I've chosen to work in a deeper medium than electoral politics: trying to change the educational system.

The elections aren't what they're advertised to be, but they still seem too important to be dismissed as an energetic, functionless game. Rather, though I never read much anthropology, it seems clear that this periodic ritual is a form of public symbolic theater, in which my culture Amerika acts out to herself what she is feeling at the quadrennial moment, her desires and fears and expectations. (This is why, in our day of documentary drama and cinema vérité, the National Drama looks so familiar there on the cathode tube. Already Mailer and others have written scripts, and soon someone will make a film.)

So I have been attending the Election Theater, watching this heavy formal drama and trying to get the message my culture is acting out. And what I have seen this time terrifies me, if I take it seriously. For what was most evident on the stage was *who was missing:* us, the young.

We have been around, increasingly. Tagged with various labels—the New Activism, hippies, Youth Culture—something massive and new has been growing in us and with us. It first became visible around 1958, with the Freedom Rides. Almost immediately, it was reflected in the Election Theater, by the tousle-haired figure of Kennedy the First, central and consummate actor on the stage. He played touch football and started the Peace Corps, and his rhetoric reflected our Noblest Aspirations.

But that was in 1960, when we still seemed tractable, when we were mostly out doing missionary good: tutoring ghetto children and getting our heads split in the South. By 1964 we had grown stranger and bolder, and had started bringing our change back home. In Berkeley the Free Speech Movement signaled the first great public outburst of the white young against their most Liberal parent institutions. And already, in the Election Theater of that year, we were clearly being pushed toward the wings and offstage.

For we were represented on the stage by Goldwater, not Johnson. This makes no sense in traditional political terms, but it does if you take the elections as symbolic theater. The voice calling for real change was Goldwater's. His campaign engendered the only youth enthusiasm. (Later, some young Americans for Freedom chapters that had campaigned for him merged with SDS chapters.) And, like youth, he was deviant, zealous, honest, concerned with moral imperatives, and greatly and blindly feared.

In the four years since then, Amerika's consciousness has centered increasingly on the strange motions of her young: the antiwar actions, the McCarthy enthusiasm, the campus

convulsions, the many voluntary youth ghettos whose pro-
totype was the Haight. Whatever is new in us announces
with growing diversity and power that we are starting to
move *en masse* out of the political and cultural mainstream
—and that our motion cannot be ignored.

Yet in the Election Theater of 1968, there was simply
no place for us on the stage. If you don't care for symbolic
interpretation, perhaps our absence can be dismissed by
the "accidents" of Robert Kennedy's assassination and
McCarthy's inability to buck an entrenched political machine. But the tableau of the election reiterated our absence strangely. The most striking thing about Nixon and
Humphrey was not that they wore cardboard masks and
played insipid roles, but that we remembered them literally
from our early childhoods, like the dear faded Tenniel
illustration of Tweedledum/dee. And Wallace crouched in
the lower right corner, snarling like some impossible cat
winking into existence from the late rabid 1930s. It was
as if the clock had been turned back, to a time before
our presence was even possible.

Wallace was the key figure on the stage, despite the
traditional political analysis that rejoices at his "poor"
showing in the vote. He was the only focus of live
energy from the audience. The strategies of the other
actors were shaped more by the Wallace Problem than by
the War or the blacks. His language decided theirs, and
all spoke in chorus of Law'n'Order. The audience mostly
assumed that they were threatening only the blacks. But
the unrecognized deep dynamic behind the Wallace Phenomenon suggests that their message was directed also,
and perhaps mainly, to the absent young.

Wallace calls his followers the "left-out people." Clearly,
they have had no national electoral outlet for their feelings about niggers, street violence, big government, and

so on. Both his friends and foes have been quite content to take this description at its political face value. But Wallace's people are the subject and vanguard of a deeper disenfranchisement whose only familiar aspect—the political one—is also the least novel and least important.

For the texture of our age is of accelerating change, and his people represent those who are falling behind Automation and new technologies are erasing their jobs, and the vocational retraining programs don't work. Three years ago the first San Francisco dance posters appeared. Now Wallace's housewife opens her paper to supermarket ads done in some weird psychedelic lettering she has to squinch up her eyes to read. She turns on the TV. Everybody in advertising smokes grass now, and the commercials which form the medium's core are getting freakier and freakier. So are her children, whose perceptions they're shaping: if not today, then tomorrow. For the new youth culture is growing rapidly in membership as well as in strangeness. Already the first wave of *lower-class* teen-age hippies have appeared in the Haight, mingling indistinguishably with the middle-class runaways.

So Wallace's people are indeed being "left-out": their familiar culture is dissolving beneath them, and their future is foreclosed, for their children will not be their own. And to the extent that this deeper dynamic underlies the Wallace Phenomenon, he represents not a cranky minority but Amerika herself, her changes and fears.

Given only the timid projections Theobald, de Chardin, Lifton and others have deduced from what has already happened, we are headlong into a shift of cultures unique in human history. Its closest parallel in depth may be the paleolithic/mesolithic transition, but its rapidity has no precedent. We have seen, in the Aleutian and Polynesian islands, examples of sudden but far less radical cul-

ture change, in which old folkways are supplanted within
the lives of their bearers. Conflict between old and young
is characteristic of such transitions, due to their speed—
and our change grows steadily heavier and faster.

Is it premature to recognize the stresses of our culture's change already being portrayed in its symbolic public
theater? The TV screen flicks from a McLuhan interview
through a Dodge Rebellion commercial to Chicago, dress
rehearsal for the Election Theater. Under her satellites
America pulled its pants down, took out his cock, and
proceeded to club their fears and our children over the
head in my street. Inside the Amphitheater, the Director
said, "Sorry, kids, we were just kidding. But thanks for
coming to rehearsal. And can't you take a joke?"
From their lost tower, from the fifteenth floor, McCarthy's
children dropped salmon of smoke to the soldiers waiting
in the street, in grave benediction. And then went downstairs to join the Yippies in the wilderness of Grant Park,
and wait for destruction.

What was acted out in Chicago had little to do with the
Democratic party or electoral politics. The conflict expressed was between the old order and its young. And
the terms of the conflict were stated clearly, from the
old order's side at least: absolute closure and violence. The
symbolic structure was so overt that even some adult
newscasters caught it. And some notable, on live camera,
flashed on this first pre-echo of a true youth pogrom and
said brokenly, "The children . . . my God, see what
they're doing to the children . . ."

In November the words of Law'n'Order and their
meaning were the same, though no machine guns were
visible in the streets. The growing strangeness of the future will be faced with refusal and violence. It is as if
Amerika had been startled to find her children on the

public stage, at about the Kennedy time, and had grown alarmed at their sudden growth and their strange freaky motions that could not fit her script. And then thrust them offstage, locked the door, and turned to speak the opening lines of this next act, in a tone of stern parental wrath and foreboding.

Amerika bends over the mirror. The children are behind her, shouting. She admits to herself that she does not like them. Their father? Once she was visited by a spirit of hope, warrior returned and weary and grateful. They embraced, heaven promised on the installment plan if only she'd work while he went off to war again. But that was before the piling withering years that brought only an empty plenitude but no peace, nor his return, nor an end to the pain. She stares at them in the mirror. No use telling her there's something wrong with her eyes. She wants only to be alone, now that everything's turned strange.

December 1968

The Context of Campus Violence

By 1969 the tides of our change were shaking every institution of higher education. In the eyes of white Amerika, provincial and racist as always, campus disturbances had replaced black ghetto rebellions and Vietnam as the Number One topic of concern. Every school and city government geared for war.

Meanwhile, among us, the slow wedding of new politics and new culture went on. After Rolling Stone *established itself as the counter-culture's leading popular arts journal, its focus began to broaden, and Jann Wenner asked me to provide its first major article of the politics of the counter-culture. I hadn't written a piece of survey journalism about education since my notes of 1966, and welcomed the chance to step back for an overview of the action on the campuses I'd been traveling for two years.*

Last month in Ohio I watched 200 Oberlin College students play with spontaneous anger and destruction in a "free environment" developed by some hip architect-travelers from Texas. Since then, Oberlin students have been suspended for a disruptive protest against Marine recruitment on campus. In Iowa, I helped teach students guerrilla theater techniques and new learning-games. At the University of Michigan, I watched leaders of rival factions of SDS—split on the strategic question of whether to lead a direct-action attack against the school's language requirement—trying to learn how to talk with one another.

Everywhere schools are alive with growth and tense with dread, at the violent intersection of old and new. Last week the University of Pennsylvania, Stillman College in Alabama, Princeton in New Jersey, Missouri, Notre Dame in Indiana, and a dozen other campuses moved into open conflict. The news media have discovered that there is another ghetto: it houses America's college youth and

is coming alive with rebellion. Each day brings new headlines, news of new gladiators. Some fans can recite the
statistics from memory: the current roster of campuses
in turmoil; the up-to-date figures this year on how many
National Guardsmen called in; how many kids beaten,
jailed, or suspended; total cost of felony bails; number
and shock of bombings; success and significance of boycotts and strikes and betrayals.

At Champaign, Illinois, plainclothes cops were photographing me while I watched 400 white University of
Illinois students debate a sit-in in defense of black brothers. The Trustees had just decreed immediate explusion
for anyone guilty of disruption. The students decided on
a new tactic: a "jam-in," to paralyze the telephone lines,
deans' offices, cafeteria, library, and so on, simply by using their own weight of numbers to overload them beyond capacity. Legal disruption, in a word, the first serious
experiment with a new tactic to replace the sit-in. I
argued for the "jam-in," which had been conceived originally in Berkeley during the November 1966 strike. The
next day an SDS traveler came down from SDS's national
office in Chicago to denounce me as a CIA agent. Simultaneously the right-wing Chicago *Tribune* was splashing
my name over its front page as an "outside agitator."
Paranoia strikes deep, sings the Buffalo Springfield, *into
your life it will creep* . . .

But I'm neither an agent nor an agitator. I'm a campus
traveler in the educational reform movement, a large but
little-known branch of that great general movement for
change among the young, whose most familiar aspects
are political activism and the hippy thing. Maybe half a
million people are involved in the "ed reform" movement
now. Most are students making free schools, trying to
change their institutions and find new ways to learn. As

movements do, this one generates travelers and spreads itself by them. My traveling takes me to many colleges, and through a wide spectrum of people, from politicos to heads.

All of them are talking about violence. Everywhere the System has been responding with violence to attempts at change (not that our own hands are clean). Since I work with people learning to make change—educational, political, cultural, personal—everywhere I move behind the surface of violence. I am sick with statistics and examples. I want to talk about what is happening in America, about why the violence will increase, and about some real reasons for fear.

The Themes of Campus Conflict

Black students at hundreds of colleges are demanding great jumps in black enrollment, special privileges and programs and the creation of Black Studies Departments which they themselves can control. At San Francisco State College, a radically successful black students' strike has now gone into its second semester with white students moving in support of black demands.

The hard edge of the white student movement has gone even harder. Since its founding in 1962 (as an offshoot of the League for Industrial Democracy), Students for a Democratic Society has grown to be the most important young white political group with over 300 local chapters and some 200,000 active sympathizers. At first, SDS rhetoric and concerns centered around "participatory democracy." Then it became preoccupied with the Vietnam War. Now, largely in response to hard-line pressure from the Progressive Labor Party (with their acrid insistence

on the importance of a worker/student alliance *à la France*),
SDS has gone over to a stance based on an updated
version of Marxism: direct attack on the total institution
of American Imperialism.

On the campuses, this ideological hardening is expressed
by sit-ins against Marine recruitment (at Oberlin),
against involvement in chemical and biological warfare
research and other university roles in the War Game (at
Pennsylvania State University), and against the university's
nature as a racist institution (at Brandeis).

Tactics and penalties for campus disruption are escalat-
ing. Black students everywhere have mastered the art of
the coercive sit-in. Since administrators are still fairly reluctant to have them beaten or expelled from school, small
groups of blacks are managing to force some real granting of their demands. At 8,000-student Duke University,
the 100 campus blacks led a boycott and sit-in that won
them a black studies program and other changes in learning and living conditions, including an all-black dormitory.

White tactics are less disciplined and effective than black
ones, and often more desperate. They range from mass
drink-ins of forbidden beer on the main quad (at Colorado
State University) to disruptive mill-ins at Berkeley in vain
defense of student leaders persecuted by the Administration. College authorities in general are becoming venomous
to white students. At the University of Massachusetts,
thirty-two protesters sitting-in against Dow Chemical's recruiters were busted by state troopers. Administrators have
become trigger-hasty to order arrests. They often, as at
Berkeley, overrule pleas or rulings from proper faculty
committees and suspend or expel student "agitators."

This fall at Sonoma State College in California I watched
two heavy black organizers effortlessly and insultingly
mobilize a bewildered group of fifty white students—who

wanted action, but had no program of their own, nor sense of their own manhood—into a support demonstration for the S.F. State strike. Whites always feel under pressure to move into direct action as radical and heroic as the blacks. A deep and natural manhood-competition thing is happening between them. It is rendered a bit sour and off-balance by the white movement's lack of a focused center or soul, and white direct-action is often clumsy, ill-prepared, and heavily punished.

Despite this, the action multiplies. There were organized student protests at more than 500 colleges in 1967/68, over issues ranging from control of dormitory rules to abolition of language requirements to the endless War. Over half involved some kind of direct action: at perhaps fifty colleges students were arrested. In late 1968 and early 1969 disruptions have been more frequent, more various, and heavier. All the awakened energy of the young McCarthy horde, shocked and blunted in Chicago, has reappeared to join last year's momentum of bitterness and impatience for change.

What all the protests have in common is this: students are demanding power, control, and freedom in the institution of higher education which shapes and controls their lives. By organizing for autonomous students' governments and free dormitory intervisitation, they are moving to control their political and social lives. By fighting against useless academic requirements and by developing new curricula in free universities, they are moving to control their education. By protesting racist admissions policies, Dow Chemical recruiters, and the Vietnam War, they are coming to use the colleges as a base and a tool to change the larger society.

Increasingly, students are coming to realize that—in ways as diverse as designing machines to help Agri-business exploit Chicano workers, and forcing their participation in a competitive grading system—the colleges participate actively in all of society's injustices, and deform them as individual people. By fighting for free minority admission policies and calling for courses that reflect their need to grow into new ways of knowing, students are beginning to demand that higher education fill the unmet needs of the people it processes.

But the colleges are an essential part of the total American system of exploitation and oppression, and are reluctant to change. If engineering departments shift their priorities to the task of producing livable cities, what will happen to the multibillion dollar aerospace industry, and the armies of young engineers with which it contends for fat government contracts? Male students must be kept to the grindstone with requirements and hurried through in four lock-step years, or else the orderly system of military deferment and obligation will be disrupted, and too many malcontents will be allowed to escape scot-free, without even paying the price of a degree and integration into the economic order.

Even as individual institutions, colleges are slow to change. Consider Berkeley, America's most prestigious public university. For five years, students' demands for political freedom and their discontent with their education have made Berkeley the nation's most protest-prone campus. Yet during this time no significant institutional changes have been made. The school goes on, average faculty teaching load has dropped sixteen percent, and now National Guardsmen patrol the campus plaza with pepper-fog machines.

As with the black liberation movement, the demand for change in the educational system grows rapidly more urgent and immediate. On every front—political, social, educational—the colleges cannot and do not want to meet the demand. Some easy concessions—like black studies programs at Duke, free dormitory hours at Denison University, pass/fail grading systems at Simmons in Boston —are finally being given. But they have come too late. They will not be enough. The student demand for real power, freedom, and control will keep growing. It is impossible to meet without deep change in the *entire* institution of American higher education.

As everywhere in America, on the campus the channels of change are clogged. Requests disappear in a maze of administrative advisory and study committees, in endless delay. On the pinnacles of power stand inflexible presidents, arch-conservative faculty councils, trustees, and often the state legislature. None wants change.

The rising desire for radical change is met on the campus as everywhere with immobility, repression, and violence. And in response, the determined and heartfelt force of the movement for change becomes violent itself, even as it continues to expand.

The State of Other Campuses

America's 2,700 colleges form a great youth ghetto with 7,000,000 inhabitants. But higher education itself is only one of a cluster of campuses now coming alive with violence and change.

After the media discovered the Haight, sister communities appeared in every major American city. The gift of the Haight's media-martyrdom was that a second great youth ghetto—a voluntary one—became visible. At first its talk was all of flowers and grass and music. But lately the rhetoric and action have gone hard in the hippy ghetto.

During pleasant nights in communes in San Francisco and Colorado, I watch friends oiling guns and learning how to load magazines; they offer to teach me to shoot. People are swiping dynamite, industrial sabotage mounts unreported in the press. In the Bay Area, we watched the unfolding drama of a year-long series of power-line bombings. The Mafia and the law have moved in on grass and acid. The dealing scene, once warm and stable, has become increasingly turbulent and ugly. Hard drugs are rising fast, betrayals and burns and shootings increase. In Berkeley last summer, narks killed a suspected dealer in a hamburger stand shoot-out.

In New York, Digger Abbie Hoffman and friends dropped handfuls of dollar bills off the balcony at the Stock Exchange, watched the avid brokers scrabble on the floor below. In a hundred cities now, digger spirits burn public dollars, stop traffic in anger and joy, pass out soup on City Hall's steps, desecrate flags into human clothing. They violate deep rituals, and anger flares at them in return. A new form of street-theater is emerging, flourishing in a thousand microdramas already passed into folklore—a new way of confronting a total system with its absurdities and people's real needs.

Spread by the example of SDS agitprop groups—who tend to appear suddenly in cafeterias, shooting Vietnamese peasants—on many campuses guerrilla theater is beginning to surface in the classrooms and libraries. It is provocative, naked, and often arrested. So is the Living Theater, which has escaped New York and is now shaking up kids at small Ohio colleges—one of many influences turning them on to notions of drama as disruptive and shaking as Aeschylus was in his time.

But the heaviest theater is still in the streets, the joint campus for the hip and political cultures. In the West, the first significant street clashes between the young and the law came in early 1967, when cops fell upon antiwar demonstrators at Century Plaza in Los Angeles, and scattered crowds of teenyboppers along Sunset Strip. Since then, at least 60,000 kids in a dozen cities have clashed with cops in major engagements, and have learned to form groups to drag each other back from the tear gas and clubs.

The issues on the street are various: the right to use it for festival, the right to a free political process, an end to imperialism. But the action is the same, and it is steadily growing more violent. Chicago was a quite typical example of the national brutality norm, shocking only because it was fairly well televised.

The classroom of Street Violence is coming to be a major shared experience among America's white young. An old Movement maxim runs, "The quickest radicalizer is a cop's club." Nothing seems to confirm people in a change of values, or push them over the edge of that change, as directly and forcefully as does a police beating. The street experience may come to have an impact second only to that of our music and drugs. In many cities bands of neighbors or brothers, initially formed for self-defense on the street, are becoming semi-political "affinity groups," learning to work cooperatively and moving underground in preparation for the repression that many see coming.

At the Intersection

Thus, campus violence is embedded in larger violence —the violence that flickers along the whole Intersection, where what's coming up meets what's going down.

Fortune magazine claims that 40% of America's college youth now pledge allegiance to the New Left. America is *splitting*. Expressed through her youth, a deep shift is occurring: a new culture with new attitudes and behavior is veering off, at righteous angles and odds to the old one.

We all sense, often with resentful hope, that something's growing in America. But the speed and variety of growth are still startling. Every large city now holds a therapeutic youth-ghetto community. National networks of communes are beginning to come together, and to generate their own economic support. Three hundred thousand students in 600 "free universities" on and off regular campuses are experimenting with new curricula and new ways of teaching, trying to build a new kind of educational institution. A diverse and independent media-network has been established. Liberation News Service, the underground newspaper wire-service, serves more than a million readers. Branches of the guerrilla film group Newsreel are appearing in major cities. The type of serious rock station whose first example was KMPX in San Francisco (1967) is taking permanent and financially viable space on the nation's airwaves.

Meanwhile, according to government estimates long outdated, at least 10,000,000 white youth smoke grass for pleasure and to change their lives. Some 2,000,000 young people have dropped acid and undergone psychotic breaks to learn that there are other ways of knowing than those taught in school. Youth has suddenly become defined as a political constituency, wooed by outside powers and beginning to generate its own leaders and programs. Youth political pressure has shifted the course of the state in Vietnam and helped to harden it at home. And in less than a decade we have generated and lovingly consumed—and have been deeply shaped by—a great flowering of music, whose sheer bulk, variety and quality compare favorably with the output of the Renaissance.

Through all these changes runs a deep unity. The children of a total system that denies human needs are moving for power and freedom to build what they want. A mass consciousness is awakening. Students, and youth in general, are becoming aware of themselves as a class. Like the black people, they are coming to see themselves as a class exploited and oppressed—forced by outside interests of power and money to labor on the colonial plantation of the campus, in preparation for their roles in service to the technological economy of capitalism. Like the black people, they are learning to recognize brothers and band together. And like the blacks again, they are developing an independent cultural identity, and moving to build in their own self-interest.

Against this wave of consciousness and building, there is coming down a System: some say in its death throes, some say merely facing the ugly impossibilities of its contradictions at last. The cities are quickly becoming unlivable, the air is choked with pollutants, the sea is befouled. Foreign liberation movements are threatening America's economic interests. A war whose frustrations will continue if it ever ends has led to political earthquakes. The economy sways dizzily and hiccoughs. Black frustration rises, the white Nixon government cuts back programs. The military grabs for the moon and extends a finger into the ocean. Wallace gets 13% of the vote, the country slides quickly right, police forces double in hard technology, Minutemen practice in the hills.

The Liberal mask America wore so well is slipping off. Her children are finding many languages to express their realization that she is an oppressive class society, anti-life and unstable—a total system that resists all real change.

And the drama being acted out along the Intersection is becoming clear. As their blind freaky growth continues, her killing response rises to the surface.

The action at the Intersection is the same in politics and education as on the streets of the city. We saw it when McCarthy kids, SDS, Yippies, and blacks converged on Chicago last August. Youth is being let on stage for rehearsals, and forced back with bayonets when it becomes clear that youth wants its own strange way. The image fled by television to China and France, where it was already familiar: everywhere a mass youth consciousness is developing. And everywhere the Authorities are terrified of losing control. Russia marches into Czechoslovakia, Daley into the Amphitheater, Reagan and Hayakawa over San Francisco State College.

But control is being lost indeed, on the campus as elsewhere. Grass and acid are entrenched and spreading, their use doubles every year. Though the War's lull seems in sight, campus draft-resistance centers are multiplying. The drop-out rate spirals. Campus travelers multiply, protest and growth spread by example, colleges flare like adjacent match-heads. The clearest avalanche warnings are given by the high schools, which are more active with protest now than colleges were three years ago. High school underground papers are so common that they are forming their own news services. Dozens of older Resistance groups are doing anti-war organizing on high school campuses. Militant high school students are traveling between schools in big cities, organizing simultaneous protests. The federal government intervened to quell high school disorders in nineteen cities last year. The Authorities grow increasingly terrified of losing control. A great repression gathers. On both sides violence multiplies its forms.

All-American Violence

Let's be frank and simple. Violence, as the good brother says, is "as American as apple pie." America is just a killer culture, that's all. In the end, there's not much karmic difference between napalming Vietnamese, creating the black American's experience, or filling the lungs of dear chubby white children with smogs and carcinogenic tars. Amerika dishes out impartial death, with more if you ask for it by challenging her.

We are used to thinking of violence as physical, but in Amerika most violence is transacted in words. And so the institutions of the word—advertising media, the educational system—are, with the military and the police, primary institutions of violence. Televised deodorant ads teach us that our natural smell is bad, everyone grows up terrified of his own freakiness, a secret nigger inside.

On the campus, students labor to raise the price of their sale into economic slavery. Their draft deferments are an essential link in a system of control, injustice, and violence. They are taught to use the intellect to fragment and divide, to legislate social control and construct engines of destruction. In the classroom, whipped on by the grading system and split sessions, students are conditioned to claw their brothers in competition for a smile. Harsh ivy grows on the ivory tower, it covers a long deep wounding that only now is beginning to break into blood.

All Amerika is a campus ripe with invisible violence vibrations. She is also a culture in unprecedentedly massive and rapid transition: a culture breaking open. Everywhere along the break, along the Intersection, violence becomes visible. It is not new, it is only translated into a different form and exposed. The growing physical violence is the last and clumsy resort of a system of quiet violence and control, as it begins to break open under the gathered pressure of changes and needs it can neither deny nor satisfy.

So violence spills over at the Intersection of black and white, at the technological interface where men's jobs vanish from their hands (haven't you noticed union action is violent again?), where the freaky young try to inhabit the streets they grew up in, at the leading edge of theater, and all along the open surface of young radical politics. Now, under the pressure of a rapidly growing movement for educational reform and political action, higher education is breaking open along the fault-line of the free university. And violence begins to appear on the campus.

But it is not simply a matter of a violent system blindly reacting to change with violence. The young have within themselves a deep and independent anger. (Will it, too, be inexhaustible?) What marks all our institutions, beneath their calm surfaces of control, is that their subjects are tense with gathered stresses and unmet needs, and are full of pains and angers, which they rarely express openly and are mostly unconscious of.

So what comes out first when we move toward freedom, along with sometimes our love, is our anger. And nowhere more heavily than in education. In loosely constructed experimental courses, 300,000 students have found that as soon as authority and control are relaxed in a learning-group, visible anger, long-conditioned and repressed, boils over, and must be dealt with *before* learning together can happen.

And in the colleges at large, every serious campus disturbance since the FSM has run on a mixture of political and educational discontent. In each we have seen groups of the best students act out a long deep fury—the living reflection of the massive frustrated boredom of the lecture hall.

Until five years ago, no one thought to connect youth discontent with the colleges themselves as the source. Since then and increasingly, students have turned against the institution itself, coming to identify it as an enemy rather than as a benevolent parent. The anti-war and black liberation movements have begun to teach them the ugly politics of higher education. Grass, acid, music and "head culture" generally have begun to tempt them with new options, alternative ways of living, learning and knowing. The stance of college authorities as stern parents in classrooms, dormitory and dean's office becomes increasingly impossible to bear.

A system of constant violence now becoming visible, an angry people growing toward freedom. Who believes that violence will not increase, or that a serious repression is not in store?

Strategies of Containment

The standard reaction to pressure for radical change is to buy it off. Across America, a strategy of campus containment is emerging, which reads: grant with relative grace the minor changes and options that don't endanger the System itself.

Suddenly there is a crucial shift of mood in the way school administrators respond to black demands. The trend is rapid toward recruiting more black students and making special programs. Yale and Duke have announced that Black Studies are intellectually worthy of honor as a separate discipline. Jerkwater colleges follow suit, and the

shortage of persons academically qualified to head Black
Studies Departments is already severe.

But those black demands that might change the nature
of colleges *as institutions of learning*—for example, student
control of curriculum, of hiring and firing, of finances;
and open admissions without entrance requirements, plus
uniform financial subsidy—are being resisted to the end.

The question now becomes: Will the thrust of the black
education movement be bought off, and the blacks satisfied by integration into an educational system breaking
down of its own non-racist accord? Or will they press
their more radical demands, and help force the system
itself to change and not merely remedy its racism?

On the front of white campus action, administrative
strategies of containment are more various, but they follow the same philosophy. Suddenly the fight for liberaliza-
tion of women's dorm hours is almost over—in most places
even before it had fairly begun. Administrators agree:
that's not the place to hold the line. Students are being
freely granted token-nigger seats on faculty and administrative committees on hundreds of campuses (but no real
power). Everywhere administrators are encouraging free
universities, for these seem to bleed off energy and pressure for reform of the system. But they carefully regulate
the nature and number of courses that can receive official
credit.

At many campuses, administrations are experimenting
with small, self-contained colleges of a few hundred students, trying to find a new form that will channel the
attention and energy of young intellectuals and activists
—one that will keep them within the system without disruption. Berkeley's 150-student "Tussman Program," begun in 1965, was a first attempt. Its teaching assistants
made the program too "unstable"; they were fired, which

made the program safer and less interesting. Currently the most attractive experiment I know of is the Residential College at the University of Michigan, in which students can paint their walls, smoke dope, and screw; and also have some real control over curriculum and evaluation. (They do not, however, control finances, the nature of curriculum, or hiring.) If state legislatures don't object, this model will spread.

But a strategy of getting all the freaks off in a safely isolated corner to play and experiment may boomerang, as may any effort at containment. At the University of Illinois' Champaign campus, organized student activism has tripled during the last three years, partly because greatly relaxed women's hours permitted students to go to meetings and talk politics over late coffee—since sex could be saved for later in the night. In the Residential College at Michigan, half of the students are activists. At Berkeley, the administration began approving a safe few student-initiated courses for credit. The students promptly sponsored Eldridge Cleaver lecturing in a credit course. The governor and the regents reacted; and the university and state were plunged immediately into political turmoil.

A few whole-system attempts at containment or inhibition of campus activism are under way. Some new campuses, like the Santa Cruz campus of the University of California, have been designed partly with a mind toward isolating students from each other in small manageable groups, making communication and mass action difficult. Such design is somewhat successful, but students there are still in the process of forcing the granting of their demand that the seventh "cluster college," scheduled to open in 1972, shall be for black studies and be named after Malcolm X.

A deeper force for the containment of student activism is now appearing, from an unexpected direction. Encounter groups, sensitivity games, and many kinds of touchy-feely play are spreading around the country, largely among the young. They involve powerful and long-neglected kinds of learning, and are potential tools for liberation. But they are being spread with the Liberal philosophy that "our troubles come not from conflicts of interest, but from inability to communicate." Encounter is being used to *substitute* for conflict, rather than to make conflict healthy and open. Thus, administrations, counseling services, and youth religious groups are all eagerly spreading encounter programs.

Some campuses, like the University of California at Davis, have become saturated with these games learned in this soft spirit. Students and administrators go through groups together, meetings are heavy with rhetoric of community. The usual result seems to be a virtual paralysis of student activism—which everywhere grows by making conflict of interest explicit. At such campuses activists seem *less* able to work well with each other in groups, despite all their "group experience"; and almost all attempts at educational change or political reform are co-opted into the structure and come to no significance.

The Gathering Repression

But the energies of change are breeding like yeast. Discontent, disobedience, and disruption are spreading too rapidly. No soft policy of containment, no matter how sophisticated, will be sufficient. A broad repression of youth has begun.

At its present pace, 1969 will see some 250,000 arrests

for grass. A few states are considering lowering the offense to a misdemeanor, but the use of selective enforcement as a tool of local community disapproval is increasing. Cops have planted dope on friends of mine—SDS and Yippie organizers, editors of high school underground papers, ed reform travelers—in Santa Barbara, Urbana, Pennsylvania, and New York, to make arrests in the course of political persecution. This is how they are martyring Jerry Rubin, John Sinclair and John Lee Otis.

A massive and single-minded Media Curse has been cast over SDS, labeling it National Whipping Boy, responsible for any old act of violence on campus or off. Already on some peaceful campuses, students are being denied appointment to committees because of their supposed adherence to "SDS ideas." National SDS figures like Tom Hayden are being damned in Congress and hauled up before the House Un-American Activities Investigating Committee.

"But how much *is* SDS responsible for what's happening?" The question is empty, even given that SDS as an organization deliberately and proudly opens many of the fronts of conflict. Though only 200,000 activists claim it some official allegiance, SDS is less an organization than a broad penumbra of feeling present in every heart. Indeed, at most demonstrations—however they begin—less than a quarter of the protesters belong to any organized political group. Young activists, like the rest of their peers, are reluctant to create formal groups. The true organization of resistance and revolution is informal and interior.

The myth that SDS is *responsible* is part of the Conspiracy Theory. Something frightening and strange is happening: there must be a simple source or cause, some conspiracy that can be thwarted. It was this need to explain everything in simple, reassuring terms that led Berkeley administrators for years to believe that all the discontent and action on their campus was caused by a *"small, hard core of non-student agitators,"* and that if these could just be cut off from the students, peace would return. Fraternity enrollment would stop falling, and the Golden Bears would win the Rose Bowl again.

These days the agitators are traveling ones. They move between campuses and cities; but the Conspiracy Theory is the same. A small, hard core minority of freak maniac antichrists are moving around the country casting spells of discontent, and must be stopped. So Yippie organizers like Jerry Rubin are also hauled up before HUAC, and are tailed and harassed constantly by the FBI and narks. Similar things are happening to campus travelers in the educational reform movement. When "traveling agitators" of any variety appear or meet on a campus, administrators go into high-level fibrillation, police patrols double and reinforcements are alerted.

A new weapon of legal repression is appearing—the felony charge of "conspiring to commit a misdemeanor," which can be used against any group of people who meet before a mass demonstration at which even trivial laws are broken. Currently, in Oakland, seven leaders of the 1967 Induction Center protests are being tried for felony conspiracy. Indictments for felonious conspiracy have already appeared in connection with campus struggles at San Fernando Valley State, Colorado State, Berkeley, and elsewhere.

Though Nixon is promising a voluntary army, jail sentences for the 5,000 active followers of the Draft Resistance are getting stiffer, mostly running three to five years. Black leaders like Eldridge Cleaver and S.F. State's George Murray are being sentenced to jail for "parole violations." Recent federal legislation against "crossing state lines to incite riots" is about to be enforced: indictments for black and white traveling organizers—Panthers, Yippies, SDS and so on—are said to be in the works, for Chicago and other offenses to America's dignity. Friendly reporters pass on word of calls from the FBI to campus Security Offices, inquiring after me. It's getting freaky.

Administrative allies are hard at work too. The influential journal *Police Chief* presents case studies of how local peace officers help deans solve their problems. In carefully timed press releases, the FBI boasts that it has thoroughly infiltrated SDS and other campus political groups, white and black. In Washington and Oakland undercover informers and provocateurs are appearing, to testify against activists. Lists of students and others in attendance at major activist conferences or demonstrations are starting to circulate among college administrations.

Reactionary state legislatures in many states are passing laws to make any kind of campus disruption illegal. In California alone, some sixty punitive bills are now pending. Private schools like Notre Dame are making participation in disruption the grounds for immediate expulsion. Mid-level administrators in state college systems are falling all over each other to see who can present the hardest line. Often hard reaction from trustees or lawmakers upsets the efforts of liberal administrators to hold the line with soft containment.

At Santa Cruz, Michigan, Denison University, and Connecticut, the contracts of young teachers sympathetic to student activism are not being renewed. At schools like Pace College of Business Administration, student newspapers are being busted or suspended.

Two years ago, control of student finances at Berkeley was taken away from the student government by the

administration. Now at S.F. State the administration, ma-
nipulated by the trustees, has taken control of $400,000
in student funds, suspended the student officers, and is
suing them for mismanagement and misuse of funds. In
the California legislature, bills are pending to take complete financial control of student affairs at all 130 universities, colleges, and junior colleges in the state system.
This pattern of financial repression will be multiplied
across the nation, as students continue to learn how to
use their own money to make change happen.

Around the nation, liberal administrators are responding to the various student thrusts with more and more
sophistication. They exchange letters, hold informal and
formal conferences, and in their academic and trade journals
publish strategies of containment presented as case studies.
At each campus, how many worried dean-hours have been
spent, together and alone, anticipating and pondering coun-
ter-measures? The style of reaction to disruptive protest
now gaining favor—to crack down early and hard—is
the product of those hours and conferences.

The possibilities for control and repression are growing
quickly more sophisticated. For several years, the University of Chicago's Admissions Office has been screening
applicants and starting to weed out activists. Since 1964,
research on student activism has been increasing rapidly,
often funded by government grants (many from the Air
Force). Leading sociologists, like Harvard's Seymour Mar-
tin Lipset, have built their reputations by studying activists.
A report from Educational Testing Services now circulating in 2,000 administrations points out that "the *absence*
of a religious preference is the single personal characteristic most predictive of protest behavior in college freshmen."

But this is a crude measure. The general psychological
types of most important activist subpopulations have been

fairly well studied, at least with a view toward description. Their profiles are now available to anyone who is interested, simply by reading the non-classified research. (Who is to know what is secret these days, in universities that train CIA agents?) To put the matter bluntly: It is now possible to prepare a battery of standard psychological tests which, properly read, will identify present or potential activists with a fair degree of certainty.

Will anyone bother? What do you think?

Action is shaping already on the national level. The National Institute of Mental Health (NIMH) granted the American Council of Education (ACE) $300,000 to do research on the nature and causes of student unrest. ACE's Director of Research, Alexander Astin, speculates—according to the February 10 issue of the influential *Chronicle of Higher Education*—that with the research "admissions officers could virtually assure that there would or would not be demonstrations on their campuses by systematically admitting or rejecting students with 'protest-prone' characteristics."

Now, isn't that a piece of paranoid news?

At first the matter was quite embarrassing to the august American Council of Education. Though the research director was hot for the grant, the ACE's president was terrified of the possible bad publicity. They considered funding the research in the same way that the CIA funded the National Student Association (NSA): through a secondary or "conduit" private institution. But details of the grant were already too public for secrecy.

So ACE accepted the grant openly and quietly. Anxious to have appear legitimate, they are trying to get NSA itself to take a piece of the action. NSA has been offered the chance to run a sub-study aimed at finding out what distinguishes peaceful campuses from campuses prone to disruption. At the moment, NSA is deciding whether to be greedy for money and a chance to keep the study "honest and relevant," or to be noble and denounce the study—and perhaps win back in the eyes of the student movement a fraction of the legitimacy lost during the CIA scandal.

What the matter amounts to is that the government is subsidizing initial counter-insurgency research against its domestic (youth) rebellion. The universities have already performed the service of research to be used against foreign liberation movements in Vietnam, the Philippines and elsewhere, and against the domestic black liberation (mostly in the form of studies of urban and riot management, and of the black family). Why should they not be used again, against their own inhabitants?

Why not, indeed? And who will understand our violent bitterness then, or now, or our growing fear, save we who feel them too strongly for words, indelibly staining our hope?

March 1969

1968–70
In Berkeley

Meanwhile, in Berkeley, the struggle to free space and to create new forms within it went on. As the Sixties wore down, the focus of our lives moved from the campus, took root in the town.

I went away to watch and work, I came back to learn to be a citizen of revolution. After seeing our investigations repeated and extended throughout Amerika, I felt less isolated: Berkeley was just like any place else, only a little more promising. Here the common energies of our change were strongest, most well-rooted, forced the door of the future open for long turbulent glimpses. Here at the Edge, where danger developed new forms, I found myself most among friends, and felt most fiercely the grim joy of wanting to survive.

For Berkeley was my home, was mine. Here I came back to quiet evenings in the cottage with my love. Here I wandered barefoot up to the Avenue with my dog, just another hairy freak lost in the friendly carnival, buying a Good Times *before taking off to the sea or the Sierras.*

Tear gas under streetlights, dope-smoke in candlelight: here where the line between public and private had broken down, I tried to knit together my life.

Why has no major novel been written about this legendary town? Alas, my art in writing—all things considered —is sociology, sometimes poetry. About fiction I feel as timid as a boy at his first dance, back in the bad old days. All I can offer of its raw material are these episodes from our lives in Berkeley, as we struggled to come together within the conflict.

Claiming Turf in Berkeley

Six weeks before Chicago, the headlines in the Bay Area undergrounds read WAR DECLARED! I forget why we called it the First Battle of Berkeley, it was typical of the time: we swarmed into the street, the police attacked to disperse us, a good many windows got broken, also some heads. July 4th was coming up, and we were demonstrating for our community's right to close Telegraph Avenue to traffic and hold a public festival. Since they weren't into shooting us yet, they gave us the street for a day. Our celebration was pleasant, and I wandered home, thinking about Independence Day, to write a piece for the paper.

There is a deeper context to this battle than one hears in the immediate political conversation, on the streets or in our forums. To begin with, it's an episode in a struggle for ghetto self-rule. For our Berkeley community, of which Telegraph is the commercial and cultural center, is a first-class ghetto. No matter that its inhabitants are young rather than black, or that membership is voluntary. (Even this may not be true, for many in their twenties feel strongly that urban life is impossible outside of our peculiar supportive communities.)

Such ghettos are new to history, and the change they portend may have properties that aren't described by any classical model of revolution. The Battle of Berkeley is more than a ghetto self-rule struggle—it is an expression of a future-oriented nationalism, an episode in our blind searching-out of forms for our growth. More than revolutionary politics or human rights of expression are involved, an emerging culture's survival is being tested out. For who can doubt that if enough of our heads get bashed senseless, a deep weariness will descend to fragment us beyond hope and into impotence, and the dawning of the new be again delayed?

A new culture, in the full strength of that term, is being born through us. Lately it has flowered in urban community, in high arts and home arts and beauty and some thought: and a glad flag has been raised in our home-seeking hearts, its emblem still seen dimly. And we have been moving to claim the heartland of its birth, our Home Turf—the campus Plaza has been shakily secured for four years, and now we move on Telegraph.

Consider the history of our intense and growing territoriality. For years our only public expression was political, and struggled for a physical toehold on the edge of the campus.

October 1964. The Administration decides to take away our space. We resist. Free exercise of political rights on the Plaza is decreed, enforced by popular support. The Plaza is ours, and we'll talk there as we please, by the laws we recognize. Our bodies on the line, to defend a public space.

April 1966. A nighttime VDC rally in support of striking Saigon students is held on Telegraph, choking the Avenue. There is no permit. Cops club the microphones silent, confiscate them. We disperse and reform at City Hall, fruitlessly.

November 1966. Police come on campus to remove an antiwar table from "our" Student Union—which we have paid for and supposedly run, but whose space we cannot control. Their arrests trigger the university's second strike, which comes off fairly well but gains us no space.

April 1967. We formed the Better Berkeley Committee and spent a year of fruitless dicking-around with the City government—committees, reports, petitions—trying for an experimental closure of Telegraph, as a mall and for festivals. Finally someone printed up 500 buttons saying simply TELEGRAPH /APRIL 9. And on that day of good music and public grass, 3,000 friendly people closed the street and played, unmolested. (The Haight beat us to the street-closing act by a week, but theirs got a bit smashed up by the heat.) We are temporarily bought off from regular trespass by the City's offer of Provo Park for Sunday rock concerts—a territory the Berkeley High kids had already somewhat liberated, where we tasted our first tear gas in 1965.

October 1967. We're trying to close down the Induction Center, we need a place to gather, to discuss and decide. The Plaza is sanctified by our use. Court order forbids us, but the university helps fudge the interpretation so we aren't molested. Why? Because the 6,000 clustered in that shallow bowl of night make it quietly quite clear once again that we will defend our right to that place against clubs, tear gas, and perhaps death.

That is the leading edge of the present feeling about Telegraph Avenue, after this latest Battle. There is no mistaking the mood that grows in Berkeley, and only much cost will change its direction even temporarily. We are acting out a deep territorial imperative—a new culture must control its birthground to control its own growth. And much of our longing for an open space which is fully our own comes from our sense that in it will crystallize that community we so strongly anticipate, and whose fragments, frustratingly incomplete, nourish us now.

In Berkeley as elsewhere we are liberating territory in which to build and play and heal and learn. Free territory for these life-functions of community and culture comes in other forms than physical space. With underground papers, rock stations and films, we have staked out a corner of Medialand, in which our control is still uncertain. And in the hundreds of free universities we begin to explore the unknown landscape of our necessary education.

As people decide to stay on in Berkeley, they build to a critical culture-producing mass. A non-campus community develops and displays itself. And the turf we decide to claim as our own expands off-campus; we move on Telegraph. The kinds of things we do on that turf, the social myths we try to act out, become more diverse and broadly humane. Creative/Joyous Community. Revolutionary Community. Are our efforts feeble? We have few models, and we're coming up from a long blind despair. Are our examples ludicrous? Don't laugh, they're all we've got. And if Telegraph is not ours, what is?

The victory of this Battle of Berkeley—to come back to that—is not in civic politics, where our quite rational arguments and allies got a few liberal Councilmen to switch votes and prevent a Fourth of July Massacre. It lies in this: the volatile edge of our disorganized community's will claimed Telegraph for our play and got it, *IN PUBLIC.* We have staked claim to our piece of turf and given notice that we will push for it; the threat of our bloodied presence and retaliation is full and credible. And this goes a long way toward shaping our consciousness, our sense of our interests, direction, and center. For some spaces of land do have special meanings and social powers.

Right now we use our turf at their mercy, and they clearly want to club the shit out of us—the broad violence of the old culture gives a clue as to how deep our change runs. Moves are under way to try to ratify our claim politically: the Peace and Freedom Party/Black Panther proposal for local community-controlled police is one such.* A good political solution seems unlikely, though to get the city to give us the street seems possible, some time in the future.

4 July 1968

* [Community control of police became the key issue of the April 1971 city elections. The issue failed, but radical Councilmen supporting it were elected.]

Huelga KMPX!!

Throw a stone into the San Francisco Bay, the ripples spread out far, far. When I got to Vermont in summer 1970, to sit in on the Alternate Media Conference at Goddard, I found representatives from 300 "underground" radio stations. It was hard to remember how unique the first one had seemed only three years earlier—and saddening to realize that the problems of freeing air-space were still unsolved, and that no one had succeeded in creating a better model since then.

I. A Testimonial

How long ago was it, when someone turned us on to that odd little station—it took a while before we could remember its name or its place on the dial—where we could turn for a few hours—and later an evening—and hear some quiet unknown friend playing all those records we'd heard of but hadn't heard because no one had them yet to borrow from, and also the best of what we had come to claim as Our Music? We knew it had to come, that now a Good Rock Station was appropriate to our dawning community and would appear; and it did, and we said, "Aha," and settled down appreciatively to listen. It was so right that we never questioned the phenomenon.

Less than a year ago, that was. Suddenly that polyglot ethnic/religious station on the edge of the dial is gone, its mosaic of private messages displaced segment by segment. And KMPX, the Voice of Community, has the largest FM audience in the Bay Area (which has the densest and livest concentration of kids in America), and our listening habits have changed completely.

We used to rely mostly on records. At first it was radio that broke us out of the classical bag: on long drives we switched back and forth between KYA and KDIA, new both to white rock and black soul. Later we kept the radio on in the house. But the commercials yammered so, and the programming was to a jangly moronic formula, really a drag. So we had to get records, and we came to rely on them, buying new ones by word of mouth, and not much using the dial at home.

And then KMPX appeared, and we put the records up for a while to give it a hearing. They're still there, though on sentimental evenings we shut the station off and late Dylan gets a considerable play from us. For KMPX is like an intelligent friend who can often surprise you, moving in the other room with playful taste through all the records you could want to hear and never afford. And KMPX is like a good classical music station with a happy sense of experiment: it treats rock music like a living art form, as it is, with its changing reaches now rich enough to be worth researching and displaying. Karen wangled us a tape recorder for Christmas from her folks. "Oboy," we said as we prepared to play, "now we can tape all the groovy new albums over KMPX." The tapes are gathering dust on the bookshelf: we seldom play them, we'd rather listen to KMPX. That's how thoroughly it's taken over our ears.

Along the way, the station kept changing. It started catching commercials. Some were as stunning as music, like the ones the Congress of Wonders did. But then commercial commercials, with their familiar sleazy jangle, started crowding in. Luckily, there were heathier changes. Programming grew more inventive. Ravi became a staple; Bach appeared appropriate; jazz and *music concrete* stumbled in, and then our childhood melodramas, segmented like centipedes. Drop-in interviews of people worth hearing happened. KMPX started semi-sponsoring things, and could pack a dance by itself.

The station started giving Sunday afternoons over to a sort of forum on matters of community interest, like the Great Pot Test Case and abortion and Vietnam. During the long newspaper strike, it picked up Ralph Gleason (in too clipped a form: better he should rap once a week for thrice the time), and presented the *Ramparts* news summary. And people listened. The politicos still haven't got it straight, that the way most people found out about the Rusk demonstration during the press blackout was through KMPX, which is why that surprising crowd was there.

A live broadcast of the Dead from Winterland, an analysis of the anti-draft demonstrations. The station's changes were linked to the changes of an emerging community, trying to find and shape its identity; and KMPX began to serve many as a Community Voice. Always its tone was the one in which we most deeply believe business should be done: taking it easy. KMPX's trademark: the programmer or someone blowing something, matter-of-factly up front on the air, backed by a chorus of giggles from the bird engineers. I remember after one song an announcement: "It's okay, Rusty, wherever you are, it's not coming in on the plane tonight, you can relax. This is a public service." Silence. Then a shocked voice from the background: "But you can't say *that* on the air!" "Well . . . guess I just did," and Procul Harum flicked on.

May I tell you other random images, how warmly I feel about that station? I never had a station to love before, or one that didn't snigger about pot. Waking up on Sunday morning to Otis Redding singing at Monterey (where we saw him), the radio left playing softly overnight. The evening the engineers ganged up and took over programming, playing their sexist music: nothing but chick singers for hours. The regular casting of the *I Ching* for us, coming up with the convenient hexagram Revolution at New Year's. Our audible Oracle, experiment in mythology.

And then strange rumblings. Happenings in the station on the air became less frequent, visitors became less welcome, calls for pizza or coffee less frequent. That kid Larry with his eccentric sometimes lovely programs was fired or something. The Public Forum programming cut out; I was away traveling when it happened. People weren't allowed to talk so freely on the air any more, "station policy," and they bitched about it audibly. Suddenly Tom Donahue was out, which meant management had nudged out the people who made KMPX into a creative center. And suddenly all the rest of the staff goes out on strike: I hear them take turns announcing one long last program. Then they cut out at 3 A.M., to join the bands and the station's lovers present in the street below: striking in protest of a Voice being strangled.

II. A Proposal

Let me cut straight to the heart of the matter by asking: Is a community-supported rock station, free to move in response to the community's needs and sensibility, possible now?

Even if public outcry forces the KMPX management to pull back a bit, allow enough freedom to cool revolt, that's still no answer. Their bit is making money, not community-building or joy; they have shitty taste, and they'll always be fucking up. To grow well, and to meet our needs, a station needs more space than Owners can afford. We need some sort of *free* station (in the sense of that word we all understand by now), a station responsive and responsible to its Community in everything from taste to politics—and to its Community only, not to outsiders (I think we can tell the difference).

KMPX has an immense, active, expanding, and partisan listener base. What can be done with and for it? The example of KPFA suggests that a community-supported FM rock station may be possible. KPFA, with 10,000 subscribers and a $300,000 a year budget, has more varied and expansive programming than KMPX had. It's a little structure-heavy to be a good model, with its Departments and Directors and Board. But some competent legal and architectural work could settle the problem of building a minimum framework to ensure that the station's audience had ultimate (and fairly immediate) control over the station's philosophy of programming, and perhaps in some ways over programming itself. (I say "audience" rather than "subscribers" because I'm convinced that it's important to let everyone who actively listens to the station have some control of it, regardless of whether they feed it directly. That's part of what *free* means.)

I'm not suggesting a hippie KPFA. The most notable thing about KPFA, aside from its considerable virtues, is that it hasn't grown or changed much at all in the last ten years, while an immense youth population has grown through rapid changes, ignoring it. But the nice thing about KMPX was that it seemed to be comfortably and naturally adapting itself to our nature and needs. We need that. And any design for a community *free* rock station should try to provide for that vital flexibility, perhaps even at the risk of not looking like much of a design at all. Anyone who wants to can think up models of how to accomplish this, or at least reasonable experiments; I won't bore you with mine.

At any rate, the place to start is with KMPX as it has been at its variegated best, and go on from there: mostly with those people, and with some sort of organized and responsive procedure for new programs and programmers to get test airings. About buying out KMPX or getting some other slot, I don't know. If people want to try to build something like this, it's probably going to take a lot of work and a lot of bread. All I know is that I'd be more than glad to lay up $20 a year to preserve the warmth of KMPX, let alone to have some control over it possible in areas in which I feel myself strongly involved, like in its public forum aspect. And be glad as well to work with it occasionally, because it's a thing of value to me and the people I live with.

I should add a word about organizing. In this day of McLuhan, electoral organizing is really sort of an anachronism, don't you think? *Bonnie and Clyde* changed more heads than the Scheer Campaign, not to mention Dylan, the televised Haight, and FSM. Locally people are plugging precious energy into the Peace and Freedom Party: it struggles, threatening to fragment, and is really only a sub-communcations network within the larger Movement, no more. Much better those energies should be put into Media Organizing. A *free* KMPX would do more to change the political climate of the Bay Area than ten PFP's, not to mention its other effects. Soon, God-father Technology, videotape will be the thing, our new medium: already kids on the educational reform frontier of the Movement are negotiating its use with the huge corporations and beginning to learn its tricks as a tool in inciting and recording change. Can you imagine a *free* KMPX of the tube: the tremendous power, the total classroom that would create? The public participation forum, the spectacular play of individual invention, and our own peculiar ransacking of the treasures of our found-ering ages. Shit, if you want to organize with scope, organize toward *that!*

And here, oddly, is where Liberals might be most helpful: in negotiating and broadening the delicate links and flows between foundations, businesses, and artistic entrepreneurs. For a lot of brash open guerrilla training in a new medium will have to go on, and many policies of media freedom must be negotiated and established— see the COMSAT case, and NET's legislation and ex-periments—before a *free community* telly station becomes possible. But it is something worth working for, and a *free* KMPX might even be a first step toward it.

17 March 1968

At the Fillmore

Opening and closing. Looking back now, from this decade in which the going gets tough, I can see how early this became a theme.

I went to the Fillmore tonight, for the first time since before they put me in jail. I'd been four months away; and, as with the puppy to whose daily change you are blind but whose different doghood you recognize after an absence, I suddenly realized how different the Fillmore was: how another of our scenes had flowered and fled. The place was full, the lights were tame, the kids were young and they wandered or listened with an empty will. No one was coming out of himself; and so the camera hung hungry at my side most of the evening, and I was too sad with observation to want to dance there alone. Would you believe it? The Byrds were playing, and almost no one was dancing.

The dance scene in San Francisco has been going for two years now. The Fillmore grew famous and New York took notice; but, like the Haight, what it was disappeared before they came to find it. Fleeting, beautiful, strange—like all our scenes of change these days. And I learned to dance at the Fillmore, and it changed my life: not a big thing, but part of the change that is upon us all. San

Francisco and Berkeley will never be the same, needless to say. Happy Second Anniversary, Dance Scene! Hail to the Trips Festival, ritual fired by Ken Kesey, Stewart Brand and others, Official Signal Go to a scene of public beauty and freedom!

Maybe that's how to get into it, though I was into what there was of the dance scene, announced only by electric word of mouth, before the three-day Carnival explosion of the Trips Festival in October 1965. Standing in the Fillmore, watching the kids, I remembered that spectacular announcement that a scene had been born. Tonight all the kids were listening or buzz-chatting. They were all young, like seventeen: casually dressed or in style but few costumes, mostly attractive but none turned on alive, and maybe three spades on the whole floor.

But that night we came with a flute and balloons up the long California Coast from Sur, late to the honeycomb elephant grey dome of Longshoreman's Hall where the first dances had already been held, the people were different. Hells Angels in force out with their old women, Rentacops, SNCCniks in denim and those heavy boots, teenyboppers teenyboppers teenyboppers, hippies in halo hair and beads, kids from the sorority scene with their sweaters and shoes, a thick pepper of spades with eyes as hungry as mine and yours and their shaming lovely loose motions, straight socialites from Pacific Heights in fancies, tree freaks down from the hills still holding something alive in their hands, tough Italian kids in windbreakers sticking together in silent twos and threes . . . wow, it completely blew my mind, as we said in those days when that phrase was still live (we learned a bit with its help before it lost its bounce).

The Fillmore—to which, with the Avalon Ballroom, the dances moved after the Trips Festival—became the barom-

eter of a freedom that appeared like a change of weather
and now seems to have expanded and migrated: first to the
Haight, and now under the surface around the whole Bay.
What were people doing that night? Dancing, watching,
talking, taking pictures, playing instruments, serving cool-
ade, painting faces and floors, dancing in rings and serpen-
tines, wigging on the light show, freaking with acid or
dazed in silent corners or running spinning wildly through
the crowd crowned with ivy and dancing alone, playing
balloon ball and passing joints and chanting and listening
and taking notes. What were they wearing? Tuxedos and
Balkan peasant finery, a zoot suit and the Angels' colors,
black chinos and clown suits, a yellow bikini and black
plastic skirt, harem garb or nothing on top, hats like Bar-
tholemew Cubbins, flag-or-bird-painted eyes, cop suits and
tired army-student. And what were they dancing, who
danced on that tight bright spotlighted floor, their senses
smashed on electric sound and the tremendous psychic
resonances bouncing from the concrete columns far
above? Fox-trot. Polka, schottische. Cha/cha. Cha. Ballet
whirls and gymnastic exercises. Bunnyhop and waltz, fragments of all those dances-with-a-name like Gulley and
Camel and Twist, and lots of touches or trips from modern
dance (thanks to the girls' high school phys-ed programs,
pride of the state).

It was beautiful, do you know what I mean? And it's
hard to talk about without getting mawkish. Through a
general wish of a young population and some skillful
catalyzing by beautiful artists, a free space was created in
the heart of the city: a space unstructured (at least to a
remarkable degree) by the surrounding society: a space in
which there were no expected roles, no outside norms of
clothing or conduct or motion: a space in which, above
their own irreducible imprisonment, the participants were

free to define themselves and their contact: to "do their own things," though the phrase hadn't then come into general use. That space has now been encroached on and is no longer the site of a center of experiment: the past that kids had to bring along to it finally made itself felt, heavily. But when they first rushed into the space they seemed to leave it briefly behind in some important way. And the test of this was the fresh feeling of a scene of newness and freedom, the feeling that takes a couple of encounters to make you know it as such, and after that is always unmistakable.

The mark of freedom is the presence of diversity (and the way you handle it is to get things actually diverse, instead of just talking about it, and then go on and see what you can do from there). That's pedantic, I know; but it was the FUCK incident that Spring and the Trips Festival that Fall that made me understand what it meant. And the most remarkable thing about this diversity of motion and costume and act was the feeling in which it was embedded. Everyone was *easy*. That night and in two years around the Fillmore, I only once saw a fight, and little tenseness. (The S.F. Police kept trying to close the Fillmore down. "A white dancehall in a black ghetto," they said, "there has to be trouble.") An air of peace, openness, excitement, vagueness, curiosity, unsureness . . . well, there were many vibrations; what can I say? People were in so many places, their own places. But it was all harmonious; any behavior that didn't push on others were tolerated warmly, and much that was. They say many hundred tabs of acid were passed out during the Festival, but that doesn't matter any more than anything else: the entire atmosphere was a high, and people were turning each other on in all sorts of ways.

That feeling migrated successfully to the Fillmore and

the Avalon, flaming now and then under the deft excitement of the Airplane or the Grateful Dead, more rarely now. The media discovered the Fillmore, the curious came, and now there's little spread or variety in those who are usually there. And they are mostly there to be spectators, on the floor where once and sometimes still the shaking air made everyone his own performer.

October 1967

All Hallow's Eve

Festival. Ritual. Opening and closing. Beginning again. Two years later our tentative commune, split by conflict, travel and overload, came together to join 3,000 brothers and sisters in practice for the future. I wrote a note for an intercommunal newsletter, about this night when children play at meeting their ghosts.

Dragon's Eye finally got itself mostly together, for Halloween Eve. Eight of us broke the bathroom sink by leaning on it to paint dominos and hearts on our whiteface, and then went out to spend the night practicing War Games in the Berkeley streets. Pretty strange: we were almost the only ones in costume or color, and certainly the only group—except for the Krishna chanters—making music on the angry street: finger-cymbals, drum, flute and dancers. Mustn't we serenade at least ourselves and maybe the pigs, even as we dodge and defy them? Shouldn't we bring as much life as we can to each nexus of coming-together and action, even the necessary ones of political anger? It was lonely to be making light on the swirling corners and in the doorways of empty shops, trying to bring together fragments of an example. But good to be there at last.

October 1969

Only after the death of People's Park did our Berkeley community choose to celebrate a holiday so grimly and realistically.

I should warn you: from here on I am following an emotional line, and not a chronological sequence, vectoring in on the matter of the Park. I come at it bass-ackwards because it left me a bit crazy with love and fear. I want to take the rich fabric of the Event and stretch it till its limits are revealed, I want to unravel just one of its multitude of luminous threads and follow it out a way further.

As I write this, People's Park is twenty months dead, the War has been coming steadily home since then. Now it has reached Laos, and our sweet Bay is full of Standard Oil as Spring comes round again. Yet against all the signs and portents of terror, and early weariness at the marrow, the Wedding we celebrated in the Park continues to begin again.

The Bare Facts about the People's Park

Somewhere else I'll tell you the full literal tale, here is enough for now:

In 1966 the police lied with statistics to brand the South Campus Area as a focus of rising crime and a target for redevelopment. A year later the university's Regents, fascinated by the "small, hard core of agitators" theory of campus unrest, decided that the worst elements of our hippy slum lived in the block running East from the single legendary heart-block of Telegraph. So they bought the block to build high-rise dorms on—in the indefinite future —and razed all the fine old apartment houses to the ground. For three seasons the great muddy field lay idle, rutted by cars daring enough to park.

In April 1969 we took the next step with our territorial imperative. In full consciousness, freaks and politicos organized an assault on the key institution of Capitalism. Claiming our turf in the spirit of the Indians who once guarded it for all without ownership, the people of the dense, grass-starved South Campus Area tried to rip off the *private property* of the Regents, the men who run the State, and put it to public use. Black people, hippies, longshoremen, working wives, children, old people, hard-line activists—here for the first time all came together in common work. For six weeks we labored, and brought forth a Park. And it was mighty pretty, as fine as what happened with us during that time.

On the seventh week there was no rest. The charade of negotiations played out, neither city nor university would even hear of *selling* us the *property;* they freaked out at the fresh dirt on our hands. At 3 A.M. the bulldozers and fencing crew arrived with 300 cops to turn it back into a parking lot. At noon we gathered at the Plaza, then marched to the fence. This time they used shotguns. One dead, several crippled, several hundred injuries, a thousand arrests. It went on for days, Reagan ordered the National Guard in to occupy the town, they gassed us from a helicopter. We ran, and planted Parks all over our Berkeley.

Memo from Spaceport Berkeley

Berkeley, mid-July in the year of Control. The military has things well in hand, at least on the surface. Today the Space Force is reaching moonward in a titanium hand, to plant Nixon's name in the vacant lot of my childhood dreams. The astronauts grin like satisfied patrolmen from the covers of national magazines. Their superiors reassure the poor: we can feed your hunger and our families of rockets too, if only there is unity. Here in Unity City the Park lies flat as lunar rubblescape, our green launching aborted; soon there will rise skyward the dorm rooms, cramped and sterile as control-cubicles, to train the flesh for the further triumphs of technological greed. On the street, wherever black or white mutter, the masks and clubs appear. Soon the air is unbreathable as vacuum. We go cough in our rooms and dream of the songs of Beginning.

We are under control, no doubt about it, ours as well as theirs. That is critical to remember. You are controlling your despair—and also, in blind confusion, your strength, which you have seen and I believe in. It continues to act through those painful moments of touching and grace which have given us the image and some of the substance of the life we might lead together and have tried to begin. You could not have believed in it five years ago. Now it taunts you with hope, though its moment's symbol has vanished, like a plant cut off somewhere above the roots.

Two thousand touched and tended that Park. Ten thousand swarmed the streets in its innocent defense, learning to walk deliberately before the tear gas and guns. Forty thousand came in carnival dress and dance, and the many faces of your love, to charm asphalt into grass. Look, let's take ourselves seriously and cut out all the cheap bullshit put-downs of our people, about how they vanish in fear and aren't for real. Everyone who drops a cap or touches flesh or goes out on the angry street has been marching to deal with his terror and rage and joy.

There are two thousand people in Berkeley now, a part of your self included, who simply and indelibly want to kill a cop, at least in the moments of seeing what is done to their sisters in the pleasures of nightstick perversion. There are all your friends, who have cried with a dozen vivid parades that they're longing to share and celebrate who they're becoming. You think the life-and-death spectrum of our gathered feelings just vanishes, maybe? That it isn't permanent growing substance? The mass of its energy hasn't diminished: river gone back under the surface, river seeking an outlet to spring forth in its singing forms, a way to destroy the constraint that closes off every open space larger than private to our growth. Not gone. Under bleak control.

How to move with it next: privately, publicly. That is everyone's question. Some first results of our experiments are becoming clear. Yes, people can learn the new cooperations of living together, to share and multiply their strength—even in a way that leaves space for the private self, which some few have truly managed. No, we don't know how to make a new politics of power. Brothers came back ghost-faced from the SDS National Catastrophe in Chicago. It is paralyzingly clear that the narrow political edge of whatever you call our Movement is headed straight backwards into a familiar dead end of splintering death that absorbs our energy.

In 1963 SDS talk centered around "participatory democracy." Now no one remembers that romance, amid screams about an anti-imperialist front and the evident growing contradictions of the capitalist state. Certainly, the power of the State of racist ABM madness must be broken by struggle in all the classical political dimensions. But that's not enough—and even for that our tools must be living fragments of our dream, in all its human dimensions. SDS dropped its preoccupation with the hope of a rich democracy before the struggle for it was well-begun, slides back into old and sterile forms. PL wants us to be pure: don't smoke dope or screw before marriage. Or they take away your membership card. Tell me, whose Revolution is that?

Only the beautiful is worth believing in or fighting for or working within—can we trust in or settle for less?—and only what is whole even in its incompleteness can be this beauty. But Amerika splits everything apart: man from his production, the self from its being. Trains us all to the shame of niggers, splits us from our sisters in long classroom years during which we're conditioned to claw our brothers in competition for a smile. Do you wonder we have trouble learning from each other? Political activists, kids into educational reform, freaks on the edge of cultural change: all hanging out in a circle of mutual scorn, refusing to learn or embody each other's tools in their own, denying a common flesh and the building of its dream. SDS now points clearly to what happens when we let our words grow narrow and live a language that does not include and build on all that we are.

That same stale death waits for any who try to move on with half their nourishment in an inadequate ship, no matter where they're sailing: they will land in a barren moon. And it waits for you personally, as you struggle with your everyday anger and love, constantly betrayed into setting them aside, denying them "just for a while" to get something done or to ease your confusion. The death that Amerika promises for any who would make her changes or free life within her now rumbles over the horizon, force gathers to make you claw your sister in factional terror, to drop your tools and new growth in the fear they will reveal you, or hinder your fight or your flight. Don't believe it, don't do it. You will need all you are even to survive in the rising wind whose violence now touches all your life's aspects.

We will need all we are and are becoming to survive or build. Somehow it must all be brought together, and nothing that does not promise and depend on this is worth working upon. This is all I know; it doesn't promise answers, but it's a strong criterion. We haven't yet begun to honor it. People are still afraid to stand by it in public when what we are building is ugly and incomplete, afraid to condemn our mistakes. Aesthetics gets last place on the political agenda or is scoffed out as romantic. (Whose politics is that?) It's hard to argue your naïve belief without alternatives to offer.

But there *are* alternatives. In various ways our new generations have made beginnings of some genuine wholeness and substance. The Mid-Peninsula Free University, the Resistance, the Free City family in San Francisco—all are forms that nourish the heart in some roundness and develop political force. You can no longer complain that there are no models, and these open the possibility of others. What is missing in general is seriousness and work, a full commitment to building what we can dream. People are still shitting around trying to get it done cheaply, or to force Them to do it for us. No use. Pay the price of your life, to learn to learn from your brothers and sisters.

It can be brought together. This belief torments many who have been through our phases and long for what is needed to move on. Watching the SDS debacle and the Park, the need gathers in us for the image of a new beginning, that embraces all our fragments. The Thirteen Points of the recent Berkeley Liberation Program are a thin and strident attempt: the people who will share that image with us have not yet come together. Or perhaps it must bloom simultaneously in a crowd of lives, in which case you are responsible and I wait for your decision.

Beyond this I don't pretend to answers other than the beginnings I share with friends, especially about the Park. I admire the holes in the fence, and think the Park's grave should become the town garbage dump as long as it's occupied by pigs. People should drop by at night with bags of debris and chuck them over the fence, then split fast with license-plates masked.

For this city is ours in ways we haven't used. Timidly people are starting to garden its soil: aside from the romance, that does in fact save money and strengthen community, as those who've tried know. Seven stores along Shattuck stand vacant and unrented; why don't we take them? Art and clothing cooperatives have formed, food ones are on the way—are we too stupid to be able to choose to buy from our own people? Each battle sends the property rates down, some estimate 25% by the end of summer near campus. Landlords are growing anxious to sell, the university can't compete with its budget bound; even in the tight money squeeze that slows the posh apartment developers, our people who've grown to earning money with their souls intact can pool their bread to lease with options to buy. If the eighteen-year-old vote comes—which is less certain as Amerika comes to fear her young, justly—this city will be ours politically.

And even now there is space to build newly, if we can clear our heads of fear and the comforting denial of our strength, if we choose to learn from each other and plug our precious energies into our own Berkeley. Where else will you put them, wandering away? If Berkeley cannot be made a safe base for our life, then no city in Amerika can, and likely no town (as the vigilante raids now threaten). We have no choice but to learn to touch each other openly through our growing fear, and build from the beginning all the aspects of a community that can take over real power here. No less will even shelter us from the hard rain that is beginning to fall, as the Official Astronauts speed back with diamonds from a moon you'll never touch if they have their way.

16 July 1969

The Mulford Act

The day they turned the Berkeley campus into an armed camp, I went out to check the action and saw these two young kids, one white, one black, walking and rapping. A competent black gas mask was dangling from the white kid's hand. I angled to get ahead of them for a front shot, but heard them talking, changed my mind, drew up and asked them where the main masses were. They figured Bancroft and Telegraph, and we decided to cut through campus to get there. When we passed Oxford the black kid dropped out. "See you later," the white one yelled as we crossed the street and went on together.

"I've gotta find my little brother," he said, "he's six, he shouldn't be here."

"Where do you think we'll find him?"

"Where the action is."

"At his age?"

"Yep. My kid sister thinks he went up with some friends."

"How old you?"

"Twelve."

"Shit, man. Kids your age . . . That gas mask yours?"

"Yep. My sister gave it to me, she's nineteen, she's moving out to go live with her boy friend."

"Is she how you come by being a radical?"

"Partly. My whole family is radical, my parents are radical."

"It sure does help to have radical parents," I told him, thirty, remembering. The first road into the campus had two squads of Blue Meanies; we didn't even bother to try. Walked past, took a reading, doubled back, took a shot, walked on. He asked me about exposure settings.

"Did you work at People's Park?" I asked him.

"Yep."

"And the Annex?"

"Yep. I had a tree there; I planted it."

"What happened to it?"

"They ripped it up. I had a patch of pumpkins in, and a patch of corn, had it coming along. They ripped it all up."

"This was at the Park?"

"Yep. Our whole family was there. It was at Dwight; they had shotguns. Some pig was gonna hit me, and my dad hit him and we split."

"Plant anything at the Annex?"

"No, it was the only day our parents went without us."

We turned in at the second path, where they were letting some students through. But they stopped us, six boys in burly blue and gleaming helmet-hoods and a short man in green exoskeleton who hurried about like a beetle. Did we have reg cards? No? Then we couldn't come on campus. "Not even to look for my brother?" "You can't go on campus unless you're a student." We turned away.

"That's cold," said my friend.

"Yeah. Let's try farther on." We headed for West Gate. "Where you go to school?"

He named a well-known public school.

"Many of the kids there radical?"

"How do you mean?"

"I dunno, however you see it. But more than just hair."

"I guess most are radical then. Either because their parents are sort of radical, or because that's just the way they want to be." The path through West Gate was clear; people were strolling in and out. We headed up the long central artery toward the Campanile. He went on, "I wouldn't of come up here today except for my brother. I'm supposed to be at home, not sposed to go out for two weeks."

"How come?"

"Well, I was up here on Wednesday with a whole bunch of guys, and I got home late and forgot to cook dinner. My dad was sore. Then yesterday it happened again; we got tangled up near the tear-gassing, and I didn't get home till six. They get home at five, and Dad saw there wasn't any dinner again and said, 'All right . . . ,' and I couldn't go out for a week. Then later my friends came by, and I shinnied out the window and down the vine, but I got caught. That made it two."

"Cooking your share of the housework?"

"Yep. I like to cook, and I don't like washing."

Three men from a clot of blue moved to intercept. Behind them was the green beetle. "I want you to arrest them," he was chittering, "they were warned by Lieutenant Flan not to come onto the campus . . ." They took my I.D., called for the booking officer on their transistors. I thought, "Shit, what a hassle, we'll miss rehearsal." The beetle kept chittering. The kid and I ignored him, went into our act: minimal, frank, good-willed. The kid explained about his brother, reasonably; I let him take the lead in handling them. "What's your name?" "Johnnie Frank." "What's your brother's name?" "Leslie." "What are you doing here, fellow?" "I was escorting him to look for his brother." "Where do you live, kid?" "He's very concerned about his little brother, sir," I said to the top cop, venturing a look of mild disapproval at how the sergeant was badgering him. The kid was quiet, reasoned, the image of self-control. Niggers to a T, precisely calculating the shade of abasement. They aren't fooled, though they can't be sure; but it pleases them if you grovel a bit, as long as you don't overdo it.

"Why do you have that camera?" he demanded. "I take pictures," I said, "it's what I do," as the one behind me started pawing through my bag. Without comment he pulled out film, lens, kazoo, hooded glasses to muffle my eyes from the tear gas, plastic bag filled with wet cloth to breath through. "Got any rocks in here?" We eyed the gas guns, their cartridges, black leather and technology, the riot guns, their shells. They looked at my necklace, my facecloth and the kid's gas mask. "Get off campus. Straight down there, don't stop. If we see you again we'll arrest you."

We stepped back smartly the way we came. "Jerks," said the kid, "they make me so mad." His voice was completely level, he was lagging a stone with his toe in the gutter. "That search bullshit." "Not worth getting busted for," I said, "not now at least." He nodded. "You haven't been in jail, have you?" "Oh yes," he said, "twice, in Oakland." "What for?" I asked, having caught myself again presuming.

"Once was for 'lewd and immoral conduct' or something; they caught me with two quarts of beer. The other was 'breaking and entering,' only what it was, I was trying to look into the window of my school after it closed and the watchman caught me. They're all the same."

"You shouldn't be surprised at anything they do, you really freak them. Me they can sort of understand, or they think they can, and kids from like nineteen to twenty-five here. I mean, we look like grubby weirdos and you can tell we're long lost; they've given up on talking to us. But seeing you must really freak them out, they can't believe you at all. Dig it, man, you look like a cherub, nothing wrong with you that a haircut and some straightening up wouldn't fix. And you're *twelve?!*"

"Yep," he said, "and there were a bunch of us out, along with the high school kids. I'm lucky he didn't recognize me from yesterday."

"You were throwing rocks too?"

"Oh yeah. Threw a choke chain, caught this pig on the head. Because he hit my dog with a rock. Burnt my hand all to heck on a canister throwing it back." He took two pull rings from gas grenades out of his pocket and held them out for my inspection. "And I broke three windows in the Chancellor's office."

We met Zelda coming up the way, fresh from the arraignment of yesterday's casualties. She was calm and full of anger, the flush of high energy in her cheeks. The tang of tear gas lingered in the air from all the shady places. I sneezed. She told us they had been coming into court all morning barely able to function, "big strong guys too, all battered. One with his teeth all knocked in. When we finally got a doctor into jail he said he had five hours to get to a hospital and save any." The kid sneezed. We looked back to see if they were coming after us. "I'm surprised," she said, "that somebody didn't throw a bomb into a knot of them yesterday." We both nodded. "So far I'm chicken to myself, but if this keeps on . . . I wish . . ." The wind stirred the delicate hair on her cheeks and the V of her breasts. Up the walk guards began drifting our way.

We almost made it through the last cordon, but it was right across from the armory and some of them were eager for games. The kid and I went through our whole bit again: worried diligent brother, disinterested protector. This time they were faster, harder, hassled us both. "You don't expect us to believe that, kid." They took his gas mask; he surrendered easily. "Where'd you get this?" "From my sister." "Where'd she steal it?" "She did not." "They're all the same. You, if you know this kid, what's his name?" "Frankie John," I said. "Kid, what's your name?" "Frankie John." "You know I can take you in for contributing to the delinquency of a minor? You know that?" "I know what contributing is." "Get caught before, huh?" "No." "All right, listen. This campus is under the Mulford Act. You know what that means? I catch either of you around here any time in the next seventy-two hours, I run you in . . ." Gave back the mask.

We started leaving. The sheriff's bully boys were playing with their gunstocks, their hair bristling like toothbrushes. One said to the kid, "Hey, little girl, what's your name?" "Frank," said the kid, coolly, "I'm not a girl." "Hey little fairy, what's your name?" said his sidekick.

We walked away. "He knew I wasn't a girl," he said. His light hair lifted rhythmically in the breeze of our motion; his face and his brow were as open and fair as a Botticelli, and as untroubled. I hugged him. "We're not afraid of them because we're learning to be not afraid of the things in our selves that they fear, at least that's the way it's been coming for me."

"I dig it," he said. "I want to kill them. I want them to get what's coming to them. But boy, do they have all the guns! It's really depressing, is what it is. But I want to kill them, I mean it, I do."

"I dig it," I said, as we cut down Alston. There hadn't been any live tear gas for hours, and we figured control on campus was tight enough so any little kids would be sent home. "But I'm glad they didn't take us in," he went on. "Dad would be furious if I missed three times in a row."

When we turned down Grove I showed him the roof of our cottage. "You ought to come visit us sometime and meet my woman," I told him, "we have a groovy place with a lot of junk and the dogs and some good people."

"Yep," he answered, "I know where it is, used to deliver papers over there."

"You into girls?"

"How do you mean?"

"I mean . . . do you pay them much attention yet?"

He laughed. "Since the third grade. My little brother now, he's been there right along. Why?"

"Oh, I dunno. We got one around our place, eleven, name of Debbie—pretty nice, though she's still childish, could use someone to help her learn some things. Take care now," I called to him as we parted, and he waved.

17 April 1970

Staring into the mirror of Time, I watched him go. I wished for a copy of my Park poem to give him, but none was left; I decided to do up a second printing. For I knew the corner of Dwight where he ran from the guns the day they bulldozed the Park and his Tree. I was there too, maybe we ran together, there where Death touched my hand with the tiniest of reminders, and send me spinning for weeks into the Well to drag up the buckets of blood that clot into metaphor.

A long poem is an albatross these days. I took it everywhere; no one would publish it.* So I borrowed fifty bucks from my dad and printed it up myself—went around to bookstores trying to get them to take it on consignment, gave it to friends, people who picked me up hitching, strangers on the street. I finally worked up enough nerve to read it in public in a few places—but never in Berkeley.

* Two years later Todd Gitlin put it in his fine anthology of Movement poetry, *Campfires of the Resistance* (Bobbs-Merrill, 1971).

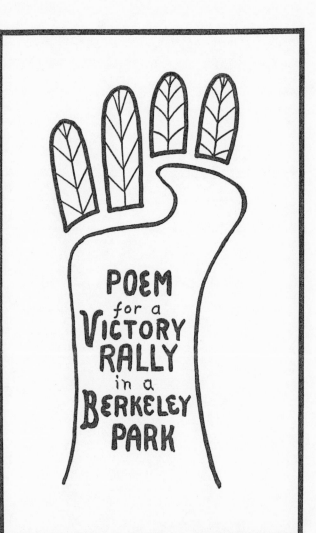

POEM
for a
VICTORY
RALLY
in a
BERKELEY
PARK

for F. J. Bardacke, who tries
to bring it together among
the members of our wedding.

It is noon in the city of fear. You are running
across endless asphalt, astonished by the sky's sweet blue,
when the centipede line of helmet and club
comes around the corner of your nightmare.
Bright in your plumage, you wheel and flutter
like a desperate shorebird through the harsh fog
of anger, and escape to a concrete beach
where your brothers wait with their wings in their pockets
together facing the wind. And some lonely freak
of your common blood stand up with a staff
in his hand to cry,
                    I planted this land with love
and confrontation in my heart, also a bit
of romantic self-consciousness. Where I started
first green, I left as fertilizer
spare locks of my hair and feathers
from my bird. They grow! it is a miracle!
I water them with rainbow tears
and the public utilities, in view of a sacrament
that commits me to experiment with foliage

on the faces their glaciers of closure
have left empty as institutions. Come clear,
choose now: we all know their response
to the flag of life, can we care any longer
that they find my eyes and your ways disturbing?
We are the changing seed, an American grain
from a season of dreams and betrayal,
with some links of our chromosome chains forced open
by a century of technology radiation,
preparing to flower in wild varieties. Soaked
in the waters of extended senses, warmed
by the early sun of our longing, your husk
has split open, the sprout of your life
swells and begins to search for its forms.
You cannot retreat to the cave
of the closed self: to live is to grow.
come watch seeds open in the ground,
attacked by the instant elements, if you think
there's a choice about confrontation.

There is rotary music in the midday sky,
skeleton birds and hornet tongues
are skywriting Death on invisible clouds
as the gardener passes the staff
to one who goes on,
                              In the night,
when my lover's fingers cling like roots in my hair,
our bodies beat soft jackhammer rhythms
on the pavements of closure, and the green of our touching
opens and covers the wounded concrete.
Under the stubborn blanket of stone, linked

at bulb and branch, the pale networks of our nerves
hum with the song of eager pain
that the blind shoots make, longing for leaves,
as they tug and shoulder the fragments
into monuments for the park of the future,
leaving space for a darkness
rich with the colors of our coming,
where weary animals collapse embraced
to dream of growing old
in the deliberate wilderness of love.

It is noon in your study of longing. You are sitting
with some other fragments of our heart
on grass beaten brown by the ignorant armies,
while the sun presides at an endless teach-in
designed to put it all together.
                              We have invented
the instant university, it exists wherever
we choose to park. With this staff, the symbol
of power and flower, I become Department Chairman.
Would you learn Agronomy? Observe the plants
teaching ignorant hands to help them grow.
Some Political Science? Trace the web of control
made visible by our resistance, examine positions
speaking like men, determine the self-interest behind
each lie, and its root in the fear of the other.
Your proper school is the crucible street: in whose arms
could you learn so clearly the nature of what is
and of what might be, or test your substance
of anger and joy? Let me read you a telegram
to our lobbyists in the Capitol:

DEMAND
NO NEW CONSTRUCTION OBSOLETE LUXURIOUS CAMPUSES,
FREEZE MISGUIDED PER-CAPITA EXPENDITURE FOR CHILDREN OF
DOMINANT CLASS, IN NAME
OF SPIRITUAL ECONOMY AND REAL HUNGER.
SOLVE HIGHER EDUCATION POPULATION PROBLEM
BY TURNING STUDENTS OUT ON STREET, CREATE
NEW CAMPUSES APPROPRIATE TO AGE OF OPEN SPACE
IN VACANT LOTS, FACTORIES. DECLARE CITY
UNIVERSITY EXTENSION. ATTACK TEACHER SHORTAGE
DIRECTLY, MOTIVATE CITIZENS TO UTILIZE
MASSIVE NEGLECTED RESOURCES BY LEARNING
FROM EACH OTHER. COMPREHENSIVE PROGRAM FOLLOWS.

The response has been encouraging
to those who dream of a revolution
in the priorities of learning, and at night by our fires
of celebration, we confess and study the fragments
of these lives, with a torn clumsy openness
that transcends the lying boundaries
of disciplines and the skin. Let me close with a text
from an eminent Eastern professor
in the college of Change:

To create knowledge,
it is necessary to change reality. If you would know
the taste of the apple of Revolution,
you must change the apple
by eating it.

It is noon at the gates of Eden
where the primeval wind blows through the orchard
 wilderness

refreshing the clustered faces, heady
with the fragrance of first fruit.
In the shadows still heavy with morning Chaos
you shiver and dream of a darker season
where the trunk and gestures of hope
stand bare above the stormfallen brothers
while a woman as slim as the staff of your spine
cries in the voice of the wind,
                              I speak for the snake,
who is our brother. The snake urges you
to plant the seed. Plant it. They lied to us
with their fairy-tales. They convinced us
to shun the knowledge of the beasts of the field
and our groins. They set us to studying
taxonomy instead, because it was value-free
and said nothing but desert lay beyond
their chaste lawns. They claimed to know it all.
They were wrong. The man and the woman
have stood naked before each other unashamed.
In forbidden vegetable ritual we have dreamed
of the great two-headed Snake of the Universe.
We have deciphered the language of our spilled blood.
It says we have but one mortal life. It is time
to stop drawing up lists of names
and tending the borders, time to recreate
the Knowledge of Good and Evil, to renew
the icons distorted by their denial.
Power to the People's Mythology!
                              It is noon
in the one-dimensional garden. Two actors

in the guerrilla theatre of our becoming
stand waiting in innocent hair, like the halves
of your common heart, in the open stage
of a sheltering tree. In the foreground
the serpent of transcendent life rises
from a sudden hole in the pavement
of repression, mounts like blind creation
through the concealing leaves. It promises
birth that is also the death of an order.
The snake offers the apple. The woman
accepts its promise, and offers the apple's body.
The man receives nourishment from the woman.
He eats of the apple. Its flesh is the lives
of his brothers and sisters. He gives the appleseeds
to the woman. Under a banner
that displays what might be a seedling
seeking the sun, or a snake coiled
above a warning, she moves with him Westward
into the wilderness of Amerika. They eat of their fruit
for life, and look for open space
to plant its seeds.

              Somewhere high in the mountains
of the twentieth century, they move through the crowd
among the tie-dyed tents of our first encampment,
handing out apples and leaflets
and plotting the overthrow of the State.
They pass you the staff. From an overhead ambush
the U.S. Cavalry focuses its binoculars
on the blushing face of your joy and defiance,
automatic fingers begin to sort for your memory,
reconstruct the essential features
of your revolt.

He is Red! cries the Officer,
redskinned like a newborn, face wrinkled
in discontent at the stuff we feed him
for the good of his system.

He is Red!
cries the Mayor, telegraphing Washington,
he's an Indian brave of some ten summers
with his dog and toy arrows, wants to pitch
his tent wherever he pleases and move on
in the morning.

He is Red! cries the General,
recalling a manual memorized for the War,
he's a high school Commie reciting the catechism:
From the State according to its Ability,
to the People for their Needs.

He is Red! confirms
the computer, sending out an all-points bulletin:
RED ALERT!!

MEMBER OF FREAK NEO-BOLSHEVIK TRIBE
HAS WANDERED BEYOND HIS RESERVATIONS. AT LARGE
IN UNIVERSE CITY, HE IS THOUGHT TO BE SEEKING THE RITES
OF HIS MANHOOD, WILL PROBABLY TRY
TO STEAL A BRIDE. DON'T LET WHATEVER
YOU TREASURE HANG LOOSE: HE IS LOOKING TO RIP OFF
MORE THAN YOUR PRIDE. SUBJECT IS ARMED WITH A STAFF
THAT TURNS CONCRETE TO GRASS, AND CONSIDERED EXTREME.
AN OPEN ADDICT, HE MAY BE IDENTIFIED
BY STAR-TRACKS IN HIS LEFT BLOODSTREAM
AND A TENDENCY TO SELF-INCRIMINATION,
AS IN THESE WORDS SPOKE AT NOON
IN THE PRECINCT OF CONTROL, DISGUISED AS AN ANIMALCULE

IN THE THIN FILM OF LIFE MISTING THE SKIN
OF A SMALL PLANET:
                    I am not ashamed
that I love the earth my mother and sister,
love learning to let her play me, as I love
to play her master, in the Tao of a dance
denied to those who taught us to see her
only as their extension. Compelled to control
who shares her comfort, they have taken the land
in a wedding of fences. They have bound her in marriage
with lying contracts that define as property
her breast and the oils of her fragrance, property,
her concave favors of vault and bay, property,
her glad production and decoration, property,
even the personal flesh of her children, property,
bewildered with separation and waving from the train
to the military academy, under court order
to learn to carry on the business
of property properly. What wonder she has turned cold
against those who treat her like dirt, or that she shrouds
her sensual ecology, befouled by the uses
of their lust? With the bitter patience
of an arsenic widow, she serves them coffee
in the drawing rooms of power, the rich harvest
of peasants in the highlands of Colombia.
She offers to mellow its dark accusations
with innocent milk from a breast
heavy with indelible chemical death,
and leaves them to breathe the smoke
that they blow in her face, engrossed in the schemes
of their anger and pride. Then she slips away

to the edge of town where our silences cross,
alive in the moon that troubles the dreams
of the burghers, and I take her in my gypsy arms
as she cries to me wild with pity,
                                They will not
let go, they are trapped in Control's illusions
where every face reflects their fear.
Alone in the private and jealous kingdoms
of power, they turn their imaginations
to machines making brick from each possible leaf
or encounter, to wall out the dreadful Chaos
of freedom. How can life possibly deal
with those who believe they have something to lose
by release?
          It is noon under the avalanche
of history, you are hanging between alternatives,
there are tears on your hands and earth
in your eyes. Equipped with the latest
in counter-insurgency chrome, and freaking
from loss of control, the tanks of the Authority Complex
are rolling through Prague with your father at the wheel,
rolling past Grant Park with your teacher at the map,
pausing for orders with your lover at the gun
where Berkeley meets the Western Sea. Under their muzzles
she cries in the voice of your frightened sister,

There's a man strung out on electric barbs
with his hands on the naked wires. His body is taut
with imperial power, he cannot let go.
When I touch him the energy flashes my mind
to the blighted lands of my isotope nightmares
and a nest in the empty heart

of what was a tree. Its entrance is narrow
with droppings, the light is dim on grown birds
crazy with magnetic derangement and some missing
genetic instruction. Stupid with the poisons
of their closing system, they squabble to death
in the failing light, in fear of the touch
of the wind. Take care, my love, the wind,
take care, they are crying your name!

In the hands of your heart is the heart
of a bird still trembling with flight, and you hold her
while the seasons spin around you and fall
through the stroboscope wheel of night and day
wrapped in each other's arms. Dizzy with that metaphysic
of polar harmonies, without shaking her you remember
to shrug off your Supergood Superman costume,
as false as reassurance, and stand naked with the wind
at the quiet wedding of joy and despair, thinking,

I've forgotten how to deny the dark twin
of my Other. In the touch of my Lover's hand
you accept my conjugate Killer, and my Teacher
blinds you with sight. When I clench my fist
I can feel my bones hum the electric song
of the man on the wires. Can I tell you now
that it's not so pure, that all kinds of freaks
will show up if you open the park of your heart,
that your flowers will die if you close the gate
to what they taught you were weeds, that you must learn
the beauty of your black selves to be free?
In the fragrance of earth, in the grass of your arms,
she stirs near sleep among fragments of light.
Ignoring your desperation of images,

she leaves you to choose some one
of her small open faces, beautiful even in the scars
of survival, to plant with the naked kiss
of your eyes and the green of commitment
that struggles to bloom in your words:
                              Nevertheless,
I confess you my love, whom I choose to begin
to invent a marriage other than ownership,
in which we are joined in the ring of belonging
with whoever creates our freedom. And what I learn
of the song of that open dance
I will sing to your rest, till you dream
of fledglings poised on the lip of the nest
with the glad call ringing in the wind,
Let go! Let go! Let go!
                     It is noon in the time
of your flight, and the guests at your fugitive wedding
embrace in a glory of banners and slogans
and wait for the sermon. You offer the staff
to the sky, alive in a festival of kites;
the green rays of its open invitation
nullify their protective charm. Through a sudden
dark corridor of air, *ex machina* Death
settles at your feet with helicopter precision.
Beneath the slowing scythes of its rotors
all the rivets retract in the iron skeleton,
joints and arms disassemble
and rebuild in the form of the bones of a man
who touches your hand on the staff and speaks
in the dry phrasing and eternal black robes
of a rector:

Rector, noun, the priest
of a parish; a teacher, usually of religion;
here the first of the white brothers
fallen for a public place. Though he watered the park
with anonymous sweat, there is some dispute
concerning the sanctity of his martyrdom, in part
because he was quiet and lately from San Jose
and you did not know him, in part
because you are new at applying the Knowledge
of Good and Evil to discover the nature
of Noble Death. You are well-experienced
in the deaths of diminishment, the meaningless
common varieties connected to Profit:
death of the drunken liver,
death of the cancerous lung,
death of the high-tension heart,
death of cholesterol arteries,
death of the whiplashed spine,
death of the unnamed embryo
from vitamin-lack in the shadow of rockets
that promise a moon whose craters of death
are towns whose names you cannot recall.
But awkward and shy with the furthering forms
of death, you struggle to come clear
within yourself and embrace their terms
at noon in the Church of our Becoming
where the bells suggest a list of examples
beginning with Goodman and Chaney
and Schwermer that gives no more hint
than the occasional flash of a bayonet
as the troops come together in a circle

with you as its focus. You cannnot escape
my fate: Death waits to define your Life,
your only choice is to learn to create
its forms and their meanings, to search out the terms
and the path of your manhood. To walk with pride
in the company of Death, you must learn to walk easy
with the hard brothers of Hate and Anger
whom the Liberal Christian Chamber of Capital
taught you to scorn as unworthy, while they sold you
insipid prospectuses for the redevelopment
of the soul, and the inner cities rotted
politely unmentioned. For it furthers to hate
the human agency of your brother's death,
the men and the systems and aspects of mind
that conspire to kill without even enjoyment
or recognition, and order the dispassionate priorities
of Amerikan murder. You are free to anger
at the waste of your living earth
in the industries of alienation, at men "reasoning together"
in the abstractions that rationalize power
and deny the dark faces of their Other, at the distorted uses
that conditioned your ego to compete for a smile
in the classrooms of greed, and left on your spirit
the indelible stain of death and anger and fear
turned inward and moving like bold saboteurs
in the work of your hands. It completes you to honor with
    anger
the full Man in the man who now appears
in his Aspect as Pig in the public street,
to enact against the open wall of History
the visible violence of the system of quiet control;

it completes to recognize him as still mostly
your extension. So accept him endowed by your faith
with choice and responsibility, grant him the love
of your hate, whom—without the unquestioning will
of a Gandhi, or a German Jew in '32—
you may choose to kill as a Man one day.
He is closer to you in his savage glee
at a club in the face of his terror
than the executives of emptiness whose innocent pens
jerk their hands in parallel blows. No, no longer,
no use to bury the selves that you fear
without names, when you know they reappear
in someone's blood. So let it all come out,
get straight with your fragments, you will need all you are
to survive and build in the rising wind
that topples the house that denies its foundations!
Let go, confess all of your spectrum of light
to see clear and accept the choice of your time:
to lay down the suicide knives
of your one-dimensional names,
to encounter the addict of Control
who administers the fascism of meaninglessness,
to plant in the soil of the present the seed
of your being, as full itself as the apple Word,
and to choose to create with your Life
a Death that furthers Becoming!

                         It is noon
in the park of the poet's life, as he wanders
through the random orchards fed by the Words
of his friends, as he dreams of building a home
in the free city of the heart, mutable

in the changes of season, and almost invisible
in the open wilderness. Wrapped in the wind
of the people, you hand him the staff:
he takes it like a woman who grants him song
and together they climb toward the numeral cliff
of thirty, that marks the end of a story
and the earth-blank page of a new beginning,
together he climbs to the lip of the nest
of the wind, to see the further land anew.

Dark with the sweat of brother palms,
the staff is the symbol of healing,
the defender of growth, the wand that creates
the open space of men speaking together
freely in turn. It sprouts leaves to promise
the kaleidoscope tree of community
that springs like a public meeting
from the universe of our soil. We were taught
to split it all apart, to live not in control
of the continual production of our selves,
to use our minds as tools of division,
to suffer the separation of things,
to cut off the hands of our hunger and fear
while the hand of Love the various joiner
withered in branch sympathy. Here the single tree
of one and many is refreshed by the blood
of your work, by the wind of announcements
from those who have been denied and are coming
together. The black man invites you
to love your secret nigger freak self,
the woman leads you to trust your brother,
the old peasant teaches you collective action

and guerrilla strategy, and the grass
tells you where to assemble
to steal back the moon. We were taught
to split it apart, we must learn from our life
to bring it together, to search out the free forms
of the Revolution of the Heart, and invent
the rituals of our Becoming. So rip up
the too-few-dimensional slogan, poster-thin memory
of wood crying HUMAN USE NOT DEATH PRIVATE
    CONTROL!
and use its fragments to kindle the fire
whose ashes of nitrate and charcoal
will nourish the green commitment tree.

It is noon in the age of our Changes.
Now the wounded are knocking on your door,
now your seasons revolve
    from Discovery through Protest to Resistance and Beyond,
now freak oratorios celebrate
    the planting of the forests of Liberation,
now the singing tendrils of our art
    free the vacant lots of the media,
now before the War
    you recover your body and love
    and salvage from China the sacred books,
now you refigure the ancient divisions
    and bring them together in this place
    where the love of struggle embraces the anger of play
    and the city of man grows with the plant of woman
    wrapped in each other's arms,
now where language is not enough,

where my heart stops, where it all comes down
and the Word of our Life is mysterious with First Action,
I ask you to admit your partnership in the conspiracy
to suspend our disbelief, and to speak these words
with me, brothers and sisters each separately in turn
and finally together:

(*alternately*)

The endless journey has slowed to halting.

The end of the circle is the beginning.

The ancient image has lost its splendor.

There is a circle whose center is forming.

Our old houses are breaking in the wind.

Our ring conspires to become our dream.

The wind cries Death to the System of Death.

We are the Life in the Park of my heart.

(*together*)

The titles we bear form weary rhymes.

I have a name no one has spoken.

We have a name no one has spoken.

24 May–15 June 1969
Berkeley

On a Wedding in Mariposa

. . . in the wilderness of Amerika
I have seen first visions, chosen
a name and a calling
of change, returned to learn
to bring together brothers and sisters
to midwife the uncertain birth
of our longing. And today,
as the first men streak
to circle the moon, on the first
day of Winter in my twenty-ninth year,
I have taken an helpmate, she whom
all my life speaks
but my song, wordlessly
sealing this time with a stone
of topaz found on a dusty road
half a life back in the map
of a name, and always held
in reserve, awaiting
a day of the choice
of the heart's society.

In the background,
in the perpetual process current

that mirrors the stream of our
difference and change, the Beatlebirds
sang *take those broken wings
and learn to fly*. And her face
lit inward, as she fell
to her knees against me,
and we stood there in softness
and stone, trying to sort out
the colors of that flash.

I do accept that tragedy
will flower through us
in its ripe young time.
Yet still am I filled
with a thin singing,
that translates its yes
fearful of flesh through these
sentimental and shaken lines.

21 December 1968

*Midway between Chicago and People's Park we married
invisibly in a Berkeley party, months later chose to make
a ceremony of our affair.*

There were seventeen different kinds of flowers in the
meadows, live surf breaking across the great rocks we
chose to marry upon, streamers and spray curling our feet.
I counted them, floating above them, mind whirling, bee

wild with the rich stink of spring. Some I knew, wild iris, shooting-star. Others, like the massed strawflowers toe-high and tangerine yellow, I'd only met at times before and never learned their names. And here all came together, to grace the theater of our wedding.

We invited the people we love, the friends of our family, our lives—how can I name the common denominator? The young professionals: social worker, teacher, physicist. Dope dealers, film makers, painters, our ex-students and lovers, comrades from eleven years of politics and life in Berkeley, sociologists, parents, millionaires and mediamen, beloved freaks from the Common Street. Most like we were late twenties, give or take. My parents were there and a handful of older others we prize, and eight small children who roamed the meadows in a pack gathering nosegays.

We brought all together on friends' land in the Sierra foothills, above Mariposa. Huge house, cottage for us, pool blasted out of the granite and warmed for the occasion, and eighty rolling acres of spring country—oak, pine and private, away from strangers and the police. So much of what unfolded was permitted by that land, and enabled by the warmth with which Danny and Hilary opened their house and helped care for the hassle. Free space, only four hours away from Berkeley! About a hundred of the 160 we invited made it. They brought maybe twenty kin we didn't know, sleeping bags, playthings and presents.

People started showing up on Thursday, came in all the next day and the morning after. Up the alarming road, park the car, find a place for stuff in the house, gossip and smoke some dope in the kitchen, from the open bowl with a clean pound of gold. Then lovers off alone, barefoot through the unbelievable meadows. It was like that; Saturday noon you couldn't go fifty feet in the upper meadows without stumbling on some couple coupling. They'd wave lazily, and later drift down to the crowded pool, where people mostly new to social nudity were mostly lying naked, chattering across microcultures or sharing the vibes like sunflowers under the benediction of the light. In the water the children played cooperative games, like trying to keep an air-ball in the air.

Karen and I were clear about the context we wanted. Some months before we'd reached another place of decision and beginning, involving confessions, time and a child. We dealt with it privately, but no life can be private now and free: and we wanted to make a public completion, a ritual of our choice to move on together. First we planned to do it in March, but by M-Day-minus-7 two feet of snow were still on the meadows. So we called everyone to say, "Cancel, we'll tell you when." There was no rush, after living seven years together and breaking up three times forever and all the changes in between, and we wanted everything to be right. So we waited till after the weather warmed, late April.

We had two ideas. One was that we wanted to be married in our society, not the old one. We are each bummed by legal marriage, which exists primarily to define each other, the goods and the kids as *property*. It's hard enough understanding who we are and each other anyway—which is why, with twenty ULC ministers beside me there, we still didn't choose to make it "legal." But what do we want marriage to be in our society, in which we are learning to share much that was private —our lives our love our children? Karen and I are still just beginning to create new terms. We wanted to confess our experiment in all we knew of home and a public, the society of our friends. And we wanted all to share in creating the ritual, for we are all involved in creating the terms. This was the other idea: that we wanted a coming-together not of us before an audience, but of us all.

Beyond these thoughts and arranging how people would eat and sleep, we had made no plans for our wedding. We were easy with this as a matter of principle, besides which there was no time: I'd just gotten back from the Midwest, a week's heavy work in a huge dorm complex with a swarm of twenty migrant ed reform workers. That was an historic engagement, the first time Women's Lib brought everything to a grinding halt in a national gathering of the ed reform movement. Six-hour fishbowl, lots of fallout and unresolved anger: as a heavy male agent, I caught at least my share. A weird preparation to marry with a woman, sort of like cleansing by fire. I came back raw and tight, pissed mainly by our work's getting blown. Karen was furious at her sisters for their timing. But it was high time. I saw us caught in the river of history, trying to learn to go with the whirling current. So much is happening, no time to move by plan, maybe enough to relax with, play it as we go. We drove on up to Mariposa drinking chocolate malts at the ratburger stands, sharing them with the dog, and as the Rambler straddled ruts up the last stretch she told me how the women had worked weekends with the men to repair the road's winter ravages: rock hard in their hands and their breasts bare to the wind and sun and the stone face of the neighbor who passed in his jeep.

For four years, with a growing web of friends in work, I'd been learning how to design events to bring people together, to create about their needs—politics, learning, festival—in deliberate painful experiments, here and there on the road. Many I'd worked with were part of the wedding. It was as if all we'd learned about how to do it went swiftly and naturally into action through us, just by our letting go. Karen wandered, determined to say yes whenever anyone asked her anything, opening situations. "Other than my role and love," she says, "I saw that as my prime gift input into making the magic/whole."

No plans. Help your people come together: that is the first principle. So we got the best environment we could, and left people free to do what they wanted. Most got a day and a half to sink into the woods and each other before anything "happened." It was heavy, seeing how free space and open time made people feel they could go off alone and still be part of the whole. Few there knew many others; they moved in and out of the gathering places bright with first contact, meeting kin known by name or mutual intimacy: the divided energy-centers of our generation, coming together.

Surely the mescaline helped. (An old student brought it with special pride and wholesale.) We'd only recently dug that mescaline helps heavy group-synch things to happen. This was an exceptionally mellow batch, so mild some took four. Only eighty caps went over the whole weekend, but between that, private stash and general relaxation, by Friday night the vibes were so dense there was no one left to catch contact high. Save a few in private sorrow.

That night in the cottage, candles and fire and musicians and wine. Carl Oglesby came down from Oregon, fresh from his first paid performance as a singer, and for a long time sang to us of our lives. Can I tell you it was magical? *"A child's idea of happiness,"* he sang,

> *reminding us our crime was very old,*
> *the ancient tales suddenly grew strange*
> *lovely children passing into exile*
> *had left us unknowingly changed . . .*

And late, not quite believing our surrender to longing, we sang as his chorus:

> *Che, Che, Che,*
> *I'm calling your name, Che, Che,*
> *I'll find my Sierra one day,*
> *I'm coming your way . . .*

Late Saturday morning people were digging the pit and chopping wood, or making music. We'd asked all to bring a cake or bread, thinking to make a mutual cake. We favored a man and a woman, but the children were building. They built their bricks into a barricade and plastered it high with sloppy frosting. Jeanie and Barbara discovered each other while hemming Karen's dress. Dad met Karen in the bathroom pissing and marveled at the cornucopia of tits by the pool, observing that one could do the research of a lifetime there. Outside on the bank Haemowitz was sitting with some people from the Floating Lotus Magic Opera, binding black and white fur to buffalo hoops, practicing ceremonial passes. We took him and got Ken and went for a walk, to talk about myth and ritual and how to divide up the Mysteries.

Sometime that afternoon Karen and I flashed together, looked at each other and decided it was time. Spitted over the fresh barbecue pits, the lambs had been roasting for hours. We went off to the cottage to plan, giddy with anticipation and mellow purple powder and everyone's touching. An hour and a half later we had the framework of a ceremony and some words to say together. We said them through a couple of times, pretty sloppily, got impatient, and went out to call people together and get it on.

We gathered everyone around the pool, while the last lovers came down from the hill, and set the context. Men and women would go off from each other for a time, to perform two tasks. The men would choose a place for an altar and build it, and find a way to deliver me up for marriage. The women would deliver up Karen, and dress her and decorate the altar. All with as little talking as possible, and without our leadership. In their hands we would come together to say our words. When? 5:32, because it was now 4:32. Right on! and it began.

I went with the men to watch them build the altar, found I had to go away to keep myself from helping overmuch. Went and sat on a hill, thought formless thoughts. But Denny, ace community newsman, taped the whole affair. You see him with mike in hand in all the snapshots, peeking out between carnival dress and flesh. His tape of the men building and gathering to deliver me is awesome. Listened to in the dark, it is a primordial record of men learning to work together. Grunts, bellows, chants. The most primitive cooperations: This, Here, Now. Heavy stone, sixty half-strange brothers. You can hear the rhythms of their intercourse shift as work takes form, nears completion.

The altar was of piled block granite and dry manzanita. They built it where the bones of the earth show through in twin granite domes. All the ranch was Indian home, but the domes are special: the top of one is pocked with grinding-pits for the acorns, and walls the Indians built still run across their faces, soft with ferns and lichens, while we try to deal with the guilt of their theft by the uses of love. On the dome the men piled the new rock, and the women garlanded it with pine boughs, roses and a pattern of pine cones focused in a star. They hung the great Yin/Yang banner Barbara made over the central stone, and the children placed their nosegays. Cicadas and guitars swelled in the wind. Someone noticed I was missing and went off to find me.

Apart from my brothers, on some high stone I sat and thought about continuity, felt the warmth of its embrace facing the absolute chill of our leap into unknowable open space. My mother's father was a Bolshevik, fled here from the prisons of the Czar; I have his blue eyes. He married his wife when I was twelve, to settle property rights. My father brought my mother home after their civil ceremony, to make their true vows on the Party Book—he told me this when I was twenty-five or so, and started to cry. The wind touched me with the cold of McCarthy winter; I grew up waiting for the knock on the door. One with the tree and the branches of manhood above me on the rock, I sat and marveled at how the spirit shifts around down time, from longshoreman to labor journalist to . . . what, technician of learning? I wondered what Karen was feeling, thought I knew, thought of how from the intimate core we've been learning together to honor our fantasies and accept their power, of how we are learning to dream and to live dream out, when dream's agent came to get me.

He brought me to where the men were milling, a quarter mile from the domes. The male dogs had come along, the female were with the women of their own accord. Each man had got himself a stick, of twisted manzanita or pine, and many had fixed lit candles on theirs. They had made a canopy of the bedspread Betty had tie-dyed for us, and four raised its corners aloft on long boughs. They set me under it, bright in peacock blues and greens, in the tunic my sister Leisa dyed in subtle faces and sewed, flapping my wings in embarrassment; I have never felt so purely beautiful. A wordless chanting began, rose up like a sudden dragon. Bass strings and flutes shifted

tempo and started to drive. The chanting quickened, fresh
with sweat. A procession formed around and behind me,
lifting and thumping their sticks, male voices ringing into
ragged exultant harmony, and we set off across the open
hills.

It was late enough for the candles to show clearly by
the time we topped the final rise, long after 5:32. Across
the meadow we saw the women approaching in symmet-
rical procession, in their colors and flowers, leading Karen
beneath an ancient tapestry of cock and dragon. The falling sun lit her through a mist of fabric, the subtle greens
of new bean sprouts. They too were chanting, softer,
silver. Across the domes we heard each other approaching, the sounds swelled as our lines converged, merged and
swirled into place around the altar. The chants grew together into a great *Om* that went on and on and on.
And then there was silence, and Karen and I went into
each other's eyes in a long moment of total surprise at
being there before the stone. Our dogchild Bull pushed
up between us, black muzzle briefly touching our crotches,
anxious to share some *together*. We took him in and
turned to begin.

"But there are no beginnings, no ends," we said together, facing the circle of our friends around the stone,
"that's just the way we speak, helplessly, or we couldn't."
Karen went on alone, from an old poem to her,

> "When you open to one thing, you open
> to all, which is why all lines,
> accepted abandoned or longed for,
> lead through this time, these selves."

And I said a poem by Robert Duncan that we had shared
for years. It appeared with a *pop!* on the desk one morn-

ing when we were talking about wanting text for a ceremony, at a peculiar conjunction of moon, expectation, and
a humming witch in the kitchen floating down morning-
after mescaline—by teleportation, as far as I could discover
by prying with a mind that was trained for science and
has seen such things happen before.

> "The fear that precedes changes of heaven
> opens its scenes; petal by petal longing
> a flower opens; its seeds   needs
> long unacknowledged,   urgencies
> as if grown over-night.   These
> voyages toward which we find ourselves,
> unbelieving,   proceeding.   Passage
> as if of death   unfamiliar.
> Coasts wrapped in unrealized light   right
> directions beyond belief where
> desire moves us.   O real mere islands,
> new lands,   bear with us,   allow
> for the heart's turning."

We turned to face each other and joined both our hands
in a Taoist clasp. Unsteadily I said, "I do not commit
myself to the death of property." "I accept you with your
body and spirit free," she said, and then, "I do not commit myself to the illusion of forever." "I accept you open
to the changes," I responded. And then we asked together,
"What then is your commitment?"

"To have you take me with all that you know of
seriousness," answered Karen, "and celebrate me with all
that you know of joy, in the process of our becoming
the world which we conspire."

"To have you walk with me as the woman of a poet and a pioneer," I answered, "and face Death as guerrillas of Life in the jungle of Amerika."

"I accept you as the father of our child," she said.

"I accept you as the mother of our work and life," I said.

We raised Mother's gift goblets of May wine to each other. Karen flashed that with them in our tunic and gown we struck the icon of the Two of Cups, which long before she had seen as the card of our marriage. A winged lion's-head rose from our hands, above the healing serpents. We tipped and sipped the goblets and started them passing from hand to hand around in the liquid circle kiss. And then shrugged, and said in unison into the lingering silence Karen's favorite line from Joyce: *"Well, as well you as another,"* our most cogent vow, and dissolved in the sacrament of laughter, digging the stunned moment before everyone joined.

When it settled we faced them again and asked them to speak words with us, grown from a ceremony we improvised early that spring at Iowa State. I said a line and the men said it back; Karen said a line and the women responded.

"The endless journey has slowed to halting."

"The end of the circle is the beginning."

"The ancient image has lost its splendor."

"There is a circle whose center is forming."

The women's voices were light in the reddening sunset, the men's were like earth.

"The voice of the answer is lost in its echoes."

"We are a question not yet framed."

Karen and I spoke the last lines together, and we all repeated them, one by one:

> "The titles we bear form weary rhymes.
>
> I have a name no one has spoken.
>
> We have a name no one has spoken."

After the silence we called the space open. George, another love once student, read the poem he had written for this time:

> A falcon circles with his eyes
> flying in rhythm with the sun
> a serpent coiled around his legs
> sliding dark
> brings round the circle.
>
> Raised out of moisture
> in an age of metallic fire
> dionysios gushes forth in bodies
> breathing into streams of crayfish
> playing in a sparkling spot near bottom.
>
> Erasing the shadow of his mother
> the spider of us all
> he clears webs of repression
> with splendid nakedness

soothing a flame to life

surrendering when not attacked
comforting when nothing is lost
to share and not to own.

Then Karen chose to throw the I Ching—we hadn't planned it, she's the custodian, when the spirit moves her. I was so spaced out by then I didn't realize what was happening till I came to with her hands guiding mine through the even tosses. The coins clinked on the stone. After the last toss she went into a huddle over the book with her occasional lover David and girl friend Barbara, while we waited for them to take turns reading the judgments.

The first hexagram was ☰☳, *I*, Increase. *"Increase,"* read Barbara, *"it furthers one to undertake something. It furthers one to cross the great water.* Sacrifice on the part of those above for the increase of those below fills the people with a sense of joy . . . When people are thus devoted to their leaders, undertakings are possible, and even difficult and dangerous enterprises will succeed. In such times of progress and successful development it is necessary to work and make the best use of the time. This time resembles that of the marriage of heaven and earth, when the earth partakes of the creative power of heaven, forming and bringing forth living beings."

"Aaah!" cried Stefan, the Savios' three-year-old son. "Aaah!" responded everyone in low wonder. "Aaaah!" cried Stefan after a moment, probing. "Aaaaah!" we cried, building our fantasy together, and he led us on and on in *Aaahing* until the pure sound of astonishment climaxed, broke and subsided. Then Barbara finished the judgment:

"The time of INCREASE does not endure, therefore it must be used while it lasts."

The fifth line was moving, and the hexagram turned to *I*, The Corners of the Mouth. The judgment: Perseverance brings good fortune. *Pay heed to the providing of nourishment, and to what a man seeks to fill his own mouth with* . . . If we wish to know what anyone is like, we have only to observe on whom he bestows his care and what sides of his own nature he cultivates and nourishes. Nature nourishes all creatures. The great man nourishes superior men, in order to nourish all through them.

Kneeling over the stones and its garlands, distracted, a candle caught Karen's hair, quick fingers flickered up half its length. She is terrified of fire, has nightmares of flame death. In the dream-slow motions of acid or ecstasy, mindless, I reached out and disappeared the fire. She didn't notice till it was all over. Then we clung to each other, shaking. Heavy icons, golden haze, the universe slipping in and out of focus. Twilight fell. We scattered over the hills, Karen and I wandering homeward clasped in anonymous silence. By the fire I ate from the lamb, didn't see her leave to go upstairs. In the basement Marilyn and Adrian labored over the cranky woodstove, discarding batch after batch of brown rice in search of a little perfection. Transfixed by the omen of flame, Karen huddled under the covers. For the only time that weekend I called her from afar, "Hey, McLellan, McLellan," and she came down out of blackness into the warmth of the living room, where some were making music before the fire. And then the fantastical candles were lit, and the children's great barricade cake unveiled with its freaky frosting. And then upstairs the sharing of gifts continued.

It is harder to take as *property* artifacts seen to have

lives of their own. I can't list all that was shared with us, play of the Children of Affluence with their tastes gone all peculiar. The refinished Goodwill rocker, the ceramic plate with a Tao of flower fields and stars, the elaborate amp and tuner, the great pillow sewn of chamois squares, the boxful of strung eucalyptus nuts, the Masai warrior wedding belt, the jar of unpoisoned morning-glory seeds, the patiently fitted crocheted lace dress, the enchanted box sent by our Illinois family, the bundle of lacquered yarrow stalks, the poster from a community strike, the paper icons and fantasy objects. The work of our hands and our hunting and play, show of affection in an open place made together. In the weaving light another Michael charmed Karen into dance with his fingers full of oranges and laughter. And later Tarney took me off and washed me with gentle hands, dried me in rough terrycloth, held me till my blood rose up, and we touched and she sent me off to the cottage. Only the ghost of Carl's singing lingered. The dog curled up before the fire, and Karen took off the wedding belt and we made slow lingering love, a little shy and a little sad with those outside who were still outside what so many had come to share together.

Do you see? Karen complains I write this as history, the magic slips through. I want to cry out: such are our people, this is how rich we are, here is a tangible sliver of how we are learning to shape and share our love. For this was half and more why we chose to make a public thing of our marriage: the sense that all around us were filling slowly with a strength of joy whose size was still unknown, because we hadn't yet gone beyond demonstration and be-in in inventing the forms that will show us what we are becoming.

We wanted to be an excuse, an occasion to focus our

energy within and beyond the unending War. Karen saw us as a sacrifice, in risk and experiment; and like the wedding couple in *A Midsummer Night's Dream*, "as if we were *presiding* somehow, both cause and irrelevant to the magic . . . The mellowness and freedom were a light of 'could be' at the end of dark 'what is.'" Me, I see us in history. We brought the best people we know together in a ripening time, and it happened. From that event lines of energy run out through many people's lives.

Long after friends were still telling us how they felt everyone actually married there at Mariposa. I lost count of how many couples confessed how it had brought them together. When she got back to Berkeley, Ann wrote us to say this of her and Ray, and more: "I had never seen the children act like that in public before, so peaceful . . . After we came down we went to People's Park and stayed there a long time. Michael, it was like the wedding, only larger, with black people and old people and hippies and plain housewives like me. I have never been political, but I know now that if they come to bulldoze the park I will be there with my children, up in front of the blades . . ."

Karen and I hung out in Mariposa alone for a few days after the wedding, letting it sink in with sun and psilocybin. Then we cleaned up the house and took off for Reno with Bull. With Tom and Russell in a pack we blew an NSA regional conference on ed reform to pieces. In the wreckage Karen and I asked people what they wanted to deal with, found it was sex, and pulled together the first version of the extended workshops in sexuality and learning, sexuality and politics, that have been the focus of our growing work together this past year. The Reno shot was our first formal work, first try at converting to teaching what we had learned in the past seven years together. Fit honey-moon.

That was a rising spring, latest of a sequence of many, rich with parallel journeys; so many people treading the common road of changes, quickening. Bad omens in the sky, since long before Chicago visible in Barometer City. When we got back to Berkeley from Reno, the Park was a legend of life, a free place where everything we embrace converged. Two weeks later the Park was a tundra, encampment of soldiers and pivot of helicopters, and Berkeley was an occupied city, five thousand in the tear-gas street. We went all together from the three houses we share, little Debbie cried because we wouldn't let her come: "I'm old enough to run." Running in the street I saw people who met at the wedding move together under attack. Got separated after the women went home, when the shooting started. Running down Dana one birdshot pellet hit my left thumb, an icy sting. Left a tiny black spot that lingered for weeks, bit of dead flesh in live, just the size of a literary grace, like a period. It started me writing the longest and heaviest poem of my life, trying to put it together, about the wedding and the Park and that little black spot.

Now Rector is dead on a Berkeley roof, and Hunter is murdered at Altamonte, and the Eight have been racked in Chicago. Our child was conceived in the back seat of a car on the road to El Paso to do our second piece of work together. It is due in mid-May, I am building a nursery for the child and the ferns, we're wondering how the dog will respond, and preparing to change. A year now since the wedding, I look at its terms and description with altered eyes. They seem to me much more clearly sexist than I'd even feared then. Or maybe not, for I'm a poor recorder of the mark of Karen's spirit on things, and I've learned that her terms work in me and around us long before I can recognize them. Whichever, we've attempted a division of the Mysteries, and if it isn't in harmony we shall try to begin again. Last month we got back from a month on the road, working together, big belly and all and the dog. Most of the campuses we stopped at were recent with conflict or about to blow. All our friends and the people we worked with were going through heavy changes, uncertain as hell but moving on as fast as they could manage. Back in Berkeley the Free Bakery has opened, capacity 2,000 loaves a day. Reagan is calling for a bloodbath. A thousand tenants are on strike. Nixon says to safeguard civil liberties the dangerous ones must be identified. Here we are planting gardens. I started to write this in Mariposa. While I've been finishing it in Berkeley someone's blown up the power line to the Radiation Lab and campus. As I write these words the plazas and streets are thick with CS gas, a thousand have taken refuge in the Student Union, the Chancellor has declared a State of Emergency, it is sunset, 15 April 1970. I sit on the porch and play on my guitar, learning to sing while we wait for the baby.

Well, I tell you it's my birthday I'm so tired of going to war, wanna

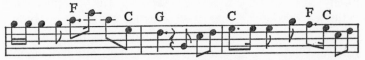

lay aside my shoulder pads for you. You know I can't be sure how late it is but

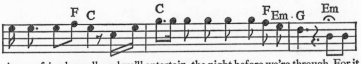

give our friends a call, and we'll entertain the night before we're through. For it

might help some to count your kin, while waiting for the winter wind.

Well I tell you it's my birthday,
I'm so tired of going to war,
wanna lay aside my shoulder pads for you.
You know I can't be sure how late it is
but give our friends a call,
and we'll entertain the night before we're through.

For it might help some to count your kin

. . . .

Well I met you on the picket line
when we were decade young,
singing, "We shall overcome . . . ,"*

and we read each other's leaflets
in the lonely downtown rain
and I said I'd trade you coffee for your name,

   Thinking it might help some to count your kin

. . . .

You were trying to write on granite
as we sat there in the hall,
a fingertip was all you had for pen,
crying "Power to the Pipers!!"
as we waited for the dawn
and the hoofbeats of the Sheriff's Highwaymen.

   And it might help some to count your kin,
   while waiting for the winter wind.

They were selling plastic sideburns
when I met you on the green,
come to count the birds that everyone became.
When you asked how many made it,
I could only tell you why
and dance with you the sacramental hour.

      . . . .
   While waiting for the winter wind.

In the streets the fog is angry
where the nimble speed the lame,
you have pulled me from the clubs of our despair.
Mind if I sit here by your campfire?
it might help to clear my eyes,
we'll play boyscouts out to brave the wilderness,

And it might help some to count your kin
while waiting for the winter wind.

And I don't know where the rain falls,
but I know the reason why,
how it wakes the seeds to struggle underground.
And I've seen the way the heart works,
how it waits to claim its time,
and it beats and beats and beats a man to death.

So it might help some to count your kin,
while waiting for the winter wind. (*repeat*)

Toward the Future

Declaration on the Birth of the Child Lorca

We will not send our child to a public school, or even to a private one in the usual sense. Together we have managed to learn much the schools couldn't teach us, and unlearn some of what they did. The heart of our knowledge is ours now, and it tells us we must be responsible ourselves for the conditions of our child's growth. This is no romantic hippy daydream. It is a full political act: grounded in theory, chosen as strategy, implemented with all the skills of our consciousness.

We chose to move on the future by freeing our child from the control of the present State. We declare independence from its essential instrument, the System of Education. We will not give our young over to be conditioned in obedience with its programs by any of its representatives, however unofficial, informal and liberal. *We will grow our own*. And we will grow them as free as we can manage, in situations where we have only to contend with what is in ourselves of the lives we are trying to leave behind.

Several years ago we left the Educational System, where we were cut off from our many selves. We sidestepped the institutions that continue it in society, and began to come together. Now we know that other lives of learning are possible. We can name them. Crippled as we are, we can create their initial conditions: we understand what is involved and have the skills and the power. For we have been learning to be what we imagine: to live in our bodies, make art with our lives, realize cooperation, and fight Fascism by any means necessary, including the creation of alternate realities, guerrilla enclaves of Life in the State of Death.

Good life learning means understanding is integrated in action. We display our knowledge of the culture of specialized roles, with its destructive systems of education, competition and authority, by how we manage to be each other's teachers, siblings and lovers, parents and children, by how we tend and heal and share each other's growth. We must focus at home through this if we are to focus anywhere else and into the future. *We will grow our own.* And we ourselves must be directly involved in what and how our children learn, for no one else can represent our interest in the future.

For this we must make our lives over: rearrange the ways we work, the styles of our play, the priorities of our time and our love; and move beyond the roles that still bind us from within. To replace what we reject, we must learn anew what we have to share, and grow to make it adequate. The price of making of our lives a school for our children is our own transformation. We believe it is possible, because it is already begun.

Our parents were forced to abandon their children to the part-time uses of the State because they were integrated into its economy and culture, because they saw no alternative, because they were isolated in marriage and privacy and could not organize their lives to be also a school. We know now that no couple can cope alone with even their own relation. We learn in a larger community. To free our young many must come together, to share their powers in critical mass and intimacy. We believe it involves all entering equal as children into the school of a larger Family.

It also means learning economic cooperation, to free space and resources. And it means committing ourselves to political identity and struggle. At present here, one elementary credential can front for up to fifty kids, leaving us with only our own limitations. But when many choose to use this freedom it will be curtailed, and that will be only the beginning. For Fascism is rising softly in this land, you have seen its sign in the black headline of the sky.

The State registered our son with a number at his birth and designs to own him. Our growing up prepared us for integration into its army, its civil and industrial bureaucracies, its systems of consumption and exploitation, decision and power. It cannot afford us to let our son grow unprepared, let alone prepared for something else. It will not give him over to the gropings of our freedom without a deadly struggle. This will take many forms. To meet them, we must realize together who we are and the politics of our necessities and choices. And prepare to resist, to fight for the cradle of the future, and to flourish in and beyond our resistance.

1 June 1970